NONFINITE
LOSS AND GRIEF
A Psychoeducational Approach

by

Elizabeth J. Bruce, Ph.D.
Counseling Psychologist
Victoria, Australia

and

Cynthia L. Schultz, Ph.D.
Honorary Associate
School of Public Health
LaTrobe University
Victoria, Australia

·PAUL·H·
BROOKES
PUBLISHING Cº

Baltimore • London • Toronto • Sydney

Paul H. Brookes Publishing Co.
Post Office Box 10624
Baltimore, Maryland 21285-0624

www.brookespublishing.com

Typeset by Type Shoppe II Productions, Ltd., Chestertown, Maryland.
Manufactured in the United States of America by
Versa Press, East Peoria, Illinois.

The case studies in this book have been compiled from
numerous sources. Names are all fictitious, and similarities
are entirely coincidental.

Excerpt from "A Sketch of the Past" in MOMENTS OF BEING
by Virginia Woolf, copyright © 1976 by Quentin Bell and Angelica Garnett,
reprinted by permission of Harcourt, Inc.

Library of Congress Cataloging-in-Publication Data

Bruce, Elizabeth J.
  Nonfinite loss and grief : a psychoeducational approach / by Elizabeth J. Bruce and
Cynthia L. Schultz.
       p.   cm.
  Includes bibliographical references and index.
  ISBN 1-55766-517-6
  1. Grief.   2. Loss (Psychology).   3. Deprivation (Psychology).   I. Schultz, Cynthia L.
II. Title.

BF575.G7 B76 2001
155.9'3—dc21
                                                                    2001035141

British Library Cataloguing-in-Publication Data are available from the British Library.

NONFINITE
LOSS AND GRIEF

CONTENTS

SECTION IV   COMPLEXITIES IN GRIEVING NONFINITE LOSS

SECTION V   PRINCIPLES AND CLINICAL APPLICATIONS

ABOUT THE AUTHORS

Elizabeth J. Bruce, Ph.D., MAPS, Counseling Psychologist, 15 Coronet Grove, Beaumaris, Victoria, Australia 3193

Dr. Bruce has an undergraduate degree majoring in sociology and English literature. She earned a postgraduate degree in social work while working as a counselor in the field of mental health. She undertook her doctorate in psychology at LaTrobe University, Melbourne, Victoria, in the School of Public Health. Her research-based thesis explored the grief and loss experienced by parents who have children with intellectual disabilities. Since earning her doctorate, Dr. Bruce has remained dedicated to exposing the impact of trauma and grief in family settings. She runs a private psychology practice specializing in loss, grief, and trauma as they present in chronic conditions and conducts regular intervention programs for families. She is a consultant psychologist for numerous early intervention agencies, has authored and co-authored a number of published articles, and is a lecturer in developmental psychology in several postgraduate courses. She lives by the sea in Beaumaris, Melbourne, with her husband, two emerging adults, and a 6-year-old son.

Cynthia L. Schultz, B.A. (Hons), Ph.D., Honorary Associate, School of Public Health, LaTrobe University, Highfields, 150 Marshall Street, Ivanhoe, Victoria, Australia 3079

Dr. Schultz earned her doctorate in psychology from the University of Queensland, with special interest in counseling, community, and health psychology. As Senior Lecturer in the Faculty of Health Sciences, LaTrobe University, Melbourne, Victoria, she authored, taught, and coordinated undergraduate and postgraduate courses in interpersonal skills, family dynamics, group processes, and loss and grief in health care settings. Her research, publications, and community involvement have focused on psychoeducational support-group programs for family caregivers. Many of Dr. Schultz's published articles and four books, co-authored with her husband, Rev. Dr. Noel Schultz, are devoted to family caregiving issues. Her contribution to distance education courses for postgraduate nurses testifies to her interest in professional caregivers. To her credit also are research and program development grants and the foundation editorship of the *Journal of Family Studies*. Now enjoying creative retirement, she maintains close links with current extensions of her earlier work and with LaTrobe University as an Honorary Associate in the School of Public Health. Dr. Schultz and her husband reside in a beautiful, leafy suburb of Melbourne. Together, they take great delight in their family, comprising three children and their partners, and five grandchildren.

PREFACE

In looking back on what led to our partnership as co-authors, you could say that grief brought us together, though not in the traditional sense. Our paths crossed out of a shared commitment to research and psychoeducation as the means for dealing with nonfinite loss and grief in a compassionate and informed manner. When one also considers our shared passion for people as individuals, our thirst to understand human nature, and our keen interest in the social sciences, a picture begins to emerge of how complementary and collegial our working relationship has been during the process of writing this book.

In more concrete terms, our partnership on this text had its inception in a 3-year project conducted at LaTrobe University in Victoria, Australia, within the department now known as the School of Public Health. Substantial funding for this project was provided by the Victorian Health Promotion Foundation (VHPF). This project incorporated two components: an exploration of the grief experienced by parents of children with disabilities and the development and application of psychoeducational support programs. The aims of the research project as stated in the grant application were twofold: First, building on the existing literature on grief, findings from this study were intended to provide an understanding of the continuing, complex, and evolving process of raising a child with an intellectual disability. Second, we hoped to contribute to a knowledge base that encourages the development of programs and services sensitive to and supportive of the needs of these families and of public health professionals in closely related fields. Specifically, the aims of the study were implemented by means of a research design that sought to

- Identify patterns and differences in parents' perceptions, feelings, and grief reactions across age-cohorts of children with intellectual disabilities

- Compare these parents' responses to those of parents with typically developing children
- Develop and test the effectiveness of a small-group program designed to increase the psychological well-being of group participants

These goals were accomplished by means of four longitudinal studies of 217 parents. Each study also included an investigation of gender differ-ences. Data were collected on three occasions at annual home-based in-terviews. Data analysis yielded many important findings.[1]

A doctoral thesis (Bruce, 1994) gave substance to the research pro-ject, paving the way for the coining of the term *nonfinite loss* and to the conviction that nonfinite loss is a concept applicable to many of life's ex-periences. This growing conviction was incipient in the closing paragraph of the final report to the VHPF in which we noted that parallels could be "drawn between the present findings and a variety of health care and re-habilitation settings" (Schultz & Schultz, 1997, p.115). We further ar-gued that a developmental component, which we discuss at length in this book, is common ground for many circumstances surrounding loss and grief and that psychoeducation has potential for use with other grieving populations. As a result of the study and report, a framework for a deeper understanding of nonfinite loss emerged, providing a catalyst for the ap-plication of the concept of nonfinite loss and grief to a much broader spectrum of society to which the text of this book bears witness.

Since the completion of the original research project and its associ-ated publications in scholarly journals, we have had numerous personal and professional opportunities to observe and learn more about nonfinite loss and the grief that surrounds it. Some of these opportunities have in-volved swift learning curves that we believe have enriched our work and strengthened our commitment to make accessible the provision of a bal-anced approach (albeit a fine balance) to all of those who grieve nonfinite loss. Through counseling and group work, we have become further ac-quainted with the traumatic life situations often faced by individuals. Working through trauma represents an extremely complex psychological task. It is made all the more difficult when 1) the trauma continues, 2) the individual is the only one experiencing the trauma, 3) the individual is isolated, and 4) the loss is not socially recognized. Hence, counseling and professional work have continued to focus on the development and provi-sion of carefully monitored and evaluated psychoeducation for individu-als, parents, families, and groups. Training workshops for professionals have become another important arm of our psychoeducational endeavors,

---

[1]For full details of research methodology, the psychoeducational program, and out-comes, see Bruce and Schultz (1994), Bruce, Schultz, and Smyrnios (1996), Bruce, Schultz, Smyrnios, and Schultz (1993, 1994), Schultz et al. (1993), and Schultz and Schultz (1997).

with a focus on psychological techniques for working through loss, grief, and trauma in a multitude of family settings.

From this background, we have endeavored to extrapolate key factors surrounding nonfinite loss and the application of a psychoeducational approach. The more we thought about and talked about nonfinite loss, the wider the circles grew, until we realized the impossibility of containing it in any single book. This realization meant that we had to be selective, because nonfinite loss is an umbrella term for so many scenarios in life. It has relevance for old and young alike, for individuals, couples, and families. In short, it is ubiquitous. To overcome the unavoidable limitations of time and space, we have taken great pains to describe as clearly and succinctly as possible the underlying theory and philosophy of loss and grief. We have also provided pertinent examples, tables, figures, and case studies to enable our readers to gain insight into their own and others' experiences of nonfinite loss and grief. Building on the traditional theoretical perspectives on grief, we place great emphasis on the framework against which loss is processed. In particular, the roles of cognitive development and identity formation stand out as crucial aspects in this process. We have designed principles and guidelines for facilitating the development of clients as strategists in negotiating their own reality and achieving a fine balance. We hope that by encouraging individuals who are experiencing loss to actively participate in the grieving process, they will gain insights and skills that will help them to better live with loss throughout their lives.

REFERENCES

Bruce, E.J. (1994). *A longitudinal investigation of loss and grief for mothers and fathers of children with intellectual disability.* Unpublished doctoral dissertation, LaTrobe University, Melbourne, Victoria, Australia.

Bruce, E.J., & Schultz, C.L. (1994). A cross-sectional study of parenting perceptions: Caring for children with intellectual disability. *Australian Journal of Marriage & Family, 15,* 56–65.

Bruce, E.J., Schultz, C.L., & Smyrnios, K.X. (1996). A longitudinal study of the grief of mothers and fathers of children with an intellectual disability. *British Journal of Medical Psychology, 69,* 33–45.

Bruce, E.J., Schultz, C.L., Smyrnios, K.X., & Schultz, N.C. (1993). Discrepancy and loss in parenting: A comparative study of mothers and fathers of children with and without intellectual disability. *Children Australia, 18,* 18–24.

Bruce, E.J., Schultz, C.L., Smyrnios, K.X., & Schultz, N.C. (1994). Grieving related to development: A preliminary comparison of three age cohorts of parents of children with intellectual disability. *British Journal of Medical Psychology, 67,* 37–52.

Schultz, C.L., Schultz, N.C., Bruce, E.J., Smyrnios, K.X., Carey, L., & Carey, C. (1993). Psychoeducational support for parents of children with intellectual disability: An outcome study. *International Journal of Disability, Development and Education, 40,* 205–216.
Schultz, N.C., & Schultz, C.L. (1997). *Care for caring parents: Leader's manual.* Melbourne: Australian Council for Educational Research.

PROLOGUE

A 30-year-old woman sits down and reflects on a recent diagnosis of a life-threatening disease:

> What does it feel like for this to have happened to me? It feels like I'm in some sort of nightmare. When I was young I used to be frightened of bad things happening, of people and things frightening me. There was one particular image and that was of an axeman. Lying in bed, I could make out his figure in a shadow that my bedroom lamp cast on the closet door. Now it is like I live this nightmare. It has come true. I am in it, and it hangs over my head—it lurks behind me.

This book is about dealing with such a nightmare—dealing with the axeman, the bogeyman—the materialization of fear.

ACKNOWLEDGMENTS

In my work as a psychologist I have been fortunate in meeting many inspiring people. I wish to acknowledge and thank these people for the ways in which they have inspired me—not only in my work but also in my life. My husband Colin, one of those rare individuals who is adaptable *and* multi-skilled, created most of the figures contained in this book. Without his continued teaching and sharing of these skills and countless, invaluable discussions, there would be no book. The artwork was produced by my youngest daughter, Jaime, an individual who brings sensitivity and extraordinary creativity to all her fine works of art. This book was further informed by the already considerable life experience and remarkable intuition of my 14-year-old daughter, Alison, while my son, Anthony, has provided innumerable examples of what the world is like for an insightful 6-year-old. I am grateful for this very special family who offers me an enviable position in life—a "secure base." Last but not least, I remain indebted to Cynthia for never failing to share my vision or to offer me encouragement.   —EJB

Working on this book has been a joy and privilege. It is the culmination of a shared dream that represents a massive extension of research begun at LaTrobe University last century. The dream developed into a project that provided scope for both authors to draw on talents and experience in a truly collaborative partnership. For this I shall always be grateful to Liz. Thanks are due to family members, colleagues, and friends, who, through their lively interest in the book's creation, have been a source of much encouragement. For me, this is true in particular of my husband, Noel. This testimony of respect and affection would not be complete without paying tribute to the many family and professional caregivers whose fortitude in the face of loss and grief has been inspirational.   —CLS

Finally, we both wish to express our appreciation for the sterling work of staff members at Paul H. Brookes Publishing Co. From its inception, the relationship between authors and publisher has been characterized by a sense of purpose and commitment. We are grateful for the highly professional supportiveness, goodwill, and expertise that we have encountered. We thank all those who have been involved in any way, especially Acquisitions Editor Jessica Allan and Book Production Editor Leslie Eckard. Their insights, keen interest in our work, and thorough attention to detail have been outstanding.

To my mother,
WHO BATTLED BRAVELY AGAINST FEAR ALL OF HER LIFE,
AND TO MY FATHER WHO NEVER RELINQUISHED HIS ROLE
IN PROTECTING HER FROM THIS FEAR
—EJB

To Noel,
WHOSE PRESENCE, SUPPORT, PATIENCE, WISDOM,
AND GOOD HUMOR HAVE BEEN ESSENTIAL ELEMENTS IN MY
CONTRIBUTION TO THIS BOOK
—CLS

"THE SECRET OF SURVIVAL IS TO EM-
BRACE CHANGE, AND TO ADAPT.... YOU
HAVE TO MAINTAIN A FINE BALANCE
BETWEEN HOPE AND DESPAIR.... IN THE
END, IT'S ALL A QUESTION OF BALANCE."
—MISTRY, 1996, PP. 230–231

SECTION I

THE NONFINITE FACTOR
IN LOSS AND GRIEF

"TO GET BETTER. TO LIVE. TO GROW UP.
TO BE LIKE EVERYONE ELSE. ISN'T THAT
WHAT WE ALL WANT IN THE END?"

—SHIELDS, 1997, P. 131

CHAPTER 1

AN INTRODUCTION TO NONFINITE LOSS AND GRIEF

It is remarkably easy to be thrown into chaos:

One minute you are radiantly pregnant, expecting your first child; the next you are told that your child will have an ongoing medical condition, perhaps be blind, have Down syndrome. "Her disability will be lifelong," the doctor tries to convince you.

Your 18-year-old son goes off on a Friday night: "See you later," he yells out from the door. Only hours later he is lying in intensive care—with an extensive brain injury. He will survive the car accident, but he will be changed unbelievably: "You will need to look after him for the rest of your life," well-meaning friends and physicians tell you.

The telephone rings; a doctor confirms that you have cancer. Following this, your life is shadowed by the fear of leaving remission and is altered irrevocably.

One of the initial responses most people have to bad news is shock, followed by the question: "Why me?" These two reactions are partly based on a naive reliance on the "taken-for-granted" world. Although people contemplate the possibility of personal disaster, the majority of individuals do not seriously entertain the possibility. For those of us who have been fortunate enough to experience a trauma-free childhood, patterns of safety become so established that they incline each one of us to think: "It could not happen to me." This position enables people to plan for the future. That is, for most people in the Western world, the future is seen as a relatively predictable entity. Ironically, the fragility of our

3

personal assumptive world only becomes apparent when it is under threat. In fact, the forced encounter with its fragile nature represents an essential part of the trauma itself. Although these moments are terribly significant, the life that follows them is even more difficult.

Experiencing personal adversity brings individuals, often for the first time, face-to-face with the issue of how to regain a feeling of personal safety and equilibrium. Facing the fragile nature of one's personal reality is very frightening and demands camouflaging. Individuals believe there must be some guarantee that they can control what happens to them—that bad luck can be taken out of the equation. In an attempt to control the misfortune that befalls them, most individuals devise their own personal formula for staying safe and securing good fortune: "The day I was to get my blood test results, I found myself hunting out an old good-luck charm: a necklace I had in childhood. It felt strange to put it on, but I actually felt a bit better."

Versions of self learned in childhood either amplify or temper the foreboding that surrounds the present situation. Those versions of self that amplify the sense of dread reflect the belief that "There is no escape; it will get me in the end!" The alternatives reflect the converse: "I can escape this nightmare."

For the individual concerned with rules, a characteristic response such as "I don't deserve this—this is so unfair" might follow personal adversity. Childhood beliefs that only bad behavior deserves punishment persist and become prominent. A friend flippantly comments, "Whose grave did you walk over?" Whether the flippancy is intended or not, even an individual who is well into adulthood might engage in the same superstitious thought, if only momentarily: "What *have* I done to deserve this?" For some individuals, this thought sequence continues to predominate for what may be an extraordinarily long period of time. Finding answers to this question may constitute a lifelong search or vocation.

The randomness of dreaded events is a hard concept to accept. In order for their lives to retain their predictability and controllability, individuals are forced to find some action or deed that can account for these events. A search may begin. Individuals may remember an incident from their past: "Life seemed to turn bad after I had the abortion. Ten years of bad luck followed this—everything started to go wrong after that! If only I had stood up to my boyfriend; if I had kept the child, things may have been different!"

Furthermore, as though there is a prescribed limit to what can be doled out to one person, traumatized individuals proclaim, "Enough is enough—I can't take anymore. When will this end?" This is yet another example of a belief constructed in childhood. The realization that bad things happen to good people and bad things do not necessarily go away is, for most people, unfathomable. There are anomalies. People who have acquired illness or disability in their early development or those people born with congenital impairment can experience life as a relentless buildup of "why me's." A response to further threat may well be, "Yes, this fits; I've always been unlucky! Who else but me?" It is not surprising that the unfairness of life resonates as a major theme throughout stories of loss.

Personal adversity, then, triggers the recurrence of childlike superstitions and childlike ways of viewing the world. When individuals are under extreme personal stress, it is not unusual for them to revert to childlike states. A number of explanations automatically resurface from childhood: punishments for risks taken and messages such as "You brought this on yourself " enter into possible explanations for the current crisis. Personal coping responses may be dormant at this point, and an individual may instinctively seek emotional and physical safety and security, usually from his or her parents. Even if the parents are deceased, an individual may voluntarily or involuntarily seek them through memories. The often urgent desire to be admitted into a setting that provides care is a measure of the helplessness that the individual feels and an attempt to secure substitute unconditional care.

BECOMING LOST BETWEEN WORLDS

The experience of waiting for a medical diagnosis for one's self or a loved one touches on the incipient fear and anxiety that accompanies a potential threat to one's taken-for-granted world. For some individuals, the first fault line in their naiveté is threatening to take form. Intuitively, the threat is sensed. Hanging by a delicate thread, individuals vigilantly attend to signs that might restore their safety: the doctor's manner, his body language, the eyes of his receptionist. A picture is forming and consolidating. In this moment, it is like balancing "between two worlds"—the world that is known and the world that is dreaded—one foot on each side of a ravine.

If the threat subsides, these feelings will be quelled and the accompanying rituals will lose purpose and, therefore, prominence. For those who receive confirmation of the threat, however, this fear and anxiety will parallel the learning experience that follows. Many individuals will feel permanently lost from their old selves. In various ways they might say, "I haven't seen myself for a long time." Yet, for some individuals, losing self is a slow, unfolding process; it will become a familiar part of their lives. A woman seeking to bear a child watches opportunities and methods of conceiving slowly slip away over time. A man who was adopted senses a vague feeling of being lost as a central or major part of his world. Another man finally able, for the first time, to reflect on a childhood of abuse chooses the word *lost* to describe the disconnection he feels as he realizes that his parents failed to protect him. These examples touch on the topic of this book, *nonfinite loss and grief*.

DETERMINING A NONFINITE FACTOR

Are you a person for whom the term *nonfinite loss* resonates, even though you are not sure what the title of this book might mean? Can you relate to it because of your personal experience with loss and grief or your professional observations of the same, or maybe both? People from many different backgrounds and experiences may see themselves in these pages. Perhaps you are wrestling with a major trauma in your own life, a major change, or perhaps the change itself has caused you trauma. Maybe you work in a health care setting and are surrounded by examples of traumatic loss. Perhaps you are a counselor or therapist to whom others turn for support in personal life crises or an educator helping your students seek answers or guidance. Or maybe you are a parent or a spouse trying to make sense of what has been lost by a loved one. Regardless of how you came to be familiar with nonfinite loss, you have probably found yourself facing the following questions and dilemmas at one time or another.

Questions Related to Nonfinite Loss

What exactly is nonfinite loss? Does grieving for nonfinite loss differ from grieving for finite loss? Is any loss able to be considered finite? Does the idea of nonfinite loss mean different things to different people and, if so, why and how? How might a child experience it, or an adolescent? Who might benefit by learning more about life experiences that occur before, during, and after nonfinite loss occurs (i.e., antecedent, concurrent, and subsequent experiences)? What therapeutic principles are available for facilitating the grieving process associated with nonfinite loss?

No easy answers exist to these and related questions, but this text attempts to broaden interested readers' understanding of nonfinite loss and how its characteristics complicate the task of grieving. This chapter introduces a framework that positions nonfinite loss within the context of an individual's past, present, and future viewpoints.

Grounded in the Past   The groundwork for the meaning and significance of the things that happen to individuals is established in the past—well before the actual event takes place (Rochlin, 1965). Drawing together developmental patterns and psychological and sociological perspectives, we trace the derivations of loss in the lives of individuals as well as in their personal grief responses. To do this, we give considerable attention to the longstanding relationship individuals have with fear and anxiety. The centrality of fear and anxiety in what an individual perceives to constitute and cause a dreaded event, as well as in his or her immediate and long-term response to such an event, is described.

Four developmental contexts are singled out, including 1) familiar patterns in relation to psychological well-being, 2) socioemotional states and learning in childhood, 3) internalized models of the "world that should have been," and 4) the public and private reputation of dreaded events. All play havoc both with an individual's ability to adapt to changed versions of self and reality as well as his or her ability to grieve. Moreover, the interrelationship between these four developmental contexts provides the basis for the therapy that is introduced.

The broad objective of this book is to present a theoretical basis that increases understanding of loss and the grieving responses, with particular reference to nonfinite loss, and ultimately leads to a sensitive outcome for grieving people and those who support them. In addition to concern for the individuals who are affected, the text acknowledges the loss, and the grieving response, of family members and significant others. Our conceptualization of loss as a dynamic and evolving entity dictates the psychoeducational approach that is described in detail.

DEFINITIONS, CONCEPTS, AND USAGE OF TERMS

In order to better understand the ideas related to nonfinite loss, it is important to introduce a number of concepts and terms used throughout this book:

- Nonfinite loss
- Threat and fear
- Dreaded events and their reputations
- Griefwork and reality testing
- Grieving ideals
- Schemata and models of the world
- Disenfranchised grief
- Emotional and cognitive knots

Each is described more fully below.

Nonfinite Loss

By far the most difficult term to define in a few words, we use the term *nonfinite loss* to refer to losses that are contingent on development; the passage of time; and on a lack of synchrony with hopes, wishes, ideals, and expectations. The term emerged from the authors' close involvement as counselors, educators, and researchers with many parents of children with an intellectual or other developmental disability (Bruce, Schultz, & Smyrnios, 1996; Bruce, Schultz, Smyrnios, & Schultz, 1994; Schultz et al., 1993). These mothers and fathers leave a doctor's or neurologist's office with a mass of foreign and frightening words, most of which threaten both their child's and their own future. Often, these words are visually incongruent with the appearance of the child. Yet, over time, the disability or the disease slowly manifests itself. In fact, it is relentless, continuing to reveal its effects throughout the life span of the parent and child. *Nonfinite* became the most apt word we could find to describe the life-span grief of these families.

In the process of working with these and other families, it became apparent that the term is equally applicable in a host of other settings. For example, nonfinite loss confronts people and their families in rehabilitation, hospital, and clinical environments. In these cases, the precipitating event may be an acquired disability, traumatic injury, or the onset of an ongoing or degenerative disease. For the family members—perhaps a spouse, a son, or a daughter—who watch the gradual decline of a loved one due to the often insidious onset of dementia, the experience of nonfinite loss is all too real. The physical presence remains while the personality slowly fragments and disintegrates. The onlooker is confronted with a painful and constant interplay of what was and what is.

Similarly, in counseling environments, cases of adoption, infertility, separation, divorce, and sexual abuse invariably present grief related to nonfinite loss. The benchmark is "what should have been." This draws on highly charged emotional ideals such as birthrights, fertility rights, marriage vows, and the right to a innocuous childhood. Often, the loss is defined in retrospect. For instance, a 35-year-old woman who is suddenly plagued by memories of sexual abuse realizes that her childhood, especially her relationship with her stepfather, was not what it had seemed—not what it should have been. As she begins to unravel her life story in this new light, there is a reweaving of past, present, and future taking place simultaneously.

Nonfinite losses have a haunting and inescapable quality. They are continuous, invariably insidious, rarely recognized for what they are, and often preceded by a clearly distinguished negative life event or episode that for one reason or another retains a vivid physical or psychological presence (e.g., diagnosis of congenital malformation, infertility, life-threatening or degenerative illness, breakdown of a relationship, disappearance of a family member in an impossible-to-reconcile circumstance such as torture or murder).

However, there are more obscure and covert or "quiet" examples of nonfinite loss that surround identity and development. For instance, nonfinite loss can germinate in a period of childhood and adolescence when an individual had a feeling of "specialness" bestowed on him or her (e.g., because of a skill, talent, or illness) but then lost that special feeling.

The place dreams and hopes take in the development of an individual's identity is pivotal to this book. When someone's dreams and hopes falter, they are often overlooked or dismissed by others. They are considered to be "part of growing up—just a part of life." But for some individuals, irrespective of their stage in life, the falling away or the relinquishment of their dreams is a cause for continuing grief. "Who I could have been," "who I should have been," or "who I should have become" are possibly the connecting themes through the losses described in this book, regardless of whether their traumatic nature is obvious.

Threat and Fear

Becker (1973) argued that our first task as infants entering the world is to contain anxiety. Much of a child's world is about overcoming fears of being alone, of life, and of death. When working with children and adolescents, one becomes aware that children have a myriad of fears even when nothing bad happens. Some children's fears are manifested by phantom characters who haunt them when it is dark. For children who experience a traumatic loss in childhood, fear is all too plainly legitimized. Invariably, when an adult's personal world is threatened, childhood fears resurface. The significance of threat and of fear is dealt with in Sections III and IV.

The *threat* instilled by a loss that by its nature is nonfinite involves relentlessness. There is an ongoing dynamic as an individual lives with a threat that he or she is helpless to fix: "It will not go away; there is no cure; there is no guarantee that it may not get worse; there is nothing I can do to change things." A *fear* of what may lie ahead is generated. "What will happen to me, my spouse, my child, my parents?" In some situations, the threat and fear can align with a personal feeling of chaos.

Dreaded Events and Their Reputations

For those receiving their first threat, such as in the first minutes of diagnosis, a world safe and predictable is now in serious doubt. In fact, despite the shock that surrounds this moment, many people admit that in that instant, part of them knew that life would be irreversibly changed. Most tragedies have well-established reputations. For instance, many of us have heard stories and wondered how people cope with cancer, multiple sclerosis, cerebral palsy, or the like. For most people the occurrence of these conditions is to be dreaded; they become *dreaded events*. The origin of the private and public reputation of dreaded events is examined in Section III, which distinguishes between those events that are publicly recognized as dreaded and those that are dreaded because they have acquired private reputations—internalized versions of self that evoke fear. "I never pictured myself as someone with a failed marriage. Can I live alone? How can I live as a divorced woman?" "I never thought of myself as without children."

These comments touch on the crux of nonfinite loss and grief. A pattern of expectations of "how I should be" is disrupted. The "me" an individual had come to picture him- or herself as, the one he or she has learned to be comfortable with over time, is suddenly destined to become someone different. To make matters worse, individuals cannot imagine identifying with a life experience that they have perhaps traditionally feared or disparaged: "I'm not *that* sort of person!"

> "I NEVER PICTURED MYSELF AS SOME-
> ONE WITH A FAILED MARRIAGE. CAN
> I LIVE ALONE? HOW CAN I LIVE AS A
> DIVORCED WOMAN?"

Griefwork and Reality Testing

The term *griefwork* embraces the intellectual and emotional workings of adaptation that take place following a significant change to an individual's view of self and the world. Griefwork involves reality testing. What is reality testing? How does one go about it? Simply put, reality testing is a process of realization and reconciliation. Following a significant change in one's life, one is more or less forced to acknowledge how this event has changed one's world. Over time, a person may come to have a realization illustrated by an interior monologue that might sound something like this: "Something has happened to me and my world. I must no longer *expect* it to be the same. Instead, I must recognize that I am different—that the world is different. Necessarily, my expectations of the world and my place in it must be modified."

This realization often involves quite drastic changes to one's knowledge structures. For instance, if I have always had two legs on which to walk, even though I may have lost one in an automobile accident, my habit will be to stand up *expecting* it to be there. In essence, my knowledge base has not been brought up to date with what has happened to my leg. Reality testing is a process of learning *not* to expect it to be there—to get it right—to reconcile my internal knowledge base, my memory, to *fit* what has happened to me.

Attaining the fit can be complicated. Frequently, there are factors that compromise reality testing: chameleon-like characteristics of the loss that suggest that the change may only be temporary. For instance, in situations involving mental health, such as schizophrenia, the loss may be unclear or uncertain. Reality testing can be held in abeyance. In Section IV we consider the salience of a loss and its effect on reality testing: "Is it clear that something has been lost?"

Updating one's knowledge base represents the *intellectual component* of reality testing; the *emotional component* adds a further dimension. The realization that we have lost an aspect of our selves and the world is painful is an extremely personal process and, depending on the individual concerned, can be exceedingly arduous and protracted. It is like retraining one's brain to accept new material after it has spent numerous years learning something quite different—while at the same time experiencing very strong emotional pulls of resistance against doing this very task.

This resistance reflects the emotional attachment individuals have to the self and the world with which they have become familiar. In the midst of all this, a feeling of vulnerability is unavoidable; integral to the process of realization is the relinquishment of who we were, who we might have been. It involves shrinking one's ideals and minimizing the devastation of this loss. Each individual will have varying needs and ways to temper this process. At some juncture, most individuals are able to integrate what has happened to them and their world into a reasonably cohesive picture of self—to adapt well enough.

Grieving Ideals

The power of ideals is a crucial factor in understanding nonfinite loss and the accompanying grief response. When we grieve, *we grieve an ideal*—the world that should or could have been—what I, or he, or she might have been, or should have been. This is a tricky benchmark. With the death of a significant other, it may be possible over time to neutralize the associated ideals. What makes us feel less bereft? Perhaps by recalling how we survived on our own when that person was unavailable? In fact, this defensive tactic can assist the grieving process. In the end, we are able to balance our perception of the lost person because of the important knowledge that we can indeed survive without that individual.

This is not always the case, however. For some individuals, this process of reconciliation with a death proves unattainable. The experience assumes nonfinite characteristics. The death of a parent during an individual's childhood may be one such example. In the absence of reality testing, a parent can be immortalized; he or she remains an ideal mother or father throughout the development of the child. That is, a child can state unequivocally, "He would have *always* been there for me." Similarly, the loss of a child whose destiny was embedded in the parents' hopes and dreams involves the immortalizing of an ideal. The family's future with that child is a lost ideal never fully relinquished: "She would have been a joy to us always!"

How do we test reality and shrink ideals in situations of nonfinite loss? The whole process of reconciliation becomes far more difficult when we are dealing with the "what should have beens." Can we so easily downplay, say, life before cancer? The life and meaning that surround having a typically developing child? Life without a colostomy bag? People do try. For instance, it is not unusual for an individual to state, "I have become a better person since this happened"; "I have learned a deeper meaning in life"; "God chose me to experience this, to make me stronger." These coping strategies or defense mechanisms must make the emerging reality bearable—the devastation less. And yet, circumstances may get worse—so the individual must constantly exert control over the management of the devastation. The tension and difficulty in continuing this management interminably are the subjects of much of the therapy described in Section V.

Schemata and Models of the World

Schemata (i.e., cognitive structures, schematic structures) are akin to personal frames of reference, belief systems, or interpretive frameworks. All personal constructions of reality, these structures that are based on formative processes and acquired knowledge play a significant, formative role themselves over time. For instance, expectations of typical developmental patterns become part of self-identity. Consider the developmental sequence characteristic of typical children, the expectations that surround typical aging, retiring, and so forth. The meaning of life is tied up with expectations that are just as much about the future as they are about the present. We naively assume that we will be healthy throughout our life; we make plans around assumptions of this nature. We become attached to a particular version of self; we fear the version of self without them.

Preconceived notions and ideals about the world as it should be produce often untenable tension for individuals. They can be seen to gather momentum and culminate into schemata that virtually take on an existence of their own and exert great pressure on individuals. How these schemata gain incredibly powerful status is discussed in Section II. In therapy, an individual's schemata are explored and skills to expose, identify, and negotiate their dominance are taught, as is outlined in Sections IV and V.

Disenfranchised Grief

Nonfinite loss embraces events that are an aftermath of varying intensities of trauma and disruption to our life patterns. With no physical death to mourn, grief is more often than not totally disenfranchised. That is, the people involved in these situations are denied a socially recognized right to grieve, a predicament described by Doka (1989) as *disenfranchised grief.* Sometimes, preferring not to appear to be complaining unduly, these very same people actually disenfranchise their own right to grieve. The fear surrounding a possible ostracizing by friends forces individuals to hide their emotions and bury their grief. The grief retains considerable power over the individual, however, and often seeps or bursts out through other avenues. A classic example here is the sometimes intense emotional reaction individuals have to sad themes in movies.

In the midst of expressing one's emotional pain, well-meaning friends and acquaintances tend to make statements designed to reassure and comfort. Consider some common statements that surround nonfinite loss: "You are fortunate your child is alive"; "You should be grateful that they found the cancer in time"; "Count yourself lucky, my wife died from a stroke—you still have yours"; or, in the case of people who have been adopted, "Think how special you must have been to be chosen."

Clearly, grieving becomes complicated: "Then—what have I to grieve? I should be grateful—stop whining." "What am I allowed to grieve? Should I feel bad, guilty for even feeling these feelings?" Instead of encouraging free expression of grief, well-intended statements contribute to distress. The feeling is not legitimized.

In order to understand the complexity of the grieving associated with nonfinite loss, the "bottleneck" that occurs in the legitimization of nonfinite loss and the emotional expression of the associated grief is explained in Section II. For example, through the expression of their own emotions parents often inadvertently teach children a complex relationship between what they feel and what they are told they are feeling. In particular, children's emotional

"WHAT AM I ALLOWED TO GRIEVE? SHOULD I FEEL BAD, GUILTY FOR EVEN FEELING THESE FEELINGS?"

and physical feelings are sometimes played down and not validated by parents. This learning becomes a central organizing feature in individuals' responses to their own experiences of loss.

Emotional and Cognitive Knots

Emotional and cognitive knots refer to the complicated and sometimes detrimental messages learned in childhood that lead individuals to actually question the legitimacy of their own feelings of loss and to institute limits on the expression of their grief. Most of the emotional and behavioral sequelae surrounding grief are learned in childhood. A child's relationship with his or her feelings, emotional or physiological, can be shared or not shared, allowed or not allowed by his or her parents.

Children may come to feel that when they are sick, ill, or when other bad things happen to them, these are the only times when they receive unconditional love and attention. They learn a unique personal pattern of how to, or how not to, show pain and feelings.

These patterns are taken into the kindergarten and school environments in which groups of children, and sometimes even educators, set similar rules about displays of emotion. There are unspoken limits to what constitutes a reasonable amount of attention. "Attention seeker" becomes a label that is to be feared. Sadly, some individuals subsequently wonder whether their illness has been an attempt to seek this feeling of being "special." The background of these emotional and cognitive knots is discussed at length in Section II.

ORGANIZATION OF THIS BOOK

Section I provides a theoretical basis for the psychoeducational approach to grieving nonfinite loss and grief as advanced throughout this book. Chapter 2 includes a discussion of the traditional theoretical perspectives on loss and grief and their application to situations of nonfinite loss. Extrapolating further, Chapter 3 draws on sociological and psychological literature to conceptualize how nonfinite loss is processed and concludes with a preview of issues pertinent to therapy.

The focus in Section II is on biographical factors, in particular the emotional and behavioral antecedents that shape an individual's response to loss and set the scene for what constitutes personal crises. In exploring childhood patterns, the central role that learning plays in an individual's ability to grieve is exposed. Chapter 4 investigates the socialization and the formation of reality and self. This learning process lays the foundation for an individual's expectations in life and the central part these expectations exert in identity formation. Considerable time is spent in scrutinizing the patterns that form within individuals and attention is drawn to the development and subtleties of comfort zones. In Chapter 5, the place of expectations—past, present, and future—in the interpretation of loss is discussed. Chapter 6 examines how learning affects an individual's emotional experience of loss throughout development into adulthood.

Section III explores the role that fear, anxiety, and dread play in the life-span development of an individual. Chapter 7 introduces a range of interesting examples that illustrate children's and adolescents' fear of the world and their attempts to overcome that fear. In Chapter 8, attention turns to the origins of dreaded events (looking beyond those that are obvious). Consideration is given to the fear of no longer being or remaining "special." Chapter 9 focuses on the private reputation of dreaded events, which represent threats to identity, and the dread that surrounds the damage to, or the losing of, one's identity.

Section IV expands on the complexities in grieving nonfinite loss. In its examination of the effect of cognitive development on grieving, Chapter 10 argues that the sophistication of the grieving process may well be beyond the capabilities of children and may be somewhat compromised by the tasks of adolescence. That is not to say that children or adolescents have no grief; rather, they may not be able to complete the grieving process. The chapter emphasizes that recognition must be given to how cognitive and socioemotional development actually shield the child from the core meaning and significance of loss. Chapter 11 develops the notion of *clear and unclear threat* and its implications for the grieving process. As illustrated in Chapter 12, nonfinite loss evolves; it has chameleon-like characteristics. A series of vignettes in this chapter illustrates how nonfinite loss can demand a "wait and see" approach. Chapter 13, the final chapter in Section IV, provides a representation of characteristic cycles in grieving nonfinite loss.

The foundation provided in Sections I to IV of this book seeks to show that the fragility of individuals and the complex requirements of therapy are abundantly clear. In adopting a sensitive approach to the position of the client, the therapist's weaving and modulation of psychoeducational tasks sometimes occur over protracted periods of time. Optimally, the therapist becomes the coach or mentor in devising strategies that are required in the mastering of nonfinite loss.

To address these strategies, Section V includes three chapters. Chapter 14 covers issues of direct relevance to the psychoeducational practice of counseling those who are grieving nonfinite loss. Chapter 15 summarizes the basic principles that client and therapist must follow in co-creating the resilience that is essential to the preservation of identity, the reinstatement of control, and attachment to emerging reality. In conclusion, Chapter 16 details eight case studies that describe the therapy as it might be applied as individuals learn to cope with disability, chronic illness, and dementia.

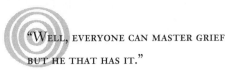

"WELL, EVERYONE CAN MASTER GRIEF
BUT HE THAT HAS IT."

—WILLIAM SHAKESPEARE, MUCH ADO
ABOUT NOTHING, ACT III, SCENE 2,
LINE 28; IN CRAIG, 1943, P. 130

CHAPTER 2

NONFINITE LOSS AND TRADITIONAL THEORETICAL PERSPECTIVES ON GRIEF

Beginning with a broad description of the grief process, this chapter presents five theoretical perspectives of grief and discusses how they might be applied to the grieving of nonfinite loss. Various theorists have described grief as an adaptive, cognitive process of dealing with loss, disappointment, and change (Jacobson, 1957; Parkes, 1971, 1975, 1988; Pollock, 1978; Rubin, 1983). The change that is forced by a significant loss is the primary dynamic in this cognitive adaptation (e.g., Bowlby, 1980; Freud, 1917; Horowitz, 1990; Lindemann, 1944; Rochlin, 1965). Essentially, this dynamic represents an interplay between two opposing forces inherent in an individual's nature: innate resistance to change versus the inevitability of having to change. When serious life events occur, they threaten a person's reality, and inner models of the world are forced to change. According to Bowlby, for an individual this "work" involves the redefinition of self and situation and is the "cognitive act on which all else turns" (1980, p. 94).

THE GRIEF PROCESS

Grief is a complex process, encompassing a range of emotional responses, subjective experiences, physiological changes, and behavioral reactions (Averill, 1968). As characterized by Parkes (1965), typical grief involves a brief period of numbness, attacks of yearning and anxiety alternating with

17

longer periods of depression and despair, and preoccupation with thoughts of the lost person or object that decline in intensity over time. An essential element of grief is the expression of sadness or sorrow (Bowlby, 1977; Clayton, Desmaris, & Winokur, 1968; Jacobs et al., 1987; Parkes, 1975; Parkes & Weiss, 1983; Rubin, 1989).

Ideally, the grieving response is sporadic: two steps forward, one step back, with time on and time off the grieving task. This rhythm protects the individual from becoming overwhelmed by the emotional nature of the task and the uncertainty of the future and provides a harbor from a head-on encounter with the magnitude of the threat to self. Optimally, for grieving to proceed, a personal minimization of the threat to self takes place and reality is reworked in tolerable amounts. This bit-by-bit approach works on a fail-safe principle. If reality is reworked in small doses, there is a greater chance of an individual receiving positive feedback that he or she can survive the loss. Such feedback, in turn, encourages individuals to proceed with the task of grieving. This process is not unlike the sequence of separation from parents and individuation that children make as they experience increasing exposure to an adult world.

A person's reality and models of the world are generated from childhood. As individuals mature, these models become incrementally imbued with a great deal of meaning and significance. In essence, they consolidate into a representation of a sense of self. Reworking of these models involves a series of compromises between the wish for what was and what might have been, and what actually is emerging on a minute-to-minute basis, day-by-day in one's life (Deutsch, 1937; Marris, 1986; Volkan, 1970; Waller, 1938).

The act of giving up a particular image or version of self to which one has become attached is a major compromise, even to the point of impasse. The threat of having to give up this version of self may be assessed as so threatening as to evoke thoughts of suicide. People struggling with such threat often set up a relationship with the idea of suicide: "I'll last just until my kids have grown up." This compromise, of giving up versions of self and the world, has been used to explain much of the emotional pain that accompanies the process of grieving (Horowitz, 1990; Marris, 1986; Parkes, 1975; Volkan, 1970; Waller, 1938). At the same time, it explains the general resistance of the individual concerned to undertake the process.

In the case of nonfinite loss, the resistance is made all the more difficult because of 1) the feared status that has become invested in some personal experiences: "Who am I frightened of being or becoming?"; and 2) the process of idealization, or romanticizing what could have been or what was, which tends to remain unchallenged because individuals do not get an opportunity to personally reality test this expectation or dream.

RELINQUISHING OBJECTS, ATTACHMENTS, WORLDVIEWS, MEANING, AND VERSIONS OF SELF

Five perspectives contribute to the present conceptualization of grief (Bowlby, 1980; Freud, 1917; Horowitz, 1983, 1986, 1990; Marris, 1974, 1986; Parkes, 1972). The perspectives of these five theorists are summarized in Table 2.1. Elements of each perspective have been presented because of the context that they provide for outlining the grieving process associated with nonfinite loss. These elements relate to the complexities involved in the relinquishment of objects, attachments, and worldviews; the intricacies of restoring meaning after personal adversity; and the delicate and fragile process of adjusting to change—that is, adapting to a change in self.

Freud and the Complexity of Relinquishing Objects

The place objects take in an individual's development are of particular relevance to the conceptualization of nonfinite loss. The analogy of a weaving can be used to emphasize the intermeshing of one's experience with these objects. When a loss occurs, a piece of thread with masses of interrelationships with others no longer plays the same part. An outcome is that reverberations are felt throughout the individual. Not only does a person lose a part of his or her self, but his or her physiological system actually is felt or experienced differently.

The functional process of mourning in adults has been described by Freud in his classic paper "Mourning and Melancholia." Mourning involves a process of reality testing wherein "each single one of the memories and expectations in which the libido is bound to the object is brought up and hypercathected" (1917, p. 245). For three principal reasons, Freud saw the process as necessarily protracted. First, Freud proposed that "people never willingly abandon a libidinal position" (p. 244); second, the emotional pain accompanying a loss predicts considerable opposition to expediting the grief process; and finally, the object embodies infinite conscious and unconscious impressions for the individual. That is, the individual's relationship with the lost object involves a variety of feelings, thoughts, and expectations related to past, present, and future. The gradual nature of the process of letting go (i.e., *decathection*) serves an important defensive function, protecting the mourner from being overwhelmed by the vast implications of the loss.

The defensive advantage of *gradually* letting go of one's expectations of self and the world is not as viable when a loss assumes nonfinite proportions. Instead, a plethora of triggers representing what is lost, both in the present and in the future, combine with the fear of who or what one might become. Take the young woman with an incipient degenerative illness who finds herself staring at a woman of the same age, able-bodied,

Table 2.1. Prominent theorists on loss and grief: Cognitive task of grieving, process, and characteristic responses

Theorist	Cognitive task of grieving	Process	Characteristic responses
Bowlby (1980)	Redefining self and situation	Phase 1:[a] Numbing	Feeling of being stunned, tense, and apprehensive; attacks of panic, anger; outbursts of intense emotion
		Phase 2: Instinctual urge to recover lost object—episodically registers reality of loss	Persistent yearning,[b] searching, intense pining, distress, restlessness, insomnia, preoccupation with loss, fantasies and intermittent hope of recovery of lost object, disappointment, anger, weeping, deep and pervasive sadness
		Phase 3: Behavior of Phase 2 is extinguished as individual learns object is lost; response systems cease to be focused on object, leading to a state of disorganization.	Disorganization, pain, despair, possible depression, alarm, anxiety
		Phase 4: Reorganization as representational models of the self and world are aligned to the new life situation.	
Freud (1917)	Reviewing the inner world and detaching memories and hopes from the lost object	Reality testing—decathecting memories and expectations tied to the lost object	Painful frame of mind, loss of interest in the outside world, preoccupation with lost object, relationship

[a]Bowlby (1980) proposed that there was no clear demarcation between phases.
[b]Characteristics of Phase 2 extend although reduced in intensity into the following phases.

Horowitz (1983, 1988, 1990)	Restoring self-organization and schemas to an acceptable accord with reality	Phase 1: Outcry;[c] serious mismatch between enduring schema and current working model[d]	
		Phase 2: Variable oscillation of two states[e]	Avoidance of reminders, thoughts, and feelings; social withdrawel
		• Denial/avoidance— increased control over ideas and feelings	
		• Intrusion—conscious reviews and recognition of significance of the loss to self	Recollections of what has been lost; dreams; reduced concentration
		Phase 3: "Working through"; frequency and intensity of states reduce	
		Phase 4: Period of "relative" completion (i.e., enduring schema are in relative and acceptable accord with reality)	
Marris (1974, 1986)	Psychological reintegration, restoration of continuity of meaning	Complex conflict between contradictory impulses. Individual wants to consolidate all that is still valuable and important in the past, while reestablishing a meaningful pattern of relationship in which loss is accepted	Numbness, somatic symptoms, preoccupation with deceased alternating with painful reminders of loss, futility, withdrawal from all relationships, guilt, hostility, anger, irritability, bitterness

[c]This phase may occur.

[d]The term *working model* applies to transient schema derived from perception of external reality. *Enduring schemas* organize this perception. Enduring schemas involve the role relationship model of the self with the object prior to the change or loss. They are activated by inner wishes and are less situationally dependent (Horowitz, 1990).

[e]Denial or intrusion states may predominate.

(continued)

Table 2.1. *(continued)*

Parkes (1972, 1986)	Process of realization that involves a reassessment of the world and how the self relates to it	Phase 1: Numbness during which fact of loss is partially disregarded	State of high arousal, autonomic disturbance; separation anxiety
		Phase 2:[f] Yearning, urge to recover lost object; permanence rather than the fact of loss is disregarded	Episodic pangs of anxiety and psychological pain,[9] restless, aimless hyperactivity; preoccupation, rumination of lost object; pining as the subjective and emotional component of the urge to search for the lost object
		Phase 3: Disorganization and despair • Permanence and fact of loss accepted • Attempts to recover object given up—no object to organize activity	
		Phase 4: Reorganization of the behavior	

[f]Parkes (1975) saw no clear demarcation between phases; individual ranges back and forth each time he or she becomes aware of another discrepancy between world as it is and internal model of it.

[9]Characteristics of Phase 2 extend into the following phases but are reduced in intensity.

walking briskly. At the same time, a fleeting image of a mother and child catches her attention. The young woman can't help but ask herself: "What will my condition mean for my life? How will it manifest itself? Where will it take me?" A man is wheeled past her. "Has he got what I have? Will I be like him?" This is a wide-angled lens. In bereavement the triggers are more discriminant and may serve a dual function. For instance, there is a strange comfort in the riveting to things, people, or places that are reminiscent of the deceased.

Traditionally, in psychoanalytic writings the main process involved in mourning involves identification with the lost object, a process that can, in part, be seen as compensatory for the loss (Fenichel, 1946; Freud, 1917; Pollack, 1961; Rochlin, 1965). That is, by taking on some characteristic or aspect (e.g., cause championed, belief, mannerism) of the deceased, the loved lost object lives on inside of the individual. In a sense, the bereaved can be seen to keep alive an aspect of the person who has died. In bereavement this can offer a certain consolatory effect, but the identification in nonfinite loss is less clear-cut and offers only an equivocal consolation. Inevitably, identification with who or what "was" creates considerable tension because the source of the grief remains. In situations of nonfinite loss, the individual is left to identify with the adversity. He or she may take on the cause of the stigmatized, join advocacy groups, or find a greater depth of self in his or her newly found empathy. Part of this process also represents a type of compensatory minimization of what has been lost; this concept is reflected in comments such as "I would never have had these opportunities had this not happened to me."

"WHAT WILL MY CONDITION MEAN FOR MY LIFE? HOW WILL IT MANIFEST ITSELF? WHERE WILL IT TAKE ME?"

Bowlby and the Relinquishment of Attachments

Bowlby's attachment perspective describes a set of behaviors elicited by the breaking of a significant attachment. An individual's attachment—or bond—with the lost object provides the foundation for Bowlby's (1960, 1961, 1973, 1977, 1980) theoretical approach to grief. Drawing comparisons between his own observations of the behavior of infants and young children when removed from their mother (1960, 1961, 1977) and ethological studies of higher animals (i.e., Lorenz, 1954), Bowlby identified a series of attachment (e.g., bonding) behaviors that he concluded had a biological function of survival in response to separation. Separation was observed in individuals to elicit the following sequential phases: 1) numbing, 2) yearning and searching for the lost object, 3) disorganization and despair when the irreversibility of the loss is realized, and 4) a period of reorganization.

Prior to the final phases of disorganization and reorganization, Bowlby (1961) proposed that there is a strong tendency—usually involuntary, unconscious, and instinctual—to attempt to recover the lost object. Because this tendency is met with repeated disappointment, Bowlby hypothesized, the principles of learning theory could apply as an explanation for the gradual extinction of this urge to recover the lost object. With no object to organize behavior, Bowlby described individuals as undergoing a phase of disorganization and despair that he regarded as indispensable to the final phase of reorganization. A sequence of emotions characterize this process. That is, whereas the first phases are represented by separation anxiety and yearning (i.e., the desire to retrieve the lost object), feelings of depression and anger accompany the acknowledgment that the loss is irretrievable.

Yearning and Searching in Nonfinite Loss   As they mature, individuals establish certain ways of *being* who they are; they gradually become familiar with an integral "version" of their self. It is important to conceptualize this attachment to a version of self and the threat to that version of self as eliciting a similar sequence of involuntary behaviors; namely, yearning and searching for ways to re-establish the previous self. These behaviors automatically are set into action when an individual's identity is threatened. The recycling of yearning and searching is likely behavior, obviously, for people who have been adopted and individuals in situations involving separation and infertility. By closely examining the behavior pattern of an individual following any significant threat, however, behaviors symbolizing yearning and searching are seen to be ubiquitous.

In later discourse, Bowlby (1973, 1980) discussed in more detail the role of cognitive theory in the mourning process. When confronted with information that forebodes loss, each individual processes the information in reference to preexisting cognitive structures, for which Bowlby (1980) used the concept of *working models of the world*. Because these models are constructed in individuals since early childhood, Bowlby proposed that these structures or models are so ingrained that they operate automatically and are largely resistant to change.

When an unwelcome situation forces the revision of such models, the task is recognized as both arduous and painful. Despite the irreversible nature of the information, the tendency is to avoid certain information and revert to old models of the world. To avoid the overwhelming nature of unwelcome information, the task of reorganization proceeds in fits and starts. Following the initial impact or numbing phase, a period of verification similar to Freud's (1917) account of reality testing occurs. According to Bowlby, the oscillation among established models and incompatible new information explains the fluctuation of feelings experienced in the grieving process.

The Difficulty in Ending the Search   The intricate development and enmeshing of one's self and one's models of the world point to the extreme disequilibrium that major change in life is likely to produce. In this state, an individual directs attention to the recovery of equilibrium. This might be likened to an instinctual urge to recover a vantage point that facilitates a sense of survival. A set of nonvolitional behaviors are signaled. The often amorphous nature of nonfinite loss means that extinguishing the searching behavior is difficult, if not impossible, to achieve. It might be useful to consider the role that rehabilitation, surgery, drugs, and new technology play in the fueling of dreams, hopes, and wishes. Continually, these aspects flirt with the notion of irrevocability. The searching behavior can organize itself around alternative aspects of the loss that might be reclaimable, aspects or abilities not yet verified as lost.

Amid this search for balance, reorganization of models of the world is obviously complex. Bowlby commented on individuals' ingrained tendency to rely on models of the world and to resist change and endeavor to revert to old models of the world. This inertia is a similar factor in situations of nonfinite loss. Depending on the circumstances surrounding a particular loss, arguably the resistance might be encouraged. Alternatively, in situations of traumatic loss, there is a risk that resistance might be broken down too abruptly, forcing an individual beyond his or her comfort zone.

As the particularities of loss reveal themselves only over time, the alignment of models of self and the world to the emerging situation has no recourse but to remain imperfect. The individual oscillates within a context of possibilities diminishing and possibilities lost. A form of separation anxiety surrounds increased distancing from being able to hold onto old versions of self and the world. At the same time, the distancing actually forces an intensification of the attachment to the old version of self. The woman experiencing physical decline through an ongoing medical condition or disability sees what she might have been. Unfortunately, the triggers often represent an idealized version of the self that has been lost. That is, loss tends to make an individual focus on the positive points, not the average or low points, of previous versions of self. Thus, the process of compensating for, or minimizing, the threat to self is made more difficult.

Parkes and the Relinquishment of One's Internal Worldview

The concept of the individual's cognitive model of the world begins to assume central importance in the theories of Parkes (1971, 1975, 1988) and Marris (1982, 1986). For Parkes, grief arises from an "awareness of a discrepancy between the world that is and the world that should be" (1988, p. 54). In describing the latter, Parkes employed the term *assumptive world*

(Cantril, 1950). Representing an individual's unique reality, the assumptive world stands for a strongly held set of preconceptions about the world and self (Parkes, 1975).

Although essentially synonymous with Bowlby's world models, Parkes (1971, 1975) shifted attention from bereavement and employed this concept to explain a relationship between major change and loss. That is, losses occur whenever there is an unwelcome major change in an individual's life (Lewin, 1935), which forces one to relinquish established assumptions or expectations held about the world and self.

As reality continues to challenge the appropriateness of previous models, the individual is forced to slowly learn of successive discrepancies between his or her inner and outer worlds. Drawing on his own study, which provided accounts of patients following the amputation of their limbs, and on Fried's (1963) study of individuals grieving for a lost home, Parkes argued that the components of this process are similar irrespective of the nature of the loss. Both involve a painful process of realization, "of making real inside the self events which have already occurred in reality outside" (1972, p. 344).

Relinquishing assumptions about the world is a principal component of adaptation underpinning the grieving process. Like Bowlby, Parkes (1986) described the phases of grieving (i.e., numbness, yearning, disorganization, and reorganization) as behavioral and emotional manifestations of this process. The protracted nature of grieving reflects the individual's resistance to giving up aspects of the familiar world. In the first instance, the individual will employ strategies to defend against the full realization of the loss (e.g., avoiding situations that reveal discrepancies). It is the strategy of avoidance that is particularly compromised in situations of nonfinite loss such as an ongoing medical condition or disability.

Still, despite eventual acknowledgment that parts of the old world are obsolete, the individual vacillates between the "lost world" and the ongoing construction of the new one. Although this tendency decreases over time, Parkes (1986) noted the persisting influence of the lost world. Events that occur years after a loss are predicted to bring the lost world to mind and precipitate the individual's return to the pining of the second phase. Similarly, Parkes (1986) acknowledged the tendency for world models to be modified incompletely. In such instances, Parkes postulated that they would exert a continuing influence (i.e., old assumptions and expectations relevant to former times persist).

Marris and the Restoration of Meaning

The processes of change were further explored by Marris (1986) in relation to personal and social contexts. He placed less importance on the loss of an object than on the associated collapse of the structure of meaning dependent on it. Marris (1986) argued that this principle accounts for the distress associated with any major change (e.g., loss of a home or neighborhood, political change). Grieving and the assimilation of loss is a process of reconstructing meaning. Marris used the concept "structures of meaning" in the same sense as Bowlby's world models and Parkes's assumptive world.

Drawing on Bowlby's attachment theory (1973, 1980) and Piaget's (1970) account of the development of conceptual abilities and relationships, Marris (1982, 1986) focused attention on the development of meaning that accompanies a child's first experiences with a principal attachment figure. Apart from providing the foundation for an individual's emotional structure, Marris (1982, 1986) proposed that innate predispositions to conceptualize and to become attached interact with experience from earliest childhood to form habits of feeling, behavior, and perceptions.

A result of the interaction between innate predispositions and early experience is a context of meaning that is psychologically integrated and represents an individual's identity. According to Marris (1986), any change that contradicts assumptions about one's world of experience disrupts one's ability to organize experience in a meaningful way and can be termed a loss. Grief represents the struggle to retrieve this sense of meaning. In adapting to the change, however, an individual must overcome his or her universal impulse to restore the past. Marris (1986) referred to this tendency as the "conservative impulse."

Yet, there are limits to this conservatism. Grief is regarded as an expression of the conflict between the despair of giving up the lost object and the impulse to escape from everything that involves reminders. Marris (1986) postulated that, in the end, the individual actually is forced to face and master the conflict itself because giving up the lost object and escaping from everything that involves reminders of the lost object create considerable stress.

The gradual resolution of this conflict is a process similar to that of identification professed by psychoanalytic theorists as the key process of mourning (e.g., Freud, 1917; Pollock, 1970, 1978). The essential meanings of the relationship with the lost object are abstracted to become a set of purposes or ideals in the present (Marris, 1986). Thus, although the object itself is given up, a type of linking object is formed in the preservation and restoring of its essential meaning for the individual. In a sense, the lost person lives on. This theme also is taken up in nonfinite loss. Optimally, meaning and purpose are extracted from the personal adversity, and ways of continuing to represent self and maintain a certain consistency are sought. As noted elsewhere, this form of identification is frequently seen in the causes that people take on, irrespective of the nature of the loss.

Horowitz and Change in Inner Models

A primary focus of the theories of Horowitz (1983, 1986, 1988, 1990) involved the psychological response to serious life events. Like the previously mentioned theorists, Horowitz (1983) conceived adjustment as a painful reinterpretation of models of the self, others, and the world. Horowitz (1983, 1990), however, paid greater attention to the role of unconscious processes.

According to Horowitz (1990), unconscious mental processes dictate much of the experience of mourning; particular emotional moods, memories, and triggers are largely subconsciously initiated by the person in mourning. Drawing on the work of Breuer and Freud (1895), Horowitz (1986) identified the task of revising inner models after deaths, personal injuries, and other serious life events as a balance between impulsive aims at mastery of the experience by repetition in thought and unconscious defensive aims at avoidance of emotional pain.

Information Processing   Horowitz (1990) proposed that it is the variation of this balance over time that leads to changes in what a person consciously experiences. Between the recognition of loss and adaptation, Horowitz (1986, 1990) identified five phases: 1) outcry, 2) denial, 3) intrusion, 4) working through, and 5) completion. Each phase can be characterized in relationship to the balance and change between intrusive experiences (e.g., thoughts about loss invade consciousness) and avoidance (e.g., reminders are avoided for fear of psychological distress). As aspects of the loss are more easily contended with, this balance reflects both decreasing intrusion and avoidance. This process represents Horowitz's (1990) model of mourning. Involving schematic change, enduring inner models (i.e., self-schemata) are matched against "working models" (i.e., models based on immediate perceptions of external reality). During the interval between the phase of outcry and completion a series of discrepancies between enduring self-schemata and working models elicit varying degrees and intensity of psychological distress.

Depending on the intensity of emotional pain and the individual's ability to tolerate it, information processing is interrupted by controls that modify the cognitive processes. The process itself reflects the underlying cognitive change required and the information processing that is forced by the review and reformation of inner models.

SUMMARY

This chapter has introduced principal perspectives on grief and their application to nonfinite loss. Focus has been given to the cognitive act that underpins the work of grieving and the adaptive use of defenses as they limit the incoming information that threatens to overwhelm the coping abilities of an individual faced with significant change following loss. Specifically, the individual is required to review and rework the view of the world as it relates to a changed reality. Through this process, the work of grieving can be seen to surround the relinquishing of an intricate attachment to an object, person, ideal, or wish that has, over time, become enmeshed to form part of a notion of self. The endangering of the attachment simultaneously threatens this notion or version of self. In Section II, prior to tracing how an attachment to a version of self develops, the complexities surrounding the grieving associated with nonfinite loss are reviewed. The section also introduces an interpretive framework against which loss is processed and the implications for griefwork.

CHAPTER 3

LOSS AND GRIEF AS COUNTERPARTS

It is generally accepted that loss precipitates grief. Historically, the term *loss* has referred to irrevocable loss, or more commonly, loss through death. Early theoretical discourse, however, suggested that the lost "object" did not necessarily have to be a person. It could be "the loss of some abstraction...such as one's country, liberty, an ideal and so on" (Freud, 1917, p. 243). Engel elaborated, describing grief as "the characteristic response to the loss of a valued object, be it a loved person, a cherished possession, a job, status, home, country, an ideal, a part of the body" (1961, p. 18). The subjective significance and meaning of the loss is of central importance to the individual. A multitude of possible scenarios for grief have emerged from the literature, for example, those surrounding elective abortion (Peppers & Knapp, 1980), stillbirth (Lewis & Page, 1978), and the relinquishment of a child through adoption (Condon, 1986; Winkler & van Keppel, 1984).

Grief also has been seen to accompany more enigmatic losses, such as those that parallel the process of human growth and development (Pollock, 1978; Schneider, 1984; Sullender, 1985), and the loss of dreams and wishes that are embedded in such development (Grayson, 1970; Shabad, 1989). Life experiences involving ongoing medical conditions or disabilities provide potent examples of how unfulfilled wishes reveal themselves over time. The concept of loss as involving a process of realization that occurs over an individual's life span has, as Olshansky (1962)

31

recognized in his term *chronic sorrow*, implications for the individual's grieving response. As established in Chapter 1, we have chosen the term *nonfinite loss* to refer to losses that are contingent on development; time; and dysynchrony with hopes, wishes, ideals, and expectations.

Both in the literature and in practice there has been a tendency to rely on the theoretical paradigms specific to death and dying to explain grief responses in general. This position is based on the assumption that these paradigms are not only relevant but also can be used to interpret a range of personal experiences of loss, such as that of parents of children who have disabilities (Collins, 1982; Robinson & DeRosa, 1980) or families of individuals with acquired brain injuries (Groveman & Brown, 1985). Widespread adoption of this theoretical perspective has led to dangerous stereotyping and unreasonable expectations being placed on those experiencing losses other than those related to death. For instance, irrespective of the nonfinite nature of the loss, individuals often have been expected to resolve their grief and accept their loss.

In cases likely to involve nonfinite loss, the traditional focus has been on an event (e.g., the time of diagnosis, the time of separation, the time of the accident). Taken as a discrete event, the loss is viewed as an entity distinct from the process that precedes or follows it (Mestrovic, 1985). From this perspective, it is often assumed that the individual absorbs the full implications of the loss at a particular point in time; failure to do so is then seen as pathological. This focus fails to take into account or legitimize the persistence of grief in the case of nonfinite loss.

According to Worden (1991), mourning involves four tasks: 1) accepting the reality of the loss, 2) working through to the pain of grief, 3) adjusting to an environment in which the deceased is missing, and 4) emotionally relocating the deceased and moving on with life. As Worden acknowledged in relation to bereavement, there is a sense in which mourning is never finished. He described the difficulties individuals encounter in adjusting to an environment in which the deceased is missing. For some individuals, it appears that loss of a sense of self and one's world looms so large that their loss converts to a nonfiniteness in nature. In most situations of nonfinite loss, however, there are clearly identifiable and recurring obstacles to each task. Characteristics of some life experiences camouflage the loss, characteristics of cognitive stages of development obscure the meaning of the loss, and the pain of grief must often be put on hold against the constant physical energy of continued caring demands. How to adapt? How to withdraw emotional energy when the source of one's grief lives on? Even the prospect can be daunting.

Departing from traditional assumptions, then, loss and grief can be viewed as counterparts: Neither can adequately be explained in isolation from the specifics relating to the other. An understanding of the complicated and evolutionary nature of loss is fundamental to a perspective on grieving that is appropriate and relevant to therapeutic practice. Some investigators have suggested the persistence of grief in specific situations (e.g., relinquishing a child through adoption: Deykin, Campbell, & Patti, 1984; Winkler & van Keppel, 1984; loss of home: Fried, 1963). In general, however, both theoretical and empirical approaches have neglected to focus on the characteristics of grief that might be particular to differing types of loss.

Certain life experiences challenge an individual's taken-for-granted identity and worldview. In cases such as chronic illness, disability, and life-threatening and terminal disease, an individual's core identity becomes fragile. When someone has cancer, for example, he or she often feels estranged from the self previously taken for granted. This may cause the individual to have feelings of disassociation, disorganization, and chaos. Yet, such a threat does not have to be of major proportions to wreak havoc. Depending on the meaning and significance one attributes to views of one's self and the world, it is conceivable that any change may contribute to such an outcome. Thus, the most urgent objectives of a therapeutic approach are first to diminish feelings of chaos and disorganization that often follow the occurrence of dreaded events and then to establish some control over thoughts and emotion.

Our conceptualization of nonfinite loss draws on specific elements found in the psychological and sociological literature base, including the individual's context of meaning, discrepancy between expectations and reality, accumulation of meaning, and resistance to change. Here, these elements are reviewed to explain the interpretive framework against which, it is argued, loss is processed. The therapeutic guidelines emerging from these conceptualizations are included in the summary at the end of this chapter. These guidelines are then used to preview issues to be addressed subsequently in this book; thus, they represent a logical and gradual progression in the transition from theory to practice.

THEORETICAL FOUNDATIONS IN
THE CONCEPTUALIZATION OF NONFINITE LOSS

The critical links between sociology and psychology in conceptualizing loss and explaining grief responses (e.g., Bowlby, 1973, 1980; Marris, 1982; Parkes, 1971) provide the theoretical framework for the types of loss and grief under discussion. That is, the meaning and definition of loss can be found in the interactions between the life experiences of an individual and the social environment in which that individual exists. In short, the significance a negative life event assumes has been established well before the actual loss event takes place.

In addition, the complex psychological tendencies that underpin the grief process are a response to multiple influences from both within and outside the individual. Specific to the present discussion are theories related to personal constructions of reality and models of the world that find their formation in early childhood (e.g., Bowlby, 1980; Horowitz, 1988; Marris, 1986; Parkes, 1971, 1975). Researchers have contended that the comprehensive nature of primary socialization (i.e., learning that occurs in the original family/caregiver environment) guarantees that the individual's worldview and internalized models are intrinsic to the human condition and that these models will have been attached with personal and social meaning and significance (Berger & Luckmann, 1966; Marris, 1986; Rochlin, 1965).

Loss and an Individual's Context of Meaning

Marris (1986) argued that an inevitable outcome of one's direct life experience is the psychological integration of a context of meaning (i.e., a framework of rules, cause-and-effect associations) that eventually accounts for a range of intrinsic expectations. This integration culminates in an ordered perspective of one's world, including "what is taken for granted about attributes of events, human nature, objects and an order of things remembered" (Shibutani, 1955, p. 163). Similarly, universal sequences of biological and cognitive development are ascribed meaning within the social world (Erikson, 1965; Neugarten, 1976; Piaget, 1929/1951). Involved also is an order of things and roles that might be expected. Merton and Rossi (1968) used the term *anticipatory socialization* to describe this process.

The context for defining loss, then, begins with an individual's assumptions about reality (Marris, 1986; Parkes, 1971, 1975, 1988), and the expectations, hopes, and wishes that are contained in his or her world of assumptions. These formative processes described in the literature provide the backdrop for a person's response to an experience that is contrary to expectations. The result of a negative life experience is a forced and altered view of the world and the perceived discrepancy with the world that should have been. The process of assimilating loss and change over time appears to be related to the amount of discrepancy that may arise between the previously taken-for-granted world and that world as it is now changed.

Discrepancy Between Expectations and Reality

Sociologists and social psychologists have identified an individual's expectations as an important reference point in their personal definition of loss (Crosby, 1982; Grayson, 1970; Marris, 1986; Parkes, 1971; Pettigrew, 1968). Adopting the theories of Parkes (1971, 1975, 1988), discrepancies with these expectations are conceptualized as continuing occasions for personal perceptions of loss. Some measure of the loss can be found in the extent to which a negative life event jeopardizes the individual's assumptions about the world. For example, Ondaatje described his protagonist's utter despair of ever making sense of brutal human violence:

> No one could ever give meaning to it. She used to believe that meaning allowed a person a door to escape grief and fear. But she saw that those who were slammed and stained by violence lost the power of language and logic....Death, loss, was unfinished; so you could not walk through it. (2000, pp. 55–56)

Those life events that threaten major postulates or schemata that help us to make sense of the world represent significant threats to an individual; in particular, his or her sense of identity is at risk. When much of the identity is threatened, it is conceivable that individuals might initially perceive themselves as completely alienated from the self and world they previously took for granted. For example, when an individual receives a diagnosis of a disease or condition that will be noticeable or disfiguring, this changes the person's self-image and seriously inhibits customary social interactions. Simultaneously, a person's sense of balance or homeostasis is threatened. The result may be chaos; a feeling likely to be experienced is that of being out of control, with accompanying physical feelings of anxiety and fear. It follows that, in cases of nonfinite loss, the threat may loom repeatedly, rendering a traditional therapeutic goal (e.g., resolution of grief) unattainable.

Indication of the extent of the threat can be found in an individual's life experiences. Although the meaning and significance of loss will have been established from early childhood, when viewed as a continuous process, the meaning will be subject to review as the individual's development offers further perspectives over time (Pollock, 1978; Rochlin, 1965). These further perspectives will evolve against the background of the numerous systems (e.g., family, work environments) that impinge on an individual throughout his or her life span. Inevitably, within this context, cumulative meanings will be attributed to an original loss. For instance, the same woman who grapples with the possibility of childlessness in her late thirties struggles with the loss of being a grandmother in her sixties. A daughter who loses her mother to Alzheimer's disease may feel this loss more acutely when she herself becomes a mother, or if she contracts an illness that creates a yearning for her mother's support.

Accumulation of Meaning and Dismissed Emotional Pain

This propensity for loss to accumulate meaning over time is not peculiar to nonfinite loss. Over the passage of time, the definition of any loss, including the death of a significant other, is constantly redefined in the present relative to what it has meant in the past and what was expected of it in the future. This is well demonstrated in relation to the death of a parent in early childhood (Pollock, 1978; Silverman, Nickman, & Worden, 1992). Often, in reaching out for counseling in their twenties or thirties, individuals who have experienced this reveal the enormous "hole" this loss continues to make both in their present life and when they contemplate the future. In many cases, the death of a father or mother gathers significance over time.

Counseling these individuals may reveal further that the grief that has accompanied their loss has not been dealt with and may have lain quite dormant. A typical example would be a man in his twenties who, when asked what he did after the death of his father when he was a 15-year-old, looked almost bemused and replied, "I put my head down to the books, and I became an academic success story!" In the final analysis, in terms of loss, *finite* appears to be an elusive term.

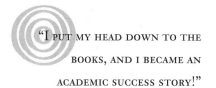

"I PUT MY HEAD DOWN TO THE BOOKS, AND I BECAME AN ACADEMIC SUCCESS STORY!"

Schemata and Their Resistance to Change

The process of shaping and modifying an individual's early schemata formed in childhood is a continuous one. In passing from one developmental stage to another, these cognitive structures are elaborated on, rather than cancelled out (Guidano & Liotti, 1983). That is, these preexisting schematic structures organize knowledge and guide what we notice and how we interpret new information. Originating in early childhood, these schemata are commonly regarded as resistant to change. In the process of socialization, such structures can be seen to be psychologically integrated to the point that they are inseparable from a notion of self. Finding their formation in early socialization (i.e., that of the family/caregiver environment), reinforced in secondary socialization (i.e., during the school years), and attributed with further meaning during adulthood, we argue that individuals become attached to these schemata or cognitive structures. Schemata and the thoughts they generate operate automatically. They provide an interpretive framework against which an individual assesses and processes single or multiple losses.

AN INTERPRETIVE FRAMEWORK

Two schemata (i.e., cognitive structures that are abstract and formative processes) at the core of identity describe the forces that propel the experience of loss. The flowchart in Figure 3.1 illustrates these schemata, which develop in parallel, play a crucial role in an individual's response to loss, and have the utmost bearing on situations of nonfinite loss. It is important to note how these formative processes are enmeshed with self-identity and how a loss event inevitably triggers a threat to identity resulting in loss of control and loss of balance.

Schema A and Schema B

Schema A refers to the commonly held and internalized expectations of what the world should be like. Emerging from what may best be described as a process of reification (i.e., regarding something as concrete or material) (see Figure 3.1), these abstractions about a taken-for-granted reality acquire a fixed and immutable quality. Having accumulated identities of their own, they seem beyond control. It is almost as if they have become embodied, no longer recognized merely as social constructions. By way of example, one need only reflect on Shield's quote that opened Chapter 1 of this book. "To get better. To live. To grow up. To be like everyone else. Isn't that what we all want in the end [1997, p. 131]?" We conclude, isn't that what we all *expect*? The working through of unmet expectations—the "should-have-beens"—is central to most counseling sessions that involve nonfinite loss.

Schema B refers to the formative process of attribution, whereby dread is attributed to certain events and life experiences. These are the internalized fears based on observation and the reputation of negative life events. Although there are common and publicly dreaded events (e.g., disability, chronic illness) that have secured a reputation since childhood, certain events (e.g., becoming divorced or unemployed) gain a private reputation and hold particular dread for many individuals. Although it may be possible to diminish their potency, it is virtually impossible to completely eradicate these entrenched fears and attitudes.

Schemas A and B provide the context against which the learning experience of the individual is pitted following a negative life event or episode (e.g., diagnosis of cancer, infertility). The worldview, intrinsic to the human condition, which has become internalized and has acquired personal and social significance and meaning, becomes the basis for defining the loss. The learning experience on which the individual is forced to embark involves a navigation through the shadows cast by the reputation of the dreaded event and unrealized expectations. This

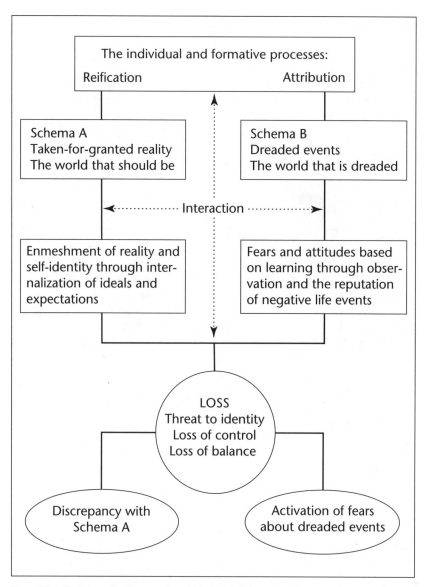

Figure 3.1.   The interpretive framework against which loss is processed.

navigation takes place within and amidst the emerging "new" reality that forms following the negative life experience. The therapeutic principles and processes introduced in this book are determined to coach individuals in achieving the best possible relationship with, and control over, their fears.

Figure 3.2. A drawing depicting the feeling of shadows associated with loss and grief. The interplay of dark and despairing and lighter and more hopeful shadows is considered crucial to an individual's ability to adapt.

Dreams, Hopes, and Shadows

Figure 3.2 is a drawing that depicts how shadows of loss and grief are sometimes dark with despair, sometimes lighter with hope and the promise of making a connection to the emerging reality. For losses that continue to be demarcated over time in one form or another (i.e., nonfinite loss), the interplay among shadows becomes a powerful force indefinitely. Because of the threat this poses to the individual's sense of identity, a connection with purpose and a balance between hope and despair become crucial factors in the person's capacity to adapt.

Any dream, no matter how far-fetched, can serve a purpose. For a person with an amputated leg, the goal of walking—however unlikely—provides protection against an overwhelming identity crisis. Proud protests such as "If *anyone* is going to walk again, it will be me!" underscore the ability to endure a looming personal crisis. Faced with the starkness of a future without

"IF ANYONE IS GOING TO WALK AGAIN, IT WILL BE ME!"

legs, such psychological maneuvers on the part of an individual may actually foster his or her ability to adapt and fuel the mastering of prostheses. Essentially, these goals, which might even be considered fantasies, might be regarded as psychological tension busters.

Even in the case of seemingly indisputable negative information, theorists have identified a crucial role for hope (e.g., Kübler-Ross, 1969; Rochlin, 1965). Against diagnoses of terminal cancer, for instance, hope fuels individuals' determination to change lifestyle patterns and undergo life-threatening treatment regimes. Whatever the scenario, whether an individual acknowledges the permanence of loss, the emerging fact of the loss itself can be seen almost to force a process of habituation. There is no escape from some form of adaptation, even if it involves only minimal adjustment to the reality that is emerging. Coincidentally, a sense of balance or homeostasis and a sense of control are slowly restored, the achievement of which becomes a basic goal of the therapeutic approach to grieving nonfinite loss.

SUMMARIZING AND LOOKING AHEAD

This chapter concludes with a summary of salient points that have been introduced in Section I. These points relate to our conceptualization of loss and the associated grieving process. They incorporate a preview of strategic elements of a psychoeducational approach to therapy, which are being introduced progressively.

Sections II–V expand further on many of these points. The impact of environmental factors on the way in which individuals learn to interact and deal with loss and grief is the focus in Section II. Through an examination of an individual's first learning environment, the origins of schematic structures are identified. Emphasis is placed on the resilience of these assumptions about reality due to the way they mesh with self-identity.

Conceptualizations Summarized

Complexity surrounds the conceptualization of personal loss. Background literature demonstrates that the origins of an interpretive framework for loss stem from an individual's biography. These early beginnings establish what factors will threaten the integrity of an individual's identity.

- In situations of loss that differ in a negative way from common expectations about life-span developments, the individual's interpretive framework contributes to the complicated nature and nonfinite nature of the grieving experience.

- The entrenched nature of schemata serve to explain why the traditional view of grieving as involving a series of clearly identifiable stages leading to "acceptance" is of limited value. Rochlin pointed out that the notion of "acceptance of loss in emotional life is probably neither a clinical fact nor a human characteristic" (1965, p. 131). This view is pivotal to situations of nonfinite loss: In respecting the magnitude of nonfinite loss, it is critical that one have permission to be unaccepting of what has happened to one's self.

Therapeutic Guidelines Previewed

- Shared deference to the loss and grief surrounding an individual's personal adversity permits therapy to proceed; ideally, this is a pervasive feature of the client–therapist interaction. Modulation of the grieving process; the appropriate timing and placement of therapeutic techniques; and close attention to an individual's affect, behavior, and cognitions are put into effect within this context.
- Therapy requires individuals to extricate their current personal experience from past learning. The management of the individual's perception of the reality that is forming following a dreaded event involves reworking entrenched belief systems, worldviews, and messages from childhood. It includes the critical examination of where ideals—the "shoulds"—have come from, what they are about, and scrutinizes the place they play in the client's world.
- Central aspects of therapy involve interactive and parallel processes: the control of information flow, the facilitation of emotional expression through legitimization and memorialization, the pacing of reality testing, and the abstraction of meaning. These areas of focus provide opportunity for positive feedback to clients and foster the development of self-prescriptive strategies and skills. The flowchart in Figure 3.3 illustrates the strategic elements of the psychoeducational approach to therapy.
- Habituation (see Figure 3.3) denotes a gradual adaptation to unremitting stress. Remarkably, individuals seem to be able to habituate to extraordinary levels of stress. Over time, a pattern of fear and anxiety mingling with a vague sense of hope can emerge. This sense of hope raises and lowers its head somewhat in concert with the changing levels of fear and anxiety. An individual dares herself to consider, "Will I regain the use of my arms, my legs? How close to a complete recovery, a normal life, can I get?"

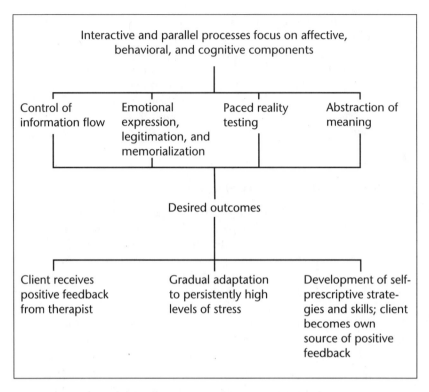

Figure 3.3.   Strategic elements of the psychoeducational approach to therapy.

- Therapy focuses on a stated goal of adaptation with the idea that emotional nonacceptance may represent a symbolic stand—a memorialization to the path individuals' lives might have taken and their place in the new path on which they find themselves. Acceptance? Never! Adaptation? Maybe.

SECTION II

BIOGRAPHY, LOSS, AND GRIEVING

"FROM THE CHILD OF FIVE TO MYSELF IS BUT A
STEP. BUT FROM THE NEW-BORN BABY TO THE
CHILD OF FIVE IS AN APPALLING DISTANCE."
—LEO TOLSTOY, AS CITED IN BECKER,
1973, P. 25

CHAPTER 4

THE FOUNDATIONS OF OUR EXPECTATIONS

An individual's awareness of loss arises from a discrepancy between the world as it is and the world that should be, its meaning and significance, and his or her attachment to it (Parkes, 1988). The world that should be represents a framework of expectations, anticipations, and beliefs. According to Parkes, what one anticipates is based on past experience and is largely a product of one's assumptive world..."the only world we know...or think we know" (1971, p. 103). Parkes's (1971, 1975) term *assumptive world* conceptualizes the personal nature of reality. It is a construction generated from an individual's own experience with the environment and does not exist as an objective fact.

Similar conceptual systems include Marris's (1986) *structures of meaning*, Bowlby's (1980) *world models*, and Kelly's (1955) theory of personal constructs and concepts involving schemas of self and role-relationships (e.g., Fiske & Taylor, 1984; Horowitz, 1988). Central to these models is the emphasis that each places on an individual's reality being represented by a series of unique transactions with his or her environment. This reality becomes the baseline from which the individual interprets a sense of loss. It can be understood usefully as comprising a set of personal patterns.

Section II of this book explores the unique transactions that individuals make with their environment and the personal patterns from which such transactions form. Intensely personal in nature, these patterns encompass the things that have to happen to make one feel intuitively safe, what an individual attributes as meaningful in life, the degree of expression of emotions the individual can tolerate, and the feelings with which the person feels comfortable. In other words, what expectations have to be met for one to feel true to one's self?

Intricate patterns are generated from the transactions that individuals have with their caregivers and world from infancy and childhood. Slowly, over time, a familiarity with one's experiences with the world emerges. Take, for example, a possible waking sequence that leads a young child to think, "The sun comes up, the birds sing, I cry, Mom comes in, Dad ruffles my hair, my brother is called...and I am fed." A myriad of senses surround the sequencing toward the act of being fed. Over time, the familiar becomes the "world that should be": a mass of intricate patterns, a delicate link between psychobiology and expectations that has become woven into a person—so much so that it becomes synonymous with a state of well-being.

"THE SUN COMES UP, THE BIRDS SING, I CRY, MOM COMES IN, DAD RUFFLES MY HAIR, MY BROTHER IS CALLED... AND I AM FED."

The "world that should be" culminates in an abstract physiological and psychological sense of being "at one" with one's self. Not only do these early experiences translate into a reality that is taken for granted, they provide definition for our later experiences and our personal conception of loss. We begin the tracing of personal patterns with an examination of the intricacies of the socialization process and the notion of a "base world." An outcome of this process is the development of comfort zones—familiarity with a way of self and a way of the world. The second part of this chapter examines patterns and comfort zones in detail.

SOCIALIZATION AND THE CONSTRUCTION OF REALITY AND SELF

Defined by Berger and Luckmann as the "comprehensive and consistent induction of an individual into the objective worlds of a society or a sector" (1966, p. 150), socialization throughout a child's development ensures that despite variations in accordance with culture and class, reality will, in large part, be shared by all members of society. The principle function of socialization is to ensure that this reality is internalized to the point that it is taken for granted. The important outcome lies in reality becoming internalized as both a subjective and objective fact (Berger & Luckmann, 1966; Mead, 1934). Although, over the course of an individual's development, his or her subjective reality is progressively modified, some argue that it is inevitable that the knowledge internalized in primary socialization will represent an original reality that persists and is firmly entrenched in consciousness (Berger & Luckmann, 1966; Marris, 1986; Parkes, 1971).

The Base World

Berger and Luckmann (1966) described this overwhelming reality internalized through childhood as *the base world*. They argued that against this reality, subsequent "worlds" often are seen as artificial. This base world embraces a sense of self, a sense of place, and a sense of balance. When talking to people, particularly older adults who have been forced or have of their own volition left their homeland, this notion appears to be encapsulated in their yearning for home.

Home draws together and actually symbolizes the intricate developmental patterns that are woven into a sense of self from day one. These developmental patterns have as their backdrop associated sights, smells, and sounds—all of which will have been absorbed and can have extraordinary resonance. For people who are grieving, such highly charged memories often provide enormous comfort. Similarly, when interactions with the outside world are no longer possible because of old age, dementia, and the like, such memories seem to locate or ground individuals. In an instant, the smell of the sea, freshly mown grass, or the sound of a train transports an individual back through time and restores a sense of self. The following depiction by the 20th-century author Virginia Woolf conveys the potency of childhood memories.

> If life has a base that it stands upon, if it is a bowl that one fills and fills—then my bowl without a doubt stands upon this memory. It is of lying half asleep, half awake in the bed at the nursery at St. Ives. It is of hearing the waves breaking, one, two, one, two, and sending a splash of water over the beach; and then breaking, one, two, one, two, behind the yellow blind. It is of hearing the blind draw its little acorn across the floor as the wind blew the blind out. It is lying and hearing this splash and seeing this light, and feeling it almost impossible that I should be here; of feeling the purest ecstasy I can conceive. (1985, p. 73)

Different "Homes"

Reality and self-identity find their formation in infancy. Both represent generative constructions based on knowledge acquired through learning (Cooley, 1902; Mead, 1934; Popper & Eccles, 1977). As the prime socializing agents (Bowlby, 1980; Erikson, 1965), parents' sociocultural characteristics, beliefs, values, and attitudes will be internalized by the child long before they are recognized as only one possible representation of the world. That is, early infancy is characterized by exposure to direct knowledge that is beyond the infant's ability to critically assess (Flavell, Miller, & Miller, 1993). An inevitable outcome, according to theorists (e.g., Merton, 1957; Merton & Rossi, 1968; Piaget, 1929/1951, 1954), is that aspects of one's world are "inadvertently swallowed whole" (Piaget, 1929/1951, p. 28).

It is evident that some children put up with insidious realities, some of which involve protracted physical, emotional, and sexual abuse. Capturing and understanding the naive state of childhood that actually tolerates this reality is extremely difficult. Many survivors of childhood abuse find it totally elusive. The fact that they, as children, yielded to an adult and allowed themselves to be abused is almost impossible to understand. It seems incongruent with their adult self. For a 40-year-old man abused by his brother from the age of 6, the unfathomable and recurring puzzle is: "Why did I let my brother go on with it? Each night he would come into my bedroom and I would just go along with it. I have never even spoken about it with him—and I'm 40!" Unfortunately, the experiences and learning that take place in childhood happen because a child has not the wherewithal, cognitively or emotionally, to question it. It just becomes what happens, the familiar.

The Naiveté Trap

To capture the naiveté of this developmental stage, with its emotional and cognitive limitations, is to gauge the potency of what an individual learns in childhood. This stage might be likened to a naiveté trap, in which children tolerate, endure, and accept things told and done to them because other options are beyond their emotional or intellectual capabilities. Simply, they might not consider there could be any options. As the work of Piaget (1929/1951) demonstrated, children take the comments made by parents or adults quite literally. A 4-year-old interprets a statement made by his kindergarten teacher, "Eat your breakfast if you want to grow big and strong," to mean, "If you don't eat your breakfast you'll die!"

"Somebody has got it in for us," a parent offhandedly comments to his 7-year-old son. The family must sell their house because the father has become bankrupt due to a run of bad management, bad luck, whatever; but, to the son, the meaning of the parent's comment is factual. In bed that night, when it is dark and late, the comment may blend together with a series of frightening images: a scary man seen on the *Goosebumps* television show, the monster who steals into his bedroom at night, and the stranger in the street who never speaks to him as he walks home from school. This combination of images is stimulated by the father's one throw-away line.

Watching television, a father talks about technical patterns in film-making to his 8-year-old daughter. He makes a random remark: "Watch what happens when the girl leaves the room. Usually this is when something bad happens." A pattern is set. For the next 3 years, Kerry warns her family when she is leaving the room: "I'm off to the bathroom. Be back soon!"

Unfortunately, such remarks can serve as a future explanation for random events in children's lives. They have the potential to become the basis for feelings of persecution and mistrust in the wider environment. The senselessness of remarks, their throw-away quality, are not apparent or questioned until later in life. In fact, it is not until later childhood, early adolescence, that children are able to understand and actually start to question the veracity of the facts that they have swallowed. For instance, an adolescent described the irritation she felt toward her 8-year-old sister: "She just takes everything our Mom and Dad say as truth. Dad's busy telling her about something to do with the Pope. She's just listening as though that's the only religion that there could ever be. I know that's all Dad knows. I feel like pleading with her, 'Question it, question it!'"

Despite the questions a child asks parents and the information that can be scrutinized, much of an individual's knowledge about him- or herself and the world is beyond scrutiny. Because the roots of much of this learning are beyond consciousness (Piaget, 1929/1951), it does not even occur to individuals that their personal knowledge is only one version of the world and that their knowledge or beliefs can be questioned.

FAMILIARITY AND THE DEVELOPMENT OF PATTERNS

The previous paragraphs begin to reveal the insidious nature of the socialization process that ensures that in early childhood, experience and resulting knowledge structures will be formed from a reality that will almost coincide with the family or first caregiver environment (Parsons, 1955). Amid a plethora of novelty, an infant must make familiar the unfamiliar. A number of crucial and sensitive patterns must be deciphered. Basically, the patterns fall into two—not unrelated—camps: survival and security. An infant must work out how to predict the world and how to secure physical and emotional sustenance.

This represents an amazing sorting out process, acknowledged in this chapter's introductory quote by Tolstoy. In this part of the chapter we look at how patterns are created, how they form an individual's expectations, and how the meeting of expectations generates a feeling of safety and balance for that individual. The patterns we specifically discuss are those of care, safety, applause, and attachment. We begin with an introduction that considers the general idea of creating patterns.

Creating Familiar Patterns

Into whatever environment a child is born: happy, erratic, unstable, or war torn, a child will start building a knowledge base. Because the child does not have the capacity to throw out information or things that do not make sense, this is quite a disturbing notion. Children use a set of observations about their caregivers and the significant people in their world to construct their own knowledge base. Facial expressions, emotional feedback, behavior, sounds, and smells will be put together; small nuances, such as eyebrow movements, will be closely observed (Marks, 1987; Stern, 1985). The child will try to extract meaning from these patterns (Bowlby, 1988). Simply put, children begin to create patterns out of their parents' behavior toward the world, them, and the routines that seem to emerge from their environment. This learning culminates in a finely tuned knowledge base that is necessarily skewed around the relationship between children and parents. Because children lack the cognitive capacity to critically assess the meaning of their parents' behavior toward them (Erikson, 1965), the learning is destined to be distorted further. An outcome is a child who actually "reads" the parents' words and behavior, but with a bias.

Many children form a pattern out of chaos. If a parent's behavior and the environment to which the child is exposed constantly change, this task increases in complexity. Greater time is required to make sense and meaning of the child's reality, and understandably there is less time to attend to other developmental tasks (Bowlby, 1988). For instance, a child who has a father who is emotionally unwell will be forming a completely different pattern through observing his behavior than a child whose father is reasonably stable.

If a child's mother is an alcoholic, he or she may be in a state of constant arousal, watching intently for her to become erratic and scary. It is only much later, as the child's cognitive ability increases, that the change of behavior becomes linked to alcohol. As an adolescent, the same child will now understand that his or her mother might be termed an *alcoholic*.

Patterns of Care: Psychobiology and the Regulation of Emotional States

Beginning with the first caregiving environment, an infant's distress from hunger followed by satiation as the caregiver responds to his or her cries forms an early sequence of security and comfort (Bowlby, 1988; Stern, 1985). Understandably, the child's action of exhibiting degrees of physical distress triggers the caregiver's response. The child cannot critically evaluate, however, why the caregiver might respond more quickly sometimes than others. The child is unable to take into account the needs of siblings or the needs of the caregiver that might actually get in the way of the response turn-around time. Instead, children seek reasons and solutions within their own behavior. "Should I cry louder, longer?" Later on, as the child matures, this consideration will become more complex and an assessment of whether one is loved will be included. The caregiver's response times will become a problem to be solved. How do I make her, or him, respond?

The Formation of a Matrix of Associations Senses (i.e., smell, sight, sound, touch, taste), cycles of time, and varying states of physiological equilibrium and disequilibrium contextualize this early learning sequence. That is, associations are being made among states of mind, states of physical distress, and experiences with significant others and the environment. These associations result in a matrix, or set, of conditioning experiences that creates the earliest knowledge structures and organizes memory sequences (Marks, 1987). The way in which these learning experiences consolidate to form self-identity is illustrated in Figure 4.1.

These interactions direct attention to a psychobiological link that theorists such as Hofer (1995) and Stern (1985) researched in their studies on the preverbal life of infants. Although these authors acknowledge the contribution of genetics on physiological and emotional constitution, their studies draw attention to this regulatory pattern between children and caregivers. Not only do early caregivers provide a pattern of inconsistency or consistency of care but also security and safety patterns translate to physiological systems. In application, this might lead to the leeway time a child can give a parent before sensing a feeling of unrest or panic, a type of learned unique toleration or comfort zone around the idea of waiting and trust.

The Place of Regulation According to Hofer "mutual homeostatic regulation" characterizes our first relationship (1995, p. 227). Drawing on experiments with infant rats separated from their mothers, Hofer (1995) transposed the notion of hidden biological regulators to the experience of separation distress in humans. Relationships with caregivers and the environment basically train and regulate an individual's biological clock and lead to synchronized states (i.e., a reciprocity between parent and child). Notably, when children are separated from their parents either through death or divorce, they describe physical sensations, specifically a sensation of discomfort or "heaviness in the tummy." The physical state reflects an intuitive lack of safety. Depending on the child's early life experiences, it also is feasible that some children will experience intense fear.

Stern (1985) talked about the development of a sense of core-self. Drawing on the concept of *attunement* (i.e., the ability of the parent to reflect the child's emotional and physical state and experience), Stern

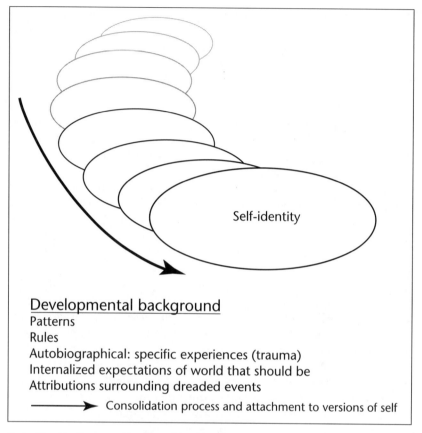

Developmental background
Patterns
Rules
Autobiographical: specific experiences (trauma)
Internalized expectations of world that should be
Attributions surrounding dreaded events
———————▶ Consolidation process and attachment to versions of self

Figure 4.1.   Identity as a matrix of consolidated learning experiences.

(1985) discussed the importance of a "closeness of match" between care-giver and infant. Regulation of stimulation in an infant's transactions with the environment is integral. To effect this, parents must make finely tuned observations of an infant's capacity to tolerate the novelty of his or her world. Too much? Too little? These important observations guide parental responses.

By being sensitive to the infant's temperament and his or her toler-ance of stimulation, ideally the infant's world can be proportionately stretched. Bit by bit the world is opened up with the principal feedback being that it is within the infant's ability to cope and master it. This in-cremental opening up of the child's world essentially facilitates positive feedback. Optimally, if a child is unhampered by enormous anxiety (by way of parents or life experiences) and gains reasonably positive feedback from his or her transactions with the environment, he or he experiences and learns without unhealthy levels of anxiety: "I can."

Patterns of Safety and Comfort Zones

Each individual develops a unique personal formula for safety. A simplistic formula for fathers and mothers might be "All the children are in bed," which means, "I can sleep now; all is safe." This can be conceptualized as a comfort zone. Deviations from this evoke vigilance; an individual's mind is elsewhere until the comfort zone is restored. It is all about states of safety—and states of unease—when key people or things are not present.

An Internal Clock or Gauge   Putting this together, all of the preceding learning feeds into the development of an internal psychobiological clock that revolves around patterns of safety and security. When expectations are met, the familiar is protected. Basically, a first casualty in loss, be it separation from a loved one or the diagnosis of a chronic disease, is the loss of this very valuable, taken-for-granted feeling of safety.

Looking at the interwoven lives of two women who are twins demonstrates this concept of a comfort zone. Throughout these women's lives, for the last 30 years from their beginnings in the womb to today, they have had daily contact with one another. Now, one of the sisters is to marry and leave the country with her new husband. The night before she leaves, she asks to share her sister's bed. The twin who is getting married is seeking comfort, security, and relief from a sense of anxiety that surrounds leaving the person who has provided most of her homeostasis.

Even seemingly imperceptible shifts in otherwise predictable patterns can create uneasiness. Thus, the temporary departure of a father who has always been at home creates a feeling of anxiety, albeit minor, in his daughter. In this case the 12-year-old girl grapples with a strange feeling of unease that she has when her father is not around: "I actually *feel different* when Dad's not around." And although an 8-year-old boy proudly exclaims, "I'm psychic" because he *knows* that his mother is coming to pick him up *before* she actually appears, it is no coincidence. This boy knows intimately the sound of his mother's car, the sound of her steps, and the turn of her key in the lock.

In situations of bereavement or separation, this intuitive sense of unbalance returns. A woman in her late twenties feels driven to call her mother every day when she is traveling. On the day that she cannot get through to her mother, her world no longer feels safe. Her emotional and physical system does not stabilize until she reaches her mother late that night. Simply speaking, this young woman is "on alert"—she feels in danger. What does she do if she cannot reach her mother? Consider the implications if a parent dies before a child has emotionally found his or her independence. The ability to believe intuitively that one can survive threat is compromised.

The Need for Consistency   Comfort zones are, however, much more complex than this. In order for individuals to feel balanced, a certain perceived consistency in both their world and identity is required. This comfort zone is made up of what people have learned to expect of themselves and others in the world, both in the present and the future. These expectations represent the culmination of the patterns that emerge from our environment and our relationship with it. A pattern may be as rudimentary as expecting the song of the sparrow each morning or as single minded as expecting and accepting only one destiny for oneself. The patterns will culminate in a notion of "me" and the confidence, and sometimes arrogance, to adamantly express, "It's just not me to get angry—it doesn't feel right."

When Expectations Are Unmet   These expectations only achieve precedence when they are endangered or are not met. Some individuals, particularly in adolescence, have quite sensitive comfort zones and are unsettled quickly. For the child who comes home from school, a rudimentary routine underpins a sense of things being okay: In the front door, to the cookie jar, then to the refrigerator for the makings of a milkshake, and straight to the television for the 4 p.m. show. But what if the television does not work? For the adolescent planning to wash her hair in the morning, the fact that the shampoo has run out may be enough to undo the day: "I don't believe this, my whole day was planned around this." Returning home that night, she exclaims, "Today was unlucky—it all started with that empty shampoo bottle." In all of these situations, the individual is thrown off course. Deviations from comfort zones can create a sense of threat and may be experienced first as a state of unease arising from disrupted patterns, followed by varying levels of anxiety. This state of unease indicates a disturbance in an individual's balance. Unfortunately, much of what one has learned through childhood can actually hinder an ability to manage and cope with disrupted patterns. These degrees of change to familiar life routines often lead children to look to a parent for verification of what they are feeling and assurance that they will be able to manage. Parents sometimes do not pick up on this need, however. Unknowingly, parents can amplify states of unease in their children. "Are you feeling too upset to go? You've been worrying about this all week. How well do you know this girl?" a parent might ask a child about to go on her first sleepover. The child's anxiety, already present, has been heightened.

Patterns of Applause: Meaning, Purpose, and the Search for Limelight

When a child's relationship with his or her caregiver is characterized by consistency and continuity of experience, one important outcome is that the child develops a feeling of inner certainty. In order for the child to experience this feeling of certainty, however, the caregiver must demonstrate a conviction that there is meaning in what the child is doing. Marris (1986) concluded that a child's experience and manipulation of the first attachment relationship 1) forms the foundation of an understanding of how to manage the world; 2) provides the first and most basic grasp of cause and effect, or predictable order; and 3) is the condition from which emotions and purposes arise. In the end, one favorable outcome is the belief in a relationship with life—that effort will reap reward.

For children to learn that they can do things there must be an ongoing reciprocity between the child and parent. That is, the child must want to gain a parent's approval or admiration in the first place and this, according to Bowlby (1988), is predicated on there being an attachment. For example, the parent's acclamation or "clapping" when certain behaviors or developmental milestones occur sets the scene for repeated efforts by the child, and so on. In these cases, the parent is responsive. The message is impregnated with meaning: "You are worthy of acclaim; you are special and loved."

These sought-after messages are foreboding in the part they play in loss and grief. Memories of being loved, of being considered a person worthy of being loved, resurface in the narratives of people who have become old, injured, and unwell. Symbols or memories of these attachments remind and reassure people that they are loved. They become extremely important to a person's ability to endure times of loneliness, as when significant others die or withdraw love or affection. An older woman with dementia searches deliberately for one card that has been signed "With love" by her father: "It reminds me that I am loved," she says.

Thus, the pattern of reciprocal contact between parent and child represents the beginning of a cognitive model of attachment (Guidano & Liotti, 1983; Marris, 1986) that extends to the child's transactions with the world. Direct links between an individual's sense of self and patterns of response and care are born from this attachment base. Generally, it is thought that insecurity develops from variations of inconsistent or unavailable patterns of care (Main, 1995). Favorable environments provide the young child with a basic trust of the world and cultivate integral components of a child's sense of self such as autonomy, control, initiative, and industry (Erikson, 1965). In situations of adversity, such as chronic illness, trauma, or injury, obviously, the parent's task becomes a great deal more complex.

Responsive parents cultivate feelings in the child that he or she is loved, holds a special and meaningful position in the world, and can control aspects of his or her world. Experiences in childhood result in images of mutual attachment and support or images of being bereft and abandoned (Bloom-Feschbach & Bloom-Feschbach, 1987). These images can become potent messages when an individual is enduring personal adversity. For one man who had been adopted as a child, the image of his mother's being able to abandon him is used to explain relationship breakdowns throughout his life. The recurring question remains in his mind: "If my mother didn't want me, who would?"

The commanding effect of the parents' applause is evident when considering the shared and almost symbiotic pleasure between mother and child demonstrated in the following example taken from Stern:

> A 10-month-old girl gets a piece on a jigsaw puzzle. She looks toward her mother, throws her head up in the air, and with a forceful flap raises herself partly off the ground in a flurry of exuberance. The mother says "Yes, thatta girl.".…It has an explosive rise that echoes the girl's fling of gesture and posture. (1985, p. 141)

The Code Behind Applause   The child keeps on listening to this applause—often throughout life. Lots of patterns to the applause will be listened for, such as a code—louder, softer, persistent, erratic, ambiguous, whatever—all imbued with meaning. Behavior to elicit certain patterns of parental applause continues in various degrees well into adulthood. For some, such behavior geared toward winning accolades is central throughout their development. Messages received that one is "being a brave boy" or "making Mom or Dad proud," both about applause, also are prone to return as predominant templates for behavior in old age or in situations of adversity.

Applause or clapping is really quite an intricate and complex piece of feedback. When given too freely, it can become too dominant. A 40-year-old woman restates her father's constant remark: "I am a child prodigy." When "clapping" is done hand-in-hand with attention it can become too alluring, and thus very difficult, almost unthinkable, to relinquish voluntarily. This is a feeling commonly expressed by talented individuals, for example, musicians, who spend a lot of time in therapy talking about how they perceive their parent's pleasure and involvement in their artistic prowess. Often, the child perceives that the parent has "given up so much—I would feel like I am letting them down—it would have all been a waste of time." The attribution that is given to the parent's involvement is that the parent has no or little life apart from the child's life or what the child does for him or her. The individual perceives that if the parent is not wholly involved in what the child does, the parent's world would be diminished.

Often the role performed while doing the activity, and this could be anything, being the "helper," being the "brave little man," "being smart," or being a "great athlete," can become enmeshed with the child. Primarily, children can struggle with whether they are loved for who they are or for the activity that they perform. So the great athlete struggles with who she will be to her mother if she contemplates giving up her sport, diving. She asks: "Would my mother love *me* if I wasn't a diver? The logical extension of this inquiry is a fear of risking the loss of her mother's love if she ends her involvement in this activity. Similar convoluted questions emanate from other tasks and habits. A woman who is used to being in daily contact with her mother wonders, "If I didn't look after her...." or "If I didn't call her every day, would I still be loved?"

Patterns of Attachment: Separation, Safety, and Confidence

Much has been written about the influence of attachment experiences on personality profiles (Bowlby, 1988; Main, 1995). Along these lines, both Bowlby (1988) and Ainsworth (1969) identified the security of the early caregiving relationship as enhancing or inhibiting an infant's confidence to explore the environment. Ideally, the caregiving relationship sets the stage for increased independence through supportive guiding of separation through infancy (Mahler, Pine, & Bergman, 1975) and adolescence (Erikson, 1965). Summing up, in the words of Kierkegaard:

> The child has to be protected against dangers and that watchfulness by the parent is of vital importance, but he doesn't want the parent to obtrude his own anxieties into the picture, to cut off the child's action before it is absolutely necessary. Today we know that such an upbringing alone gives the child a self confidence in the face of experience that he would not have if he were overly blocked: it gives him an inner sustainment...that allows the child to develop an ego-controlled and self-confident appraisal of the world by a personality that can open up more easily to experience. (1844/1957, p. 72)

The process of separation and individuation from the parent is a fragile one. Handled sensitively, it should provide the child with a sense that he or she can survive in the world. Thus, it is not purely about physical separation. Rather, it is played out through the juggling of physical separation and the messages that parents give about the child's ability to master the environment and the safety of the world. Mahler et al. (1975) described the intricacies of this process for the infant. Once again the ideal model involves the mother slowly freeing and guiding the child to navigate and master the environment. Here, the parent is a source of emotional fuelling, nudging, coaching, and clapping.

The emotional maturity of the key caregivers is integral—the child's wish to separate must be supported and the child should be surrounded with quiet confidence. The confidence must be instilled in the child as well as the idea that the world is generally a safe place. "You will be fine" can be grounded by the teaching of things a child can "do" if he or she feels unsafe. It is important that the same messages from the parents should be reiterated whenever the child needs emotional refueling. Equally, the same principles come into play when an individual suffers personal trauma, be it through the loss of a significant person, place, or the onset of chronic illness or disability. Appropriate therapy, particularly with regard to the relationship between the individual and therapist, aims to mimic a harbor from which a replay of the sequence of separation can be guided. Unsure of the way they might manage the world, sometimes with changed bodies and depleted self-confidence, individuals require the same emotional refueling and quiet, confident barracking that ideally was experienced in childhood and adolescence.

Impaired Autonomy: The Delicate Comfort Zone   The task of the parent is to support the child's courage to conquer anxiety. It is apparent, however, that for some parents, there is an unconscious sabotaging of the child's courage to separate. Still afraid of the world themselves, these parents can convey the message that the world is too scary: The child will not be safe without his or her parents, Mother or Father will be sad if the child leaves, the child will forfeit the parent's love if he or she leaves, or at the far end of the continuum—the parent may not survive if the child leaves. These messages are learned and set a template for the separation–individuation process that may be replayed in adolescence.

In some cases the child remains unable to successfully separate. Feedback from the parent, coupled with the child's experiences with his or her world, fails to provide positive information to the child that he or she can survive independently. The consequence of impaired separation is the undermining of the achievement of autonomy. The comfort zone for these children, instead of expanding incrementally over time, can remain quite static and is oversensitive or particularly sensitive to new experiences. Signals of separation difficulties are illustrated in the experience of a 17-year-old boy who is taken out on a boating day-trip with his father. His father, whom the young man describes as a stranger, left him and his mother when he was 4 years old: "My dad took me out on this boat, and all the time I'm thinking I want to be back with my mom. I mean, I, like, got really worried and got strange feelings as this boat started to leave the shore. The further away from shore it got, the worse I got. It wasn't until it turned around that I began to feel a bit different."

The young man's description of his relationship with his mother amplifies the dependency: "She comes in each night and helps me get to sleep. I just feel really worried if she doesn't do this. I worry that I can't get to sleep. When she's angry with me, I worry about it and sometimes when she worries about me, she cries and that is when I feel the worst—to have made her cry like that."

Impaired autonomy spawns inadequate coping skills and a lack of strong self-image. Sadly, if the parent dies and separation is thereby forced, even adults can be left with no evidence that they can survive on their own. A 35-year-old woman, whose mother died 18 months previously, repeats the statement: "I don't know how I can live without her." Apart from questioning her capacity to live without her mother, it is also implausible to this woman that she would *want* to live without her mother: "Why should I want to live?" These are the serious outcomes of an enmeshed relationship in which mother and child have become inseparable.

"SHE COMES IN EACH NIGHT AND HELPS ME GET TO SLEEP. I JUST FEEL REALLY WORRIED IF SHE DOESN'T DO THIS. I WORRY THAT I CAN'T GET TO SLEEP. WHEN SHE'S ANGRY WITH ME, I WORRY ABOUT IT AND SOMETIMES WHEN SHE WORRIES ABOUT ME, SHE CRIES AND THAT IS WHEN I FEEL THE WORST—TO HAVE MADE HER CRY LIKE THAT."

As a testimony to the love for her mother, this same woman persistently contemplates a reunion with her mother. In an ironic twist, this contemplation actually enables her day-to-day survival of the extremely frightening months that follow her mother's death: "I could so easily be with her, and when I think about this I feel strangely comforted." In fact, interestingly, she actually feels safer when she speculates about a reunion with her mother.

The theme of securing safety is integral, but it can be perceived as a matter of survival for individuals whose autonomy is impaired. The fear of the death of parents is then too central. Amidst this fear, the search for a partner for single adults in their early fifties can be more about securing safety in case their parents die than about anything else. A 50-year-old woman protests: "Here I am, a 50-year-old, and all I worry about is what I will do when my parents die."

SUMMARY

Although self-organization as a process continues throughout an individual's life, the primary socialization associated with early childhood generates major postulates about self and the world that will be attached with meaning and significance. Out of this will evolve a set of thoughts or understandings about who one is, whether one is loved, what one is loved for, and what things about oneself or what behaviors elicit care and love. Also, this period of socialization underscores the ability to tolerate the anxiety associated with change, the assessment that individuals make of their ability to survive change, and the relationship individuals have with the expression of emotions.

Obviously, there is an advantage for those individuals whose emotional development has been founded on secure emotional bases, with parental encouragement of autonomous functioning and the availability of strong messages for internalization. Although the ability to draw on strong and capable versions of self is important in grieving the death of significant others, it is equally crucial to the grieving and mastery of adversity.

The presence of a strong sense of self greatly facilitates an individual's therapeutic progress. The problematic aspects of this progress are expanded on in the following chapter, which examines the developmental foundations and psychological role of expectations. Culminating in a sense of "Who I should be," these expectations create an individual's formidable resistance to change.

AN 18-YEAR-OLD ATHLETE RELATES, "THE COACH TOLD ME ALL ALONG THAT I WOULD BE A TOP HURDLER. ONE DAY HE SAID THAT HE WOULD GET ME TO THE OLYMPICS. I REMEMBER THAT DAY SO CLEARLY. I FELT AWESOME. TWO YEARS LATER, HE TELLS ME THAT I 'DON'T HAVE WHAT IT TAKES.' SO WHO AM I NOW, WHAT AM I? CAN I CALL MY-SELF AN ATHLETE?"

CHAPTER 5

FORMING EXPECTATIONS AND THEIR PLACE IN LOSS

Anxiety is part of human nature. It is interesting how exacting or in-finitesimal change need be for individuals to experience states of unease or anxiety. For one 15-year-old, Graham, a haircut tipped the balance. Graham had been invited by his new and first girlfriend out to dinner to meet her parents. Although his haircut was a little bit too extreme for Graham, it was not the cut itself but rather how it rendered him unable to place and angle his sunglasses on his head exactly as he had before that had upset him. "I really liked how the sunglasses looked, how I looked with them on my head—it felt right. I've been trying to get them right on my head ever since but it's just not the same," he remarked. According to Erikson (1965), adolescence is a time in which issues surrounding identity are integral. For Graham, the haircut with its resulting effect on his sun-glasses had created a sense that he did not look "cool" or okay. This per-ception made him anxious; it took him out of his comfort zone. He longed for his old haircut and the familiar way it made him feel.

As discussed in the preceding chapters, a sense of predictability and the security it brings equates with a psychological experience of equilib-rium or homeostasis. Thus, change can be extremely threatening. Human beings need perceived stability; this accounts for much of people's aver-sion or discomfort toward change, particularly change that is nonvoli-tional. The idea of comfort zones extends to individuals' sense of who they are, who they should be, and who they would like to become in the future. That is, all individuals are made up of a matrix of expectations and dreams about themselves. When these are unmet, they may be personally construed as representing a loss.

This chapter explores the formation of an individual's expectations and dreams, the place these expectations and dreams take in an individual's identity, and their relationship to loss. We begin by exposing the intricate nature of patterns and the inevitability of the resistance individuals feel toward change in these patterns, particularly change that is forced on them.

THE INTRICATE NATURE OF
PATTERNS AND THE RESISTANCE TO CHANGE

The mutuality between the development of inner certainty and outer predictability for a child has been illustrated by numerous theorists (Bowlby, 1988; Erikson, 1965; Parsons, 1955). Through an individual's development and experience with his or her environment, the world becomes understood as working in a certain way. Individuals believe they are able to predict the outcome of others' behaviors as well as their own; they construct expectations and have meaningful exchanges with their world. These transactions with the environment form structures of knowledge. Developed since early childhood, these knowledge structures provide meaning, safety, and control that are synonymous with well-being and a sense of self (Becker, 1962; Marris, 1982, 1986; Mead, 1934).

Providing mental templates (i.e., scripts for action), these original knowledge structures or cognitive schemata are slowly revised and elaborated over time rather than cancelled out (Guidano & Liotti, 1983). That is, as people tend to make incoming information or data fit their existing knowledge structures, these structures *organize* ongoing knowledge and shape what is perceived and recorded in memory (Fiske & Taylor, 1984; Horowitz, 1988). According to Fiske and Taylor, these knowledge structures can be described as filters that process incoming material.

A self that represents a composite of these structures of knowledge emerges. Over one's personal development, these early structures of knowledge are fleshed out. Representing integral building blocks, a certain consistency to the notion of self is basically a *fait accompli*. It is this consistency of self that aligns with emotional well-being. This process might best be symbolized as a slow interweaving and merging of self and reality that is almost imperceptible except over large tracts of time. A parallel to this almost camouflaged learning is to be found in physical change or decline. As an individual ages it is almost imperceptible at the time but is apparent when the person looks at photographs of him- or herself taken a decade earlier.

The consolidation process of "becoming" accounts, in part, for the difficulty individuals may have in integrating drastic changes in themselves.

Innate knowledge structures molded slowly over time cannot accommodate the degree of variation. That is, information that is way out of the normal range of what an individual has learned about him- or herself cannot be routinely processed. Interestingly, change in itself may not be integrated until a sufficient amount of consistent information compounds to a point in which it forces a presence (Marks, 1987). The issue is even more complex; although feedback from others and comparisons and contrasts with others form part of one's reflective self (Mead, 1934), a plethora of personal defenses guarantee that the reflection back to one's self from others is not clear-cut. Because individuals build up a personal armory over their lives, the ability to *see* inner changes or to see *clearly* what is happening around them is slow to take effect.

Thus, obvious change to the onlooker often is not as stark for the individual. Even individuals who look back at pictures of themselves undergoing chemotherapy do not recall the changes at the time as having been so grim: "I can't believe I walked around like that!" For some people the changes concurrent with pregnancy are similarly obscure, certainly not as starkly seen, at the time. If a woman returns to view pictures of the process she might herself reflect, "Was that really me? Did I look as big as that?"

The degree of change that threatens one's self is highly personal. Threat to self can be gleaned in the anxious exclamation of a 4-year-old who is wearing his first suit for a wedding: "It doesn't look like *me*!" It can also be illustrated by reference to a most salient threat to self and reality, namely, in chemotherapy for the treatment of cancer. No amount of knowledge prepares individuals for changes of the magnitude involved with chemotherapy. Amid the process of physical change, it is apparent that the individual is struggling with retaining a consistency of self. Almost unrecognizable to themselves, "shipwrecked" individuals hold tenaciously to the remains of the self that is being threatened.

A nurse observes an older woman who appears to cling to one remaining consistent aspect of self during chemotherapy: "Looking at the older woman—no hair, frail, and pushing a walker—I see that she is wearing a slipper on one foot and a stiletto-heeled shoe on the other." The shoe is symbolic—perhaps the last bastion of self resists a total takeover by the treatment.

It is precisely because one needs a certain consistency of self that certain degrees of change are threatening. This enmeshment of

"LOOKING AT THE OLDER WOMAN— NO HAIR, FRAIL, AND PUSHING A WALKER—I SEE THAT SHE IS WEARING A SLIPPER ON ONE FOOT AND A STILETTO-HEELED SHOE ON THE OTHER."

identity and reality almost predicts that individuals will resist information that threatens their established view of the world (Fiske & Taylor, 1984; Horowitz, 1988; Marris, 1986; Parkes, 1975, 1988). That is, the enmeshment of self-identity and reality predetermines that certain amounts of change will simultaneously threaten one's sense of self: "Who will I be? Who would I become? This is not *me!*" As Marris (1986) proposed, the impulse to resist radical change may be identified as essentially a fear of psychological disintegration.

WHO I AM

What one expects, as well as the meaning and significance attached to an expectation, emerges in the process of primary socialization. Drawing on the work of Kelly (1955), the "world that should be" might be described as a construct that has become internalized to a point in which it has become part of self-identity. It is indistinguishable from the notion of self—"who I am." One becomes one's expectations. In recognizing the developmental process that underpins and generates such expectations, there is potential for these to have become ingrained so as to operate automatically (Bowlby, 1988). These expectations can be characterized by two features: First, they will be internalized as part of one's self; and second, they will be drawn on automatically as referents. Inevitably, they will persist as an interpretive framework that parallels an individual's life and makes change a potential threat to self.

The expectations that one has become large and integral parts of identity. Certain roles, role expectations (e.g., parenthood), developmental tasks, and family transitions become a type of prescription for behavior. A single mother forced to work full time berates herself: "I should be a better mom; I should be at home." A wife unhappy with her husband gives up her desire to leave him because of her model of what a family should be: "Parents should stay with their children; I couldn't live with myself if I took my children away from their father. It's about family!" The same themes hold true for a woman who was adopted as a child. Expectations of her biological family, what it would have been like had her biological mother not relinquished her as an infant, affect her ability to embrace her life. Her family experience with her adoptive family is correspondingly diminished: "It just was never where I felt I should be. I always wanted to be somewhere else."

WHO I SHOULD BE AND
WHAT SHOULD HAVE HAPPENED TO ME

For Parkes (1971), any negative difference from our expectations constitutes a loss; in conceptualizing loss, the world that should have been remains the relational context. This world, against which outcomes in personal life are measured, is a powerful benchmark. Ironically, although very fragile, the models and schemas that make up our assumptive world have themselves become reified. That is, despite being constructed, they become almost fixed and immutable, practically an entity. In sum, these models and schema define loss as representing what a person has come to believe "should be" (see Figure 3.1):

An older man who takes care of his wife who has dementia watches another older couple in the park and reflects "We should have been like them, you know, just a typical couple enjoying retirement."

A childless woman in her fifties states, "I should have been a mother."

A young woman, having contracted multiple sclerosis, protests, "I would never have imagined my life turning out like this! I thought I'd just be like everybody else."

A father of a boy with a disability recognizes that his younger child, a daughter, is missing out on what life could have offered her: "She should have been able to enjoy having a brother; instead, we rarely go out. She misses out on so much because of Sam."

The notion of a correct life sequence (Berger & Luckmann, 1966) is a principal referent. Developmental pathways and their value are established throughout childhood. Through primary socialization one learns the correctness of one's life program and socially defined learning sequences, such as "at age A the child should learn X, at age B he should learn Y, and so on" (Berger & Luckmann, 1966, p. 156). Similarly, stages are biologically and socially demarcated. The concept even extends to such fallacious ideas as "firstborn children should be taller and stronger than their siblings always and despite minimal age difference!"

"WE SHOULD HAVE BEEN LIKE THEM, YOU KNOW, JUST A TYPICAL COUPLE ENJOYING RETIREMENT."

According to Neugarten (1976), the outcome of these socially defined learning sequences is a series of age-graded perceptions that define expectations of adult development and that exert strong societal pressure. That is, every society is age-graded and has a system of social expectations regarding age-appropriate behavior that provides a large measure of predictability (Neugarten, 1976). This is well evidenced in the rites of passage surrounding 18th and 21st birthdays, when it is perceived that children should start going to college or working. The following statement of a mother of a 20-year-old son with a severe intellectual disability indicates that such expectations apply even when they may be inappropriate given the child's condition: "This year, we had the option of getting Jerry into a house. At first I was very keen, but I rethought it again. He's still very young. He'll only just be 20. You wouldn't expect a typical child to be leaving home at this age now. They tend to stay for longer. So there's all this guilt of pushing him out at such an early stage."

Along a time line shaped by these expectations, Neugarten (1976) argued that plans and goals are set and reassessed. The value of such pathways is further subscribed to in the school; in adolescent environments, and far beyond, to finally include versions of maturing relationships among aging parents and middle-age children. Differences with the desired life program may be subjectively perceived as a loss. It follows that in cases in which developmental milestones are persistently unmet, the experience of loss is revisited over and over again and hence, becomes nonfinite. This is well demonstrated in situations of acquired or congenital disability. Despite an initial diagnosis that forecasts a life with permanent disability, the expectations that make up the world that should have been remain a persistent context against which the loss is reassessed. By way of example, take the comments made by a father of a child with autism and severe intellectual disability. His comments are made in relation to an emotional experience he had while walking. A group of boys, around 18 years old, the same age as his son, were enjoying a game of football:

"The fact of my son's disability suddenly comes to the forefront of my mind and I'm wondering what he would have been like, wondering what he would have been like if he had been typical, what our lives as parents would have been like, and what our relationship with him would have been like? As he gets older and is no longer a child, I feel increasing sadness."

Thus, apart from technical yardsticks, these developmental and societal expectations are steeped with significance and meaning. Surrounding these expectations is a quality of life that "should be had," and "should be enjoyed." The mother of a child with AIDS protests, "He should have been enjoying the best years of his life."

The daughter whose father has had a stroke protests, "They [mother and father] should have lived out their old age together."

Not only do such prescriptions for normative expectations define what will be different and less desirable, they form a basis for hopes and wishes. An outcome is a context consisting of ideals invested far into the future. Some prolific examples of lost ideals are found in the experiences of people who are adopted, who faced the losses of infertility, who have an ongoing medical condition, who have or care for someone who has a disability, and who have lost a parent in childhood. As the world that should have been remains the benchmark, prospective loss and prospective grieving surround the discrepancies experienced throughout the life span. The parent of a 1-day-old baby with Down syndrome finds herself lost in thoughts of the future as it may turn out. She finds herself imagining her daughter as never being able to get married—and she, the mother, as being denied the opportunity of becoming a grandmother.

WHO I WILL BECOME

Dreams and hopes play significant roles in the formation of our identities and expectations for ourselves.

The Role of Dreams and Hopes

According to Marris, the identification with "hopes about the future...what we will become" is sometimes more meaningful than our identity in the present (1986, p. 108). For example, an individual might strive for something from early childhood. An occupation or vocation might be a driving force, but when that dream is achieved the reality is far from what was envisioned. Take the case of one young woman, a nurse, who arrives at therapy because nursing has not turned out how she wished. Her anxiety surrounds her being, her existence: "Who am I if I don't enjoy nursing?" she asks. "When did you decide to become a nurse?" the therapist asks her. "All my life, I have wanted to be nothing else," she responds.

Who an individual might become can be a thread winding through his or her development. Becoming rich and famous is a common fantasy in childhood; however, ongoing transactions and experience with the environment create a gradual modification of these dreams. Individuals slowly pick up on changes in themselves: They assess their abilities, they position themselves and their chances of success according to feedback they have received, and they evaluate the feasibility of the dream, which gently guides the dream as it merges into something else—ideally into some other dream!

A young girl who dreams from the age of 7 of becoming an actress, for example, might over time, with increasing knowledge about herself and the world, assess that it may be too difficult. At the same time, her broadening knowledge enables her definition of "rich and famous" to be fleshed out. She becomes able to evaluate alternatives. What other dreams allow her to have her needs met? Perhaps she could be a director, a model, or a singer. This is not a conscious decision but instead, an outcome of broadening knowledge about herself and the world.

For some individuals, a dream slowly emerges and becomes apparent. Little by little an individual learns of different potentials and a different version of one's self emerges. Either way, a certain consistency of self is able to be maintained and the dreams are psychologically friendly. Through early adulthood, while the dreams begin to merge with reality, different goals or dreams mark the future. They may become more "pedestrian" and less grandiose—dreams of having children, marrying, or buying a house are a few examples. However, the dream may become too central, too important; almost everything is pinned on it. One's identity seems to rely on it coming to fruition. With no other aspect of identity being groomed, the failure of this dream can become a personal threat. The following case of a young adopted man illustrates the power of the dream, the part it plays in identity, and the threat should it fail.

A young man comes to therapy. He describes himself as always having been angry. "I should be, shouldn't I? I am adopted." He states that he has always contemplated suicide; that a vision of "getting a hose from the hardware store and fixing it to the exhaust of his car" frequently comes into his mind. When asked how he got through adolescence, he states that the dream of finding his biological parents actually "kept him alive." Each night he would lie in bed and fantasize how it would be—*the* reunion. In some cases, it would seem that elusive dreams may be more psychologically friendly than those realities that can fail. For, when this young man met his parents their reaction was not what he had expected, and his survival dream faltered. "It was all about them—what they wanted from me!" At this point, at the age of 20, he has no dream. Without the dream, he feels lost.

The Psychologically Friendly Dream

What might a psychologically friendly dream look like? "I want to be a rock singer. I could sing as well as that girl on television," a young woman thinks. Never tested, the dream remains intact, protected; it is vastly different from the experience of those primary school children or adolescents who road-test their dream early on. Athletes these days adamantly correct you when you talk about fantasies: "Concentrate on goals, not fantasies—dreams that can be realized with work and effort," they urge. True, but still, such goals can become threats if they are the only goals supporting you. As one physiotherapist remarked, an athlete might be "one injury away"; the risk of losing one's dream is apparent.

As discussed previously, for some children who are made to feel particularly "special" because of some talent very early in their development, ongoing fear surrounds the loss of this specialness. The young athlete whose comments open this chapter illustrates the conundrum that surrounds a notion of self that is based on a skill that must be guaranteed for the individual to continue to feel special; "My dad says I have a special skill, but what if I am not *really* an athlete?" The corollary is, "Who am I, if I am not this?" Sadly, the adolescent who cannot regain the glory she enjoyed as a preteen swimmer states: "I get jealous of *me* back then!"

The Dream at Risk

In mid-life and old age it is common for individuals to realize the possibility that they may not pull off what they thought they would. Time left and the consequences of aging force individuals to come face-to-face with limitations and the realization that some of their hopes, in all likelihood, will not be met; this psychological context in itself can create threat. Between the ages of approximately 40 and 50, males typically fear that their dreams are just fantasies. They speak of being trapped, having to pay mortgages or college tuitions for their children, and other burdensome responsibilities. Underlying this is the realization that "jumping on a motorcycle and riding away" is no longer an option.

Strangely enough, what by some is described as a feeling of hitting a brick wall has actually been gathering momentum slowly over time. It is often, however, perceived as coming out of the blue. Small, incremental changes like drops of water building up behind the walls of a dam suddenly amount to making an impression and burst through day-to-day existence. At the age of 40 or 50, and earlier for some, a sense of resignation that "this is it" can come into the foreground. "You only have one life," is the warning a father hands down to his 20-year-old son. "Make the most of it !"

The Fading Dream

Dreams and goals become precarious subjects for the 85-year-old man. As transactions with the present world decrease because of his lack of mobility, so too do new experiences. He is sometimes left with the task of generating versions of himself from his past transactions with the world. His mind may play, or fantasize, with what might have been. He works backwards, idealizes times in his life and the roles he has played. Possibly he rewrites his life story, putting a different spin on it.

Frequently, the older person has no recourse but to become lost in his memories. Amid the routines in his life, earlier incidents, highly emotional, sometimes traumatic, will stand out in his memories. For instance, in the long periods of time he is alone, a recently bereaved older man finds himself compulsively returning to the death of his mother. He thinks of the long journey home to try and see his mother before she died. Feeling the physical limitations of old age, he finds empathy with his mother's limitations and the struggles she had to bring up six children. He begins to feel disappointed in himself: "I should have looked after her."

Left with many hours to himself, this older man is unable to distract his mind away from such memories. The lack of busy transactions with life and the company of other people prevents him from sharing his thoughts. It results in an inhibition of the ability to contemplate his memories differently. In his isolation, his memories are more difficult to work through, and they become potent.

At the same time, the dependency that is forced by physical decline often leads to a yearning for the care and protection offered by parents often long-ago deceased: "I am thinking of my mother, how I would like her here now. I find myself thinking of this like never before in my life." An outcome of the isolation and long periods of time with one's thoughts may be an intense regrieving for one's parents. In this environment, earlier patterns that make up an individual become predominant. When an individual is able-bodied and experiencing a fulfilling and independent life, these patterns are more likely to be dormant. However, in situations of dependency, these early patterns become activated and can operate very much in the foreground.

SUMMARY

In summary, it is clear that the potential significance of any loss has been established or scripted well before the loss event has taken place, due to internalized expectations of what the world should be like. Expectations, dreams, and wishes form central parts in an individual's identity. Sometimes, because they have become almost pivotal, the individual perceives it to be impossible to relinquish them without creating a great deal of personal threat. Although it is apparent that dreams can become psychologically friendly, different life experiences and age contexts threaten their viability. For some individuals, this will be experienced as a dreaded event. Yet it is apparent that many individuals are unable to acknowledge their loss or give themselves permission to grieve. In the following chapter, attention is directed to the emotional and cognitive scripts learned in childhood that might sabotage the grieving of nonfinite loss.

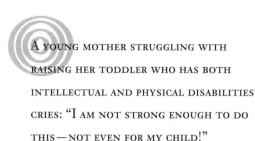

CHAPTER 6

THE ROLE OF MESSAGES AND THE DEVELOPMENT OF KNOTS

This chapter is concerned with exposing the rules and messages children learn from parents and other significant people about personal adversity, their ability to master their fears, and the expression of emotion. This knowledge base culminates in the ways individuals make meaning of what happens to them, what individuals actually allow in terms of the emotion they express about personal adversity, and how individuals restore feelings of safety should they experience personal adversity.

Certain developmental histories make tasks more difficult for some people than for others; some people find it difficult to perceive or even fantasize themselves as capable. Tracing through their background, these individuals habitually line up all of their experiences as evidence of their inability. The young mother in the opening quote is experiencing this: A disarming thread in her biography is taking over. A learned message from childhood is sabotaging her ability to deal with her current personal crisis.

Such individuals cannot conceive of a notion of optimism. This idea is borne out by theorists (e.g., Ainsworth, 1969; Bowlby, 1988; Main, 1995), who have pointed to how the relationship between caregiver and child affects disposition, notwithstanding the interplay of genetics, and generates the development of optimism. The parent's support of a child's confidence and self-esteem is, in this respect, critical. Picture a little boy off to school on his first day. The parent who displays confidence in the child, implying, "You can do it—you will be all right," obviously begins building far more self-confidence than the child whose parent anxiously asks, "Will you be all right?"

According to Horowitz (1988), such information from parents and the early environment forms schemata that are used to organize knowledge about self, role-relationships, and reality. Over time, the perception children make of parents' messages forms a potent thread in the person's biography. Individuals in therapy often return to such messages, both verbal and nonverbal. A message has two components—fact and feeling—but it is not always clearly sent and clearly received for a host of reasons. Senses, thoughts, emotions, interpretations, and actions affect the messages learned in childhood from caregivers.

In childhood, associations among the words and actions of adults and how the world works are constantly being made. Considering some of the clichés and proverbs that adults themselves have learned and use about why things happen, sometimes almost unintelligible connections about the world are made. For instance, a mother replied to her child's concern about the future, "It will all come out in the wash." Although such comments may be relatively harmless over time, less so are some other messages. A plethora of individualized messages from parents provide personal dictionaries for children. A 28-year-old man seriously injured his legs at a building worksite. Later, he talked in therapy about when the incident happened and his immediate fear of being seen as stupid and deserving of a reprimand. This self-evaluation led him to feign unconsciousness; he lay motionless on the ground with his head down when his boss returned from lunch. The man's perceptions of childhood and memories of his father reprimanding him before checking any injuries he sustained dominated his actions.

What behavior provides safety? What degree of emotion can an individual express before he or she is considered to be a complainer, an attention seeker, and the like? More to the point, what has an individual been permitted to express in his or her past, and about what? What is he or she comfortable in expressing? Has a child's intuition about his or her physical and emotional sensations been legitimized? Have a child's feelings been shared, talked through, and acknowledged in situations of personal loss—or have they been dismissed or belittled? All of these messages from caregivers to children condense and culminate into a series of conspicuous rules for how the child should present and judge his or her feelings. Constricting the child's own appraisal of the situation, these rules might usefully be described as emotional and cognitive *knots*. These knots can actually bestow or deny to an individual permission to express grief.

THE IMPACT OF LEARNED MESSAGES

Underscoring an individual's life, sometimes one feels there is a personal register with a stipulated number of good things and bad things that should happen to people. A parent reflected after his daughter's death: "We had just arrived at a place in our lives where things had settled. Finally, we were happy—and then this happens. Dare to be happy!"

Cracks, Ladders, and Lines: The Rules on How to Stay Safe

Why does "bad luck" happen? What are the rules that allow an individual to exclaim, "Surely this is enough. I've had my run of bad luck!" Where did those proverbs, such as "Bad luck runs in threes" come from? Who decreed that 7 years of bad luck should follow the breaking of a mirror? Gen-eralized rules about how life and relationships work are formed, learned, and stored in memory systems (Crittenden, 1995). These include rules on how to keep safe and the behaviors that a child might take to mean that he or she is "good" and deserves a reward versus those behaviors that might mean he or she is "bad" and deserves punishment (Harris, 1989). These rules foster suppositions such as "Bad things *should* only happen to bad people." From these types of associations meanings emerge, beliefs are constructed, and familiar patterns and automatic responses are learned (Flavell, Miller, & Miller, 1993). A supposed set of guarantees surround sensible behavior. If one eats sensibly, exercises, does not do anything wrong, then misfortune or punishment will not be invited. Punishments surround foolish behavior. If things go wrong, it is your fault, something you did, something you did not do. The message in childhood is that if it is bad, you deserved it or caused it. A 6-year-old lies under her bed eating sweets. She had bought them behind her mother's back. Her mother had warned her against eating sweets. While gulping them down, one lodges in her throat and she has a coughing fit. She becomes frightened. An association is produced between disobeying orders, that is, being bad, and punishment.

Conscience plays a large part in this equation, so much so that individuals may actually track back through time to search for the misdemeanor in their backgrounds that might explain and account for the misfortune. The message is clear—one can have some control over whether bad things happen. For some people, their childhood has been

> "WE HAD JUST ARRIVED AT A PLACE IN OUR LIVES WHERE THINGS HAD SETTLED. FINALLY, WE WERE HAPPY—AND THEN THIS HAPPENS. DARE TO BE HAPPY!"

thwarted with abuse. An individual might end up judging his or her whole self to be bad—it was his or her fault. A 13-year-old girl watched the long, grueling course of debilitation in her grandmother, who had dementia. She sought an explanation for this suffering and wondered, "Did Grandma do something bad in her life to have this?" Implicit in this statement is, "How could I avoid having this happen to me?"

Sometimes inadvertently, parents teach rules about how to stay safe. The naiveté trap of childhood allows the child's learning to be incontestable and absolute. "Take vitamin C and you won't get sick," a mother advised her child. Later on, a 12-year-old who had stopped taking vitamin C and became unwell reflected, "I was not sick when I took vitamin C—I should have done what she said." Because a child takes his or her parents' statements literally, some parents introduce a jail of fear. One mother tells her son that bad things will happen if he does not eat all of the food on his plate. Another child learns that bad things will happen if she eats fatty food. An 8-year-old lies in bed listening to the radio. The radio announcer is talking to a medical practitioner. Much is being spoken about, but the 8-year-old girl hears and interprets only one statement: "People get sick if they don't sleep." As the girl lies awake worrying about the radio announcement, her mother comes into her room and warns her that she may not make it to school if she doesn't get to sleep. The fear becomes amplified: "What if I don't get to sleep!"

The Construction of Emotional and Cognitive Knots

Learning to know and interpret one's own body represents an important skill easily thwarted and impeded by parents and a child's interactions with others in the environment. Unwittingly, a parent often can undermine the development of this skill.

In the following scenario, the potency of the naive world of the child discussed in the preceding chapter is apparent. It highlights the colliding of realities as a son translates his parent's perception of his experience.

Perspective of the Son   William, a 50-year-old carpenter, became depressed because he had lost his job. Feeling sad and granting himself permission to stop and take it easy seemed quite alien ideas to him. William went to the doctor. When the general practitioner told him that he was understandably depressed because he had suffered a major loss, William bursts into tears. It seemed that he was relieved that his feelings were believed. He had not realized how important it was to be believed that he felt this way. Memories followed, and he recalled the length to which he had to go to stay home from school when he was young:

Feeling unwell just wasn't good enough. My mother would always say, "You'll be all right when you get there." One morning I remember feeling strange. She said the same thing, "You'll be all right." I guess in retrospect, I probably just hoped she was right. After that, I was running late. My friends were waiting for me. My mom waved as I ran up to them. At school I collapsed. They called my mom. It turned out that I had meningitis. All I can recall was that she seemed angry and she said that it [meningitis] was my fault because I ran after my friends. But she did look after me then. I was put on the sofa in the living room, blankets wrapped round me, and she really looked after me.

Hearing Both Sides   To fully understand this complex scenario it is worth looking at the sequence described here from an adult perspective. The mother possibly had an appointment or had to go to work. She, herself, might have been feeling unwell. It was morning. She was flustered, facing different demands from different children. Lunches were being made. She perceived her son as looking okay—not wonderful—but okay. His brother started a friendly scuffle. William responded. She reassured herself—yesterday he seemed okay, he'd eaten, not much, but eaten—and she assumes that he had slept fine. She reassured him by telling him that he was okay; the feeling would go away. Possibly she saw him run to meet his friends. The fact that he could run validated her actions—possibly reassuring her. Her decision had been right. He *was* okay. She was able to quell her discomfort that perhaps she should have kept him home, not gone to work—whatever.

The call from the school and the subsequent doctor's report that her son has collapsed made her feel extremely sad and perhaps guilty. She railed against this feeling of guilt and blamed her child—intimating that he made himself sick: "You ran after your friends!" At the same time she knew her son was ill and needed her. She became protective, in part to atone for sending him to school. Days of nurturing followed. Her son recovered. She returned her child to school. His protests to stay at home were possibly met with the words: "You're better now. Stop playing on this." The attention was over. His "special" time with his mother ended.

The Learned Messages   The 8-year-old child knew nothing of this backdrop. Instead, William had gathered a plethora of possible learned associations, all of which had implications for the grieving of nonfinite loss. First, his mother had told him whether he was unwell, whether it was a *real* feeling. The corollary to this is that possibly he was amazed when it turned out that he was, in fact, really unwell. Second, his mother's statement drew an association between running to the bus and becoming ill.

The corollary is that he caused the meningitis and was to blame. The up-shot is that he should be grateful, therefore, for her care.

The Relevance of "Being Special" to Personal Adversity

The last sentence of William's statement ("she really looked after me") introduces the rather insidious learned associations between being sick and becoming special. Becoming special through sickness seems to be a universal association. Specialness is conferred. Apart from the parents emerging as consistently caring, the giving and receiving of presents dur-ing sickness can strengthen these associations. Becoming special is a yearned-for feeling (Rochlin, 1965). This is evident in the daily struggle between siblings to gain the limelight from their parents. When one is sick, the struggle is over. The "choice" is obvious. But there seems to be a limit, and once the sickness has run its course, the message can shift. Parents return to their typical behavior.

"You're milking this for all it is worth" is a comment that represents the delicate balance surrounding the limits of attention deemed appropri-ate should an individual be unhappy, unwell, or injured. The rules are subtle and reflect a confluence of individual biography, cultural heroes, and group and personality dynamics. The complex context surrounding the notion of specialness is replayed in groups and society. Poor "so and so" all of a sudden becomes the "attention-seeker," the "complainer."

Such labels can be poison to adolescents. The message is clear. Do anything but do not be an attention seeker. In the case of a 16-year-old girl whose brother was dying of leukemia, her friends had reached their limit of hearing about it. Her sadness had gone on too long. Her friends warned her that she might be "using it." For a 14-year-old girl with bu-limia, her friends in whom she confided warned her that they had had enough by co-signing a letter that they left in her school backpack: "We want you to get better but we think this has gone on too long. We now want to get on with our lives." She came to feel that her strong feelings must be bottled up and her recovery must be soon if she was to keep her friends.

Individuals come to believe that, evidently, there are limits to sad-ness and helplessness. To keep the group on one's side, one must recog-nize when to return to normal. If the situation is related to an ongoing medical condition or disability, this intricate social skill necessarily be-comes particularly difficult to manage.

"Will my friends get sick of my wheelchair?" a 15-year-old asks. Anxiety related to losing companionship led her to offer to do special favors for her best friend. The nuances of help-seeking behavior can be-come strategic. Can help-seeking behavior still be deployed? An 80-

year-old female resident in a senior home commented on the behavior
of an older man up the hall who constantly rings his bell for the nurse's
attention. Although the older man is paralyzed, she assessed and judged
his behavior: "He won't get anywhere going on like that. He wants too
much attention. I don't ask for too much or complain too much."

In fact, someone may take personal rules to extremes. This older
woman only tolerated a certain degree of emotion in herself. Emanating
from her childhood, the foundation of this personal rule she derived from
the admiration a boarding-house owner had bestowed on her. This
woman had praised her for being brave, for not crying, for being strong
when she was left by her parents; "You're such a strong girl, much braver
than any other little girl I've ever known." Times in her later life that were
sad or traumatic may have challenged her to keep the rule. But somewhere
in her background, a certain pride began to surround this behavior that *she*
has since proudly owned. Today she may even flaunt it, boast about it.
After receiving a painful injection she arrogantly stated to the hospital
nurse, "I never cry—it's not me to cry. I'm not like the rest of them."

These learned associations between being ill and becoming special
with its attendant feeling of enjoying specialness and therefore enjoying
being unwell, or the pairing of being strong with personal adversity, are
enduring models of great import for the concept of nonfinite loss and
grief. The relevance of these associations can be seen in the case of a 45-
year-old woman with a degenerative illness. One of her main concerns
was that she felt she got some perverse pleasure out of having this chronic
condition. During therapy she actually brought up the following sorts of
questions: Was she "playing on it"? Was she making it a big deal? Did
she, in some way, like having it? Was she a malingerer? Throughout this self-doubt, she was experiencing disbelief that her condition was
so serious.

The same individual later states that her illness had somehow made
her feel special. She asked, "What's all that about?" Perhaps, similar to the
80-year-old previously, the illness has become her opportunity to be brave
and demonstrate coping skills that others will admire. It may hark back to
her mother applauding her for her courage when she was hurt or injured
as a child: "You are my brave girl!" Bravery is admired but may be expected in males. An 18-year-old boy severed his arm while using an elec-
tric chainsaw. His arm was surgically repaired. Despite the pain he
endured, he did not need to be enticed to return to the scene of this horror. He was defiant: "I went back to that house. I stared at that chainsaw—
looked it right in the eye. You're not going to scare me. I'll be back to get
you!" To most, his bravery would be considered admirable. Conversely,
negative connotations surround what might be construed as helplessness
and the securing of attention.

Thus, when a person has cancer or another life-threatening disease, those individuals who do not seek abundant attention by way of demanding people's sympathy or help are admired. It is not difficult to understand why many people force their emotions and grief underground. The following quote represents this dilemma, which actually prevents people from exposing their true feelings about personal adversity: "I don't want to be seen as somebody who complains. I don't want other people feeling sorry for me. I don't want them to see me as helpless. It actually makes me feel weaker. I feel uncomfortable to hear myself talking like that. I feel I have to pull myself together and be brave."

"I DON'T WANT TO BE SEEN AS SOMEBODY WHO COMPLAINS. I DON'T WANT OTHER PEOPLE FEELING SORRY FOR ME. I DON'T WANT THEM TO SEE ME AS HELPLESS. IT ACTUALLY MAKES ME FEEL WEAKER."

Legitimacy: The Fear of Being Phony

Gauging whether it is legitimate to receive a lot of attention seems to play a large part in whether individuals give themselves permission to grieve. As was discussed in earlier chapters, a delicate skill indeed is that of ascertaining how to manage attention. For a primary school student, failing to recognize the limits of attention he or she is entitled to may be stigmatizing, and, similarly, an adolescent might forfeit his or her membership in a group. Gauging the legitimacy of attention continues into adulthood and becomes a common pastime. Correspondingly, it is a preoccupation of those with acquired injury to convince the outside world that they are not "pretending"; they are not "malingerers." Sadly, a 68-year-old woman seriously injured in an automobile accident spent much of one therapy session trying to prove that she was a hard worker: "I'm a person who used to sweep and clean and dust and get my groceries. I was really happy with that. I worked hard every day. I would never not work unless I was really sick. And even when I had a bad work injury, my boss, she would say, 'Nell, don't come in to work like this.' She would have to *tell* me to go home."

In effect, the threat of being perceived as malingering is so potent that individuals often are forced to hide behind the authority of others. If time is taken off for day-to-day demands or responsibilities, blame is shifted to another party, most often and ideally the doctor: "He says I *must* have time off or he will put me into the hospital—my doctor said he had never seen a blood pressure reading as high as mine. He *ordered* immediate bed rest. If I had my way...." When hospitalization is required, legitimacy is conferred without a doubt!

LEARNING DISPARAGING LABELS

Some disparaging labels directly affect an individual's expression of loss and ability to grieve openly. It is relatively easy to glean the delicate balance between when behavior or an emotion is perceived to be legitimate and when the behavior reaches limits that puts it in danger of being labeled negatively. A paradoxical situation is created. Although individuals may deeply want others to empathize with their feelings, they do not want to risk being thought of as a pain in the neck.

Table 6.1 fleshes out some of these labels, including the fear of being weak; the fear of spoiling others' enjoyment and becoming "the wet blanket"; the fear of going over the top and becoming "the attention seeker"; the fear of overexpressing emotion and becoming "the pain in the neck"; the fear of only having bad things happen, feeling jinxed, and becoming "the loser"; and the fear of others regarding what has happened as deserved and as just punishment for being irresponsible, not trying hard enough, and so forth. The latter association seems generated by some people's need to see illness or adversity as controllable, in which case the responsibility for illness or personal adversity becomes divested in the individual. Broadly speaking, some might take the attitude that if anything goes wrong, an individual didn't do something or enough of something they should have (e.g., take enough vitamins, do enough exercise, visit a faith-healer early enough).

Emotional Learning

Early on, parents or caregivers establish limits to the intensity or type of emotion that can be tolerated or is deemed personally or culturally acceptable (Stern, 1985). Stern pointed out that parents inevitably have a selective bias in their attunement of affect (i.e., their ability to tune in to the child's feelings). An outcome of this selective bias is that the child's reality or experience of something is not shared by the parents and, therefore, the child's experience of something is not confirmed; the child may experience strong feelings of sadness that the parent has never experienced and, therefore, cannot validate. This is also true of a range of emotions including positive affect such as enthusiasm or perceptions of pain. This by itself may alter parts of what the child actually experiences and create the beginnings of a template that alienates or disavows certain aspects of one's own experience.

Parents may make negative statements about their child's strong emotions, which could lead to the child's withdrawing or subverting his or her feelings. As explosions of strong emotions are pronounced unacceptable or denounced as evidence of a "lack of control," children may learn to hide their feelings. As a result, they may decide to make their

Table 6.1. Development of messages, labels, and their effect on individual's ability to express loss and grief

Childhood experience of loss or grief	Response of child	Response of parent	Outcome for child experiencing loss	Possible learned associations
Child experiences a loss (e.g., change of school, house, pet).		Parent may camouflage loss with promises or statements that indicate that the loss may have blessings: "You'll love it at the new school. You'll make new friends." "You might be able to get that pony you've always wanted."	A feeling of unease (anxiety and sadness) about change of routines and loss of friends accompanies a feeling of excitement. The excitement is associated with receiving a present, becoming special, and getting attention from friends.	Mixed and complicated emotions (e.g., guilt associated with conferred specialness or failure to be grateful for "blessings") surround experiences of loss.
Child experiences an injury or illness.	Child presents behavior or emotions that parent perceives as true and legitimate given the situation.	Parental caring becomes unconditional and singular.	Child perceives that behavior considered legitimate confers unlimited attention and feeling of being special.	Emotional expression (e.g., fear, anxiety, sadness) is okay if the situation is judged to be valid. In chronicity, as specialness becomes permanently linked with disability, the child may question the value of being special.
	Child's reaction is restrained.	Parent admires restraint. "You are such a brave boy." Attention is given to the child for the characteristic of being brave and for the injury.	The child perceives acclaim to be associated with restraint.	Individual seeks to earn continual praise for being brave and blocks or hides expression.
	Child presents behavior or emotions that the parent perceives to be not legitimate (e.g., anxiety,	Parent queries, assesses, and disqualifies veracity of child's illness or feelings: "You are well enough to be at school." "Once you are there it will go away." "You're	An unsettled or strange feeling in one's body accompanies a fear of being a phony if the illness is found not to be serious or if the feeling state is deemed to be "over the top."	Difficulty in critically assessing or legitimating states of mind or states of feeling physically unwell. The role or expression of feelings

	playing on this." "You were fine a second ago."		such as anxiety and sadness becomes stigmatized (e.g., fear of being a phony or an attention seeker).
fear, illness, crying judged to be cause).	Parent puts limits, both in terms of time and intensity allowed, on what is considered acceptable expression of feelings and behavior. "Don't carry on like that." "Go to your room." "Stop complaining." "That's enough."	Feelings of shame and embarrassment accompany a child's expressions of strong and persistent emotions.	Regulation of expression to within limits that are acceptable. Fear of becoming a complainer, a wimp, or a "pain in the neck"; feelings of being seen as a "drama queen."
Child experiences misfortune.	Parents and others attribute misfortune as having been caused by the child (e.g., "If you had been more sensible, this would not have happened").	Incongruence between feelings, emotions, and feedback from others. Being irresponsible, not sensible, or bad provides explanations for bad luck and punishment.	Expression builds up inside and may become translated into behaviors (e.g., suicide, self-injury) or kept secret to punsh the nonlisteners. Individual is unsure of legitimacy of experience. Experiences feelings of self-doubt.
	Parent is oblivious to the experience or dismisses that it has taken place and/or its intensity.	Feelings unheard and/or dismissed.	Randomness of misfortune is doubted. Seeks explanation for misfortune in self. Fears being seen as bad, damaged, unlucky, or a "loser."
		Personal experience is not validated, not explained, or made sense of for the child.	

(continues)

Table 6.1. (continued)

Childhood experience of loss or grief	Response of child	Response of parent	Outcome for child experiencing loss	Possible learned associations
Child experiences repeated misfortune.		Parent puts limits on the "amount" of bad things that can happen to the child. "It just can't happen like that, you must have done something!" "You attract bad luck."	Confusion as to whether the misfortune was orchestrated.	Searches for explanations to account for bad things happening. Frequently finds reasons in self. Blocks expression. Tries to convince others of the veracity of losses. Superstitions are evoked. Experiences fears of being jinxed.

emotions and feelings a secret from their parents. A 10-year-old-girl talks about her decision to hold back her feelings from her mother: "I had promised myself not to tell her as much as I did. It's my secret. She does not deserve to know. I'm surprised she got it out of me." At the same time, the expression of emotions becomes unpracticed. As talking about feelings becomes uncomfortable, an individual's perception of living in an all-too-private world in which "Nobody understands me—I am like no one I know" gains in intensity.

As Table 6.1 outlines, it is evident that parents or caregivers often inadvertently miss the intensity of a child's experience related to an incident. Implicit is a lack of validation for the child's strong emotions. Unac-knowledged, almost rejected out of hand, the child's feelings go unexplained. He or she might describe his or her resulting feelings in terms of a "black hole." A great deal of confusion surrounds this lack of attunement. Specifically, the child is unsure: "Have I made something out of nothing?"—a sort of "crying wolf" feeling. This creates a type of dissonance. The feelings are there, but are they valid? The experience happened, but was it *really* that bad? Eventually, the child is forced to question whether the experience did actually take place—was it imagined?

In this case, the adolescent or adult is left to try to justify or seek justification of his or her feelings. How to deal with a feeling? Running away, becoming ill, or committing suicide represent alternative routes to demonstrate the feeling and the pain. At the same time these responses might be seen as an effort to hurt the person, parent, spouse, or sibling who minimized or dismissed the pain or emotional intensity of a personal experience. "I often find myself fantasizing about suicide. I think that then they [the parents] would see my pain. Then they would know how bad it had been for me. Then they would be sorry!" the person in pain might think.

Conversely, parents may offer children unlimited time to talk—they might continually intervene and save their children from working out what to do when they feel strong, intense feelings. As an adult, this relationship may continue in the form of daily contact, in which an individual picks up the telephone in the middle of the night to have emotionally overwhelming feelings regulated by his or her parents. What if something happens to the parent? For such adults, it is the fear of how to tolerate strong emotions that first and foremost might leave them grappling with a series of panic attacks. Teaching children how to manage and thereby survive their own strong emotions of sadness, frustration, or anxiety coupled with helping them learn that they can be alone with their thoughts are skills that are important to acquire. They are central attributes for the ability to grieve personal loss.

Emotional Knots

As in the case of William, mentioned previously, contradictions between feelings are learned in childhood. Often, emotions coexist. For instance, excited anticipation and a feeling of sadness or being frustrated might easily be partnered in a child whose parents are relocated by their business. Anxious to protect their child from the pain of leaving friends, the parents offer enticements, and the child's sadness becomes confused with excitement or a feeling that he or she should be grateful for the enticement. The scenario becomes even more complicated if parents tell the child an incomplete or untrue story. A 10-year-old boy who is asked by teachers or friends if he is sad to leave his friends and his school replies almost offhandedly, "Mom and Dad say I'm accepted into one of the best schools, and I'm going to get a pony where we are going!"

In adolescence, the complexity of the feelings surrounding leave-taking conceivably become clearer. Adolescents sense other nuances in their own feelings and are better able to anticipate what relocation might mean than a younger child. Not as naive, adolescents' feelings are mixed with sadness, unease, anxiety, and a feeling of helplessness. Young adolescents usually have no recourse but to go along with the move. When she was 14, Barbra returned from a 12-month stay overseas. One year is a long time in adolescence. She did not feel at home with her old friends. They had changed, as far as Barbra was concerned: "They had become snobs." Although initially yearning to return to the United States, Barbra now began to miss her friends overseas. Actually, schematically, this young girl can now be seen to have been "between" two homes, idealizing the one she had wanted to leave and feeling alienated from the one to which she had returned. Barbra tried to talk about her mixture of feelings with her old friends.

Missing the emotional complexity, Barbra's friends admonished her for her sadness and angrily persuaded her that she was lucky to have experienced new things: "We'd give anything to have been where you have been." There is no room here for the expression of sadness. The message is that she is ungrateful.

The nuances of social conversation are difficult to learn and decipher. The difficulties become more pronounced when no one shares your feelings or comments. In order to keep her friends, Barbra had been separating from her inner feelings. They did not hold any meaning with her friends. In therapy, she found it immensely difficult to talk about her feelings. It was apparent that much of Barbra's inner experience had not been articulated and shared with anyone. In fact, for this young girl her feelings actually were unintelligible. Like a lot of other adolescents struggling with their emotions, she called her feeling "a big black hole." Her incapability to converse and share her thoughts with her friends was clear: "I don't know what to say, how to express myself. It seems to take me a long time to work out what to say, how to say it—and by then the opportunity is lost!"

Encouraged not to discuss her thoughts, Barbra had carried her feelings of disappointment around with her through various stages of her life: disappointment over not being able to finish her final year at primary school with her friends, confused feelings related to leaving home and going to a new country, and then mixed feelings again as she returned home. Instead of these complicated feelings being opened up and legitimized, they went underground, gathered momentum, and confused her. Two years later, these unexpressed feelings had created a wall: Barbra did not know where to start and had no practice in freely conversing about feelings. An emotional rift between Barbra and her friends had been created.

Barbra had not had an opportunity to master her strong feelings by talking them through. It was clear that she was feeling disconnected from her peers. The ability to express emotions is an important skill. Without it, the feeling often gets expressed in behavior. This can be where self-mutilation behaviors and eating disorders find their way into an individual's life. Early environments that allow or accept the practice of talking about feelings seem important but are not always available. Sibling dynamics, life experiences, peer-group relationships as they interact with an individual's disposition all play important roles in an individual's life. Thus, although a child–caregiver environment usually offers the modeling and the permission to show and practice expressing and explaining feelings and thoughts, an individual's peer-group or one's siblings may not. This may be exacerbated by the gender makeup in the family (e.g., being the only daughter in a family with five boys or vice versa).

SUMMARY

The enigmatic messages sent among parents, caregivers, and children lend meaning to children's behavior and the things that happen to them. Parents interpret what can be construed as loss and what is permissible in terms of reactions to loss. By becoming angry, sad, frustrated, scared, even expressionless, parents model behavior for their children. By putting conditions on children's experiences and their emotions, parents send mixed messages. Often, children do not learn to respect or legitimize their own emotions that surround loss and illness. These learned messages not only become tacit expectations and rules for other people's behavior but also they become rules for individuals themselves. In adulthood, they continue to conspire against an individual's ability to express strong emotions or even admit to an experience of loss.

Section III delves further into the components of identity. Identity is composed of a range of learning experiences; from early childhood, individuals establish who they would dread becoming. Chapters 7–9 trace the central role of fear, stigma, and the internalized dread that surrounds the reputation of certain life experiences. This knowledge base is a further acquired interpretive framework in conceptualizing nonfinite loss: Who or what an individual dreads becoming has significant implications for the ability to grieve nonfinite loss.

SECTION III

FEAR AND DREAD

ORIGINS AND ROLE
IN NONFINITE LOSS

CHAPTER 7

FEAR, ANXIETY, AND DREAD

We all remember childhood fears. Which of us cannot recall the bogey-man of our childhood, invisible, yet visible, the co-mingling of anxiety and imagination? What's under the bed? In the cupboard? In the corner? A man with an axe, poised to "get" us? It is not difficult to frighten a child or an adolescent. Anybody who has worked as a therapist would add that it is also very easy to scare an adult—many adults become frightened children when faced with the loss of their jobs, appearance, or abilities, let alone faced with a life-threatening disease. Fearing that "all is not what it seems," the suspicion that danger may lurk seems to play out in an individual's dreams. A 9-year-old boy describes a recurring nightmare: He sees a stretch of dirt road between his parents' house and his grandmother's house as turning into giant holes that attempt to swallow him.

If the world actually reveals its danger in an individual's life—through disease, an accident, even a regular inoculation—and validates the person's fears—then dreams reflect those fears. Thus, an older woman undergoing chemotherapy talks of nightmares that revolve around her walking on wooden piers that slowly start to erode and collapse around her. A 12-year-old boy whose father has recently committed suicide dreams of a blue bedroom carpet transforming into a sea of sharks, and an 11-year-old girl undergoing extensive and invasive medical testing describes nightmares about walking through a forest that suddenly reveals itself to be unsafe; it becomes "full of poisonous snakes."

Integral connections exist between innate fear and anxiety about danger and the materialization of such fears. In this chapter we reveal the innate role these two emotions play in childhood and adolescence and the sometimes inordinate lengths to which individuals are forced to go to secure a feeling of safety. Patterns surrounding securing safety as well as of superstition and rituals often are forced to resurface when individuals are faced with situations of personal adversity, such as when they are grieving or experiencing a loss.

PATTERNS OF FEAR AND ANXIETY

Central to an understanding of human nature are two basic fears: the fear of life and the fear of death (Heidegger, 1949, as cited in Becker, 1973; Rank, 1931/1961). For children, this translates into anxiety surrounding the "overwhelmingness of the world, the real dangers of it," and a fear of being alone and helpless (Heidegger, 1949, as cited in Becker, 1973, p. 46). According to Becker (1973), an ongoing task for parents, starting in their child's infancy, is containing his or her anxiety. Obviously, the task is significantly more difficult if the child has an ongoing medical condition or disability—or the parents themselves have not reached a stage of development where they have mastered *their* fears. The fact is that in the end, the ability to master one's fears may be the biggest hurdle and the most precious skill to have learned in dealing with nonfinite loss and in facing one's own death.

The Regulation of Internal States

Very minor changes to a child's body can create large degrees of anxiety. The reaction young children have to their first wound or skin blemish attests to this. It also illuminates the enormous part a parent can play in limiting a child's anxiety. Following a fall, a child races to a parent for affirmation of recovery: "Will I be all right?" "Will I get better?" "Will the sore go away?"—all are typical questions children ask their parents. For some children, a mosquito bite will raise a degree of alarm. Until the child has learned the cycle of the bite, the child will be preoccupied with its "out of placeness" on his or her skin. In fact, young children provide salient demonstrations of the anxiety that implicitly surrounds disability, illness, or major disruptions to assumptive worlds.

As a child, one has to *learn* that many changes, even in bodily functions, do not endanger survival. A 4-year-old boy's first experience with the sensation of perspiration is one example. While sitting next to his mother in the front seat of a car with the sun streaming in, the boy cautiously leans forward and very tentatively feels his back and stares at his hands. His hands and back are wet. He anxiously exclaims, "Mom, there's water coming out of my back, there's water coming out of my hands!" Reassurance from the parent is demanded. Only then does this boy return his attention to other things. This scenario could just as easily describe a child's first experience with a bout of diarrhea or with separation. All of these kinds of experiences create anxiety or fear. All require an adaptation process that will be facilitated by the knowledge that things will return to normal. Buoyed by the parent's assurance, the child first noticing his per-spiration is able to understand that his body will return to what he per-ceived it to be before. In such instances anxiety and fear slowly subside, and the physiological systems described in Chapter 3 by the work of Hofer (1995) drop back to normal or a state of balance.

Although the parents' assurance quells the boy's anxiety, it is often the case that parents' anxiety undermines children's development of trust in their own ability to read their bodies. Instead of downplaying chil-dren's anxiety about their bodies and allowing them to experience and learn to tolerate their vagaries, the parents themselves panic. The situa-tion of the 17-year-old boy described in Chapter 4 who has difficulty get-ting to sleep without his mother is a good example of a parent subverting a child's self-confidence.

The following example shows the possible outcome of a mother's continual involvement in her child's bathroom habits beyond the typical toilet-teaching years. A 14-year-boy had sought counseling because he could not go longer than 2 hours between toilet breaks. Counseling re-vealed that the boy's mother's habitual statements such as "Don't forget to go to the toilet. Have you been to the toilet?" were, it seemed, persis-tent reminders throughout his development. This mother's perceived lack of confidence in her child's ability to master his body was intimidat-ing the 14-year-old. He had become frightened that he would soil him-self. Not surprisingly, his confidence was thwarted. In therapy, he described a procedure of clearing the path to the toilet at night, a ritual that actually prevented him from having friends stay overnight because if a friend stayed over, all would be revealed. The ritual of safety could not take place.

The Regulation of the External World

The tasks of feeling and being all right are far more difficult than parents imagine or remember. Fears are a natural part of childhood (Marks, 1987; Rutter & Rutter, 1993). What begins for young children as a cer-tain manufactured tension that is somewhat exciting—mental images surrounding the cellar or the trapdoor and what may be lurking behind it—can easily escalate into real fear. The feeling of fear is much harder to conjure away in the dark. Many children introduce a cast of nasty characters who threaten them when they are alone or go to bed at night. According to Warner (2000), such "bogeymen" materialize fear into some kind of living shape. For some, the bogey character might be the classroom teacher with the "hairy face and evil eyes" whom the primary-school child feels is "picking on her." When a child describes a terror, the idea of surrounding blackness is conjured up, as well as its inescapability. One 4-year-old boy describes "scary pictures" that appear in front of his eyes at night—an arm that floats above him and a light that falls down and tries to stab him. A 6-year-old girl relates a similar fear. "There's a small hole in the roof," she says. "Something scary is behind it, waiting for nighttime." She pulls the covers right up under her chin. This will stop "it" from "taking blood from my neck."

At age 12, a girl describes a range of behaviors that she has to carry out to protect herself from "a tall, dark-haired guy, wearing old jeans, a bomber jacket, and black boots." Before she can go to sleep she has to inspect and close drawers and cupboards. Is he hiding in her room? To ensure a quick getaway, all clothes and objects are meticulously shifted from the center of her bedroom.

The sense of continuing peril is graphically portrayed in the form of the axeman. Even when the axe itself stays in a fixed position, there is a pervading dread it may fall. The axeman symbolizes the psychological context that characterizes nonfinite loss—fear, anxiety—the dread of what might happen to us, what we might become. An 8-year-old and an 11-year-old introduce their versions of this character—as illustrated in Figures 7.1a and 7.1b. They believe this daunting figure will "smash" through their bedroom window at night. Wielding a big axe, he will "cut them up into little pieces." A 10-year-old girl is prevented from entering the bathroom because of her fear of a disarming image behind a mirror, which she calls "Bloody Mary." Apparently, to see her image in the mirror, the girl must chant "Bloody Mary" 100 times. Figure 7.1c shows one child's depiction of this character.

Escaping Fears

Some children cannot imagine escaping the axeman—they perceive that this is not an option. This is not always the case, however. Some children have an escape route planned: "I would climb out the window, jump onto the roof, down the side of the house. He would never be able to catch me," one child says. As the introductory quote to this chapter illustrates, other children may go into quite elaborate thoughts of how to protect vital organs during sleep. The 5-year-old, full of bravado, acts out the attack that would take place should he be faced with an adversary. Holding

Figure 7.1. Drawings of frightening bogeyman characters by children: a) "The Axeman" by an 8-year-old (E. Fehring), b) "The Axeman" by an 11-year-old (J. Bruce), and c) "Bloody Mary" by an 11-year-old. The ability to escape images such as these, and to believe it is possible to do so, is central to a feeling of safety and a positive self-image.

a toy sword high above his head, spinning, he becomes a Jedi warrior from the film *Star Wars*. Anything seems possible—from his wheelchair a young boy with diplegia plays out an attack with miniature fighting men.

An individual's ability to escape these images, and to believe it is possible to do so, is central to his or her feeling of safety and helps to foster strong self-images. According to Seligman (1995), this optimism is largely generated by the primary caregivers and learned by the child. Alternately, the parent can have the opposite effect and instill pessimism. The following example shows how a negative, anxious mother's beliefs had insidious effects on her daughter, who is now 50 years old:

> My mother spent some time in a boarding school in England. She was left at a very early stage, maybe just 6 years old, to look after herself and her 4-year-old brother while her parents traveled the world. I don't exactly know the facts about her life there, though it is not hard to imagine the anxiety that surrounded what possibly felt like an endless abandonment. But to me, she seemed to always have this black outlook. It was as if every time I left her side, something bad might happen. She would stand anxiously watching me, almost pleading with me to be careful. Even when I could drive, she would stand at the car window trying hard to not let me leave her; I would be unsafe—she would be unsafe. Now, as I sit here, I realize that I have her thoughts about the world myself—it is unsafe.

Optimism can be enhanced or diminished, certainly tested, by the transactions children have with their world. Some children secure proof of their ability to escape; others secure information to the contrary, in which case there is no escape. Their attempts are fruitless. Often, they learn from parents that the world is too unsafe—even when they have not experienced that reality for themselves. Parents often inadvertently miss their child's need to establish a positive estimation of personal safety. In the case of children with chronic conditions, this need to establish a positive estimation of personal safety is necessarily amplified.

All Is Not What It Seems

Two sisters, now both in their early thirties, have sought therapy at separate times in their lives. Both are dogged by fear of the world. One night, while lying in bed with the nightlight on, one of them hears voices. Tracing back, a therapist finds out that they had a mother who unwittingly sent them the message throughout their development that "all is not what it seems." A spiritualist, the mother introduced a world that could not be seen. During their childhoods their mother's mention of spirits, good and bad; seances; auras; and the like diminished the girls' ability to convince themselves of safety. What might guide a feeling of safety for a child when there are things that cannot be seen? Certainly for these young women, their habit of checking cupboards before they go to sleep can be seen to be illogical and sadly futile.

In a situation of traumatic bereavement, the issue of "all is not what it seems" becomes amplified. A 13-year-old whose brother had recently been murdered was becoming what she termed "spooked." She felt her dead brother's presence. Although this felt comforting, she could never be sure when he was observing her, so she was understandably unnerved. "He might be watching me. It makes me feel real guilty if I am doing something wrong and I know he is there," the girl said. The candle flickering at night, a tape turning off seemingly by itself—all were interpreted as messages from her brother. He was trying to tell her something. "Is he all right?" she wondered. Even the answer to this question is surrounded by doubt.

"WHERE IS HE? DO YOU THINK HE IS IN HEAVEN, OR DO YOU THINK IT IS A BIT LIKE SANTA CLAUS—THAT HEAVEN IS SOMETHING THAT IS MADE UP TO MAKE US FEEL BETTER?"

For adolescents in particular, what the world had seemed to be during their childhood loses its psychological guarantees. They begin to question heaven and such beliefs presented to them by adults. This bereaved teenager checks her emerging view of reality with an adult: "Where is he? Do you think he is in heaven, or do you think it is a bit like Santa Claus—that heaven is something that is made up to make us feel better?"

For this girl, it is crucial that she make connections with reassuring adults who are willing to calm and guide this emerging, frightening reality.

Thus, acquiring confidence in the world is important. Losing teeth, even hair, is frightening, but it is also normal. The experience can build confidence if handled with reassurance. A child of 4 will anxiously state, "But I don't want my teeth to fall out." The 8-year-old anxiously checks with the parent, "This was a baby tooth, wasn't it—I'm all right then, aren't I?"

Of course, there are differences in extremes, with some children more able to tolerate loss and change than others. One child might be distraught and unable to be comforted at the loss of a balloon while another child seemingly is unaffected by the same scenario. Some children may be emotionally able to withstand moving each year; other children may be so distressed by their first move that they become emotionally overwhelmed.

The variables involved in this are impossible to decipher. Although the interaction between one's socioemotional, cognitive development, and knowledge and experiential base is one foundation, the roles and importance that people, places, and things (objects) play at particular points of an individual's development also are central. For instance, the words "We are leaving—we'll return" that accompany a family's year-long relocation to another state are almost unintelligible for a child without a fully developed concept of time. For a 6-year-old, leaving friends can be far less traumatic than it is for an 11-year-old who is experiencing the first feelings of being special through being a leader in school. Friends also may have become integral. A child's reaction to a loss of a balloon may be proportionately less if he or she has learned that balloons can be replaced. However, although appraisal of a situation is directly affected by cognitive development, all reactions can be tempered by individual differences in attachment, temperament, and stress reactivity (Howe, 1998; Marks, 1987).

RULES SECURING SAFETY

A group of 5-year-olds plays a game. "You're dead if you step on the lines." One child decides to disobey the rule. Deliberately, he jumps on top of the lines—daring danger. Without further ado, his peer-group confers certain kudos to what might be regarded as a display of courage. Although the daring of death may retain some status of bravery throughout childhood, as children get older, the possibility of being labeled "an idiot" or an "attention seeker" becomes equally feasible.

Fascination with playing games that revolve around danger and death (Opie, 1993) results from the creation of a certain exciting tension between daring death and staying safe (Warner, 2000). A 5-year-old waits for his friend to come over. For the boy, the highlight of the visit is showing the friend the cellar door at the side of the house. Similarly, fascination with magic, rituals, fortune-telling, and the like revolves around this tension. However, when fantasy becomes reality, that is, when danger blatantly enters a child's life either through injury, illness, or death, the child is challenged to restore safety. Equally, the same applies for an adult encounter with a real threat.

This need to restore safety is apparent in the type of rules children develop for themselves. A 10-year-old girl claims: "It's like this. Every day that I have worn this necklace nothing bad has happened to me. If I don't wear it, something bad will happen." Originating from the time she broke her leg, this rule is about creating ideas that make the world feel safe. In fact, these rules and rituals can take on magical or religious proportion (Piaget, 1962), or they can fail and pull the rug out from under the child's feet. If the ritual fails to create a feeling of safety, the child may be forced to create tighter rules. The converse is that the idea of safety has to be dared—reality must be almost frightened away: As described in the quote at the beginning of Section II of this book, defenses become "scare-crows" (Ortega y Gasset, 1957). These scarecrows continue to play an inordinate role in an adult's experience of threat or trauma.

> "IT'S LIKE THIS. EVERY DAY THAT I HAVE WORN THIS NECKLACE NOTHING BAD HAS HAPPENED TO ME. IF I DON'T WEAR IT, SOMETHING BAD WILL HAPPEN."

For some individuals the scarecrows, or defenses they build up against their fears, become very complex and intricate. A daunting task of reestablishing a feeling of safety was set for a man whose mother had died of cancer when he himself was in his early teens. Now 55 years of age, he came to therapy seeking help with panic attacks. Tracing back through his development, he described a feeling like being struck by a "lightning bolt" when his older brother told him that his mother had died. Later in therapy, he was asked whether he had any superstitions. Reddening from his neck up, he recounted an elaborate set of behaviors that had become integral to supplying a feeling of safety in his life. One such behavior involved his hands, which he would clasp and unclasp. In this therapy setting he felt anxious; his need for this behavior was thus amplified as it would create a temporary distraction and diminish the fear: "I clasp my hands, it's okay. Unclasped, not okay." Not long after his mother died, he had developed a safety ritual—his act of placing his hands "just so" was about making sure bad things would not happen again.

Adapting to a world that becomes too scary can transform children into a mass of rituals. Often, children's rituals involve religion and attempts to ensure that God will protect them from further adversity.

Alternatively, in adolescence, an individual who feels encumbered with adversity may perceive no such protection. There may be no recourse but to adopt a different tack. He or she may become a person who dares danger and takes on numerous risks; as a type of protest, previous cautionary behaviors will be discarded. The individual may run away from fear—camouflaging the dangers and unpredictability of the world by drinking alcohol or taking drugs. Perhaps an early intimate relationship with another person will provide a temporary feeling of safety. None of these behaviors are exclusive to childhood and adolescence—any individual, particularly when he or she is experiencing a relentless personal siege, will exhibit a variety of them.

It is clear that even if nothing serious has happened, the issue of protecting a certain degree of naiveté is, in today's society, actually being undermined. Many children currently are watching and hearing a multitude of things from adults, personally or by way of the media. Their world now embraces knowledge about every known threat—from spiders in Africa and televised, gruesome details of murders to graphic and intimate knowledge of how the body works and what happens when it fails. The depiction of a stroke in the news media is graphic, full of foreboding. Some children will be frightened; others will be forced to ignore or defuse the threat. "Would that happen to me?" a 9-year-old child inquires. Adolescents, although still frightened, may react with more ridicule to the threat. For example, they might rate the horror scenes they see on television: "Did you see that—that's a 4, that's a 2!" Scoring, jeering, deriding the believability of the actors, mimicking the drama—the scariness of the scene is covered up. Now, at least, an attempt may be made to explore the world!

SUMMARY

This chapter has examined the nature of anxiety and fear and its roots in early childhood. Children and adolescents are frightened of bad things happening to them. Fear is at the basis of all superstitions, as is well illustrated by the children Dill and Jem in the novel *To Kill a Mockingbird*:

> Haven't you ever walked along a lonesome road at night and passed a hot place?" Jem asked Dill. "A hot steam's somebody who can't get to heaven, just wallows around on lonesome roads an' if you walk through him, when you die you'll be one too.... But if you hafta go through one, say 'Angel-bright, life-in-death; get off the road, don't suck my breath.' That keeps 'em from wrapping around you. (Lee, 1960, p. 41)

Parents have the potential to amplify or deemphasize the dangers of the world. They also are in a position to help their child believe that he or she can manage danger. Later on, these learned messages play a pivotal role in the handling of personal adversity. The following chapter explores the origins of dreaded events and the part they play in the interpretive framework of nonfinite loss.

A 5-YEAR-OLD BOY POINTS TO A FLOCK OF
SEAGULLS SCRAMBLING AROUND SOME
SCRAPS ON THE SAND. AMONG THEM IS
ONE WITH A DAMAGED WING. HE SAYS TO
HIS MOTHER, "I WANT TO BE THE MOST
COLORFUL BIRD IN THE WORLD. I DON'T
WANT TO BE THAT ONE!"

CHAPTER 8

DREADED EVENTS
Public Reputation

This chapter is devoted to the dread associated with the fear of disease
and disability and the difficulty such dread casts on the process of grieving and adaptation. Perhaps the dread surrounding certain situations and
where they might lead originates in experiences similar to that of the boy
looking at the seagulls. The child easily recognizes which bird he would
choose *not* to be. He would not want to be the one with the damaged
wing, but he does want to be special. Naturally, he chooses the colorful
bird. Thus begins comparisons and attributions that surround being different: I am "better off" or "worse off" than someone else.

PUBLIC REPUTATION
AND PERSONAL MEANING

Certain life events acquire reputations that represent an accumulation of
negative images. The malignant power of these images should not be un-
derestimated. Fear of dreaded events can be attributed, in part, to models
of life imbued with negative properties. The assignment of dreaded properties to certain life events is the result of a learning process—what we
see, hear, and are told over time—that begins in childhood. According to
Rochlin (1965), by the age of 3 or 4 years, a child has attributed vital importance to bodily functions. From early elementary school days, the origins of fear surrounding disease and disability are set: "Can you catch

those germs?" "Could I catch that?" the child anxiously asks her mother. Frightened of the possibility of contracting a disease, a child in a late elementary school grade refuses to use the pencil of a child who has spina bifida: "I might catch 'leg germs,'" she protests. Apparently, these sets of preconceived and entrenched scripts, pregnant with extraordinary foreboding, form very early in life. One of the reasons why people reject those who have a disease or a disability is learned fear.

Personal experience varies greatly and has the potential either to modify or attest to the dread that surrounds certain events. The reputation of disability, disfigurement, and chronic illness, however, seems to possess unqualified and universal dread. In his novel *Three Dollars*, author Elliot Perlman described a scene in which Tanya, one of the characters, has an encounter in the street with Rachel, another character, who has a significant disability. Rachel is in a wheelchair and appealing for help. "I didn't want to talk to her," Tanya says. "I was angry with her.... Her existence was causing me pain. I didn't even want to look at her. I told her I had to go" (1998, p. 91). Ironically, if someone who initiates this kind of rejection acquires a disability then he or she will recall rejections of this type all too well. Invariably, when an individual envisions personal reactions to scenarios such as a diagnosis of cancer or of blindness or the prospect of parenting a child with an autism spectrum disorder, this immediately forecasts a number of threatening and projected future realities. Should a negative event of such magnitude befall an individual, the difficulty in extricating oneself from preconceived scripts is clear.

Preconceived scripts are laden with well-learned awareness of the attitudes that being different (e.g., through disability, impairment, divorce) arouse in others (Goffman, 1963; Mead, 1934). Often, they are embellished with disturbing and vivid images. Hallmarks of such images include scenarios of human helplessness, abandonment, dependency, pain, and, often, humiliation. They also contain some sad evidence of the indifference of the world to such human conditions. In place well before the event has occurred, this representation derives from a number of sources (e.g., recollections of childhood, personal experiences, storytelling, myths, media). This representation will be complicated further by values and attitudes that children acquire from their parents, significant others, and cultural symbols and icons.

Fear of Being Different, Fear of Rejection

By and large, biographical experience itself contains some confronting memories of one's own behavior and attitudes toward differences in others. Peer pressure and the need to conform affect behavior toward people who are perceived to be different (e.g., impairment, disability, illness)

(Erikson, 1965; Flavell, Miller, & Miller, 1993). A slightly overweight kindergarten student, Michael, was labeled as fat, slow, and clumsy. A number of boys in the kindergarten taunted him. This might not have revolved around a conscious decision to tease Michael. Children often just simply "find" themselves joining in a taunt. A 5-year-old recounted his experience to his mother. The boy and Michael had been working together on a kindergarten project when some of his peers began making comments. "Mom, I didn't *want* to call Michael 'stupid,'" the boy said, "but James and Jack began and then I was calling him 'stupid' too. I tried once not to, but then I was calling him 'stupid' again. They made me say it."

Much of this conforming behavior reflects an unconscious or conscious desire to be one of the "in" group. This behavior is the way *in* to that group. Because no child likes looking as though he or she is friendless or alone, being a member of this group and *not* being "a Michael" becomes critical. The group gains its own momentum (Canetti, 1973). Not surprisingly, aligning with Michael had become risky. For the 5-year-old concerned with his group membership and its guaranteed (although short-lived) feeling of safety and security, even finding one of Michael's pictures accidentally placed in his bag would be judged as risky, a type of contamination fear. "Will you give this to Michael?" his mother asks. "No!" the boy replied. Although the memory of rejecting Michael will most likely fade, later on the same rejection of those who are different will begin to gain clarity and momentum. He will begin to understand what it is about.

Most adults are readily able to name the child who they would not have wanted to be. One young mother recollects her school days, when she and her friends would make fun of children whom her group called "spastics." She finds it painfully ironic that she has given birth to a child with cerebral palsy and wonders whether the birth is a punishment.

The antics of childhood, the need to be liked and accepted, and the need to avoid being an outcast drive a lot of discriminate behavior. In fact, the fear of being alone and its association with being "friendless" drives individuals into all manner of situations. A teenage boy recounted with amazement his participation in the theft of a car: "I am a thief—how did this happen?" Therapy revealed that the answer could be found in the teenager's need to hold on to his best and only friend, who on that occasion wanted to have some fun. The prospect of "becoming a Michael" remains a frightening proposition for individuals, so much so that being dislocated from the mainstream remains a central aspect of the trauma surrounding personal adversity.

Memories provide individuals with empathy and perceptions of the generalized response to differences and impairments. So, if one becomes an outcast, an outcome resembles a two-way mirror; individuals with heightened empathy and sensitivity to the attitudes and behaviors of others experience a stigmatization process of which they are acutely aware. This is aptly demonstrated when considering the unique position in which parents of children with a congenital disability find themselves. Unlike their children, the parents can predict a range of ostracizing situations that will parallel their child's development. Typically, they forecast horror stories for their children at school based on what they saw and experienced as children themselves: "When I think of her at school, I can see, almost as if it were yesterday, the behavior that was meted out to a little girl with a disability. I can't imagine how she endured it in the sandpit, she would sit and let us fill her underpants up with sand."

And seemingly, the prediction of terrible scenarios is not necessarily a figment of imagination. Some adults with disabilities validate these concerns. Consider this statement made by a 40-year-old man with a lifelong disability: "There are endless horror stories of my years at school. Countless times I would be fighting someone behind the gardener's shed who had goaded me until I exploded. "I will never forgive my mother for not finding some operation to make my disability less of an object of derision." This man has since become the father of a child with physical disabilities. As an adult, his need for personal revenge continues. Even though he has had an operation to reduce the outward manifestation of his own disability, the man seemed driven by a need to redress what happened in his childhood but now from a different vantage point. Wheeling his child down to the suburban shopping center, he tracked the stares of shoppers passing by: "What the hell are you staring at?" he demanded. In therapy he admitted that he looks for any opportunity to berate people who stare. Albeit less aggressively, a 45-year-old woman with a skin condition had a similar need to protest. She stated a need to demonstrate the pain she experienced in what she termed her "nightmare childhood." This woman's skin was red and sore, almost bleeding at times. It was so raw that looking at it took one's breath away. What children might have felt about it was not difficult to envision. The school reunion 10 years after graduation represented an opportunity for her to observe her peers revisiting their childhood: "I want them to see me now that they are adults and remember how they treated me. I want to stand in their faces."

"I WILL NEVER FORGIVE MY MOTHER FOR NOT FINDING SOME OPERATION TO MAKE MY DISABILITY LESS OF AN OBJECT OF DERISION."

Why did this girl's classmates treat her so badly? Basically, because they were frightened of the disease she had. Perhaps, as Marks (1987) theorized, it was a primitive reaction to the fear of being contaminated.

Again, being a member of the group would have been a crucial component for most children. What would have prevented these children from "ganging up" on this girl? Certainly, learning that they are safe, learning through ongoing transactions with her that she is an individual first and that the skin disease she has cannot threaten them, would be a key. Yet, many individuals have never come into close contact with such differences in people. For many Caucasians, even darker-skinned people can be feared or vice versa. Children who have not been familiarized to the range of different types of people that make up society can become frightened on their first visit to a cosmopolitan marketplace. The outcome for children with salient differences is to spend their time in elementary and secondary school environments representing a misunderstood symbol of fear. It is this fear, the fear of being different, the fear of not being liked, and the fear of being feared, that necessarily often keeps certain diseases (e.g., HIV/AIDS) undisclosed. Without learning and the resulting desensitization that convinces individuals not to be afraid, ostracizing is guaranteed.

The paradox for some parents who have a child with an ongoing medical condition or disability becomes clear. A 25-year-old father of a child with a rare syndrome that has distorted many of his child's physical features cried out within a group of other parents of children with a disability: "I am not one of you—I am not just a parent of a child with a disability!" A fear of contamination as in childhood had surfaced, but now this man will have to align and support what traditionally he might have feared. A lack of personal experience sometimes prevents the desensitization of negative feelings (e.g., fear, repulsion) that may accompany some behavioral and physical outcomes of impairment of function. Ironically, very similar words were proclaimed by an 84-year-old woman about other older adults: "What would I want to be stuck with a whole lot of old people for?" The images from childhood that create a fear of old age are rampant. Preschool children huddle together to talk about their classmate's 92-year-old grandmother: "Uh-oh, she touched you!"

Desensitization and Sensitization to Fear

Desensitization can result from firsthand and childhood exposure. Individuals who have obvious physical disabilities do not have a choice but to face the crowd, the stares, and the questions. Sadly, the only alternative, which is taken by some, is to avoid the crowd. Individuals who face the crowd, however, often begin to devote their energies to educating the community about the experience of being different. When a member of one's family has a frightening condition, such as bipolar disorder or alcoholism, desensitization can simultaneously begin. Knowing someone who contracts and recovers from the disease is likely to reduce fear of that condition. With good outcomes, such as when a girl's sister recovers from leukemia, it is likely that the girl will have less initial fear of other life-threatening conditions she encounters throughout her life. Similarly, if an individual has not caught a sibling's illness despite living in close quarters for 5 years, he or she will have learned that not all illness is infectious.

However, desensitization is not always the outcome of exposure to certain conditions. For instance, it is apparent that many siblings are extremely frightened of, sometimes terrified by, brothers or sisters with behavior problems related to an intellectual disability or autism spectrum disorder. Rather than being inured they become sensitized, that is, their feelings of fear are continually realized. The often erratic behaviors of their siblings overwhelm them emotionally and physically. Sam, an 8-year-old boy with a brother who has autism, knew intimately the "change" in his brother's eyes that signaled a rage or what Sam has learned to term an "episode." In order to maintain his personal safety, he needed to perceive this cue; by learning to read it, Sam knew when to hide. How does one respond when one's sister or brother does not seem to understand limits? There is no reasoning, no comeback, no common ground to sort things out. Obviously, the home environment without the shelter of the parents can become a frightening place. Often, a child has no recourse but to remain continually vigilant.

Personal life experiences provide an information source that has the potential to modify or magnify what one thinks about things that happen to them. Apart from differences in outlook, generally, there are origins to an individual's response to personal adversity. Representations of conditions exacerbate personal experience. In particular, some individuals must embrace a life that is contrary to their expectations and one they might have traditionally feared. Research (Ganiban, Barnett, & Cicchetti, 2000), which has found complications in attachment among mothers and their children who have disabilities, has identified the possibility of unresolved maternal grief. Bruce and Shears (2000) suggested that some parents are traumatized by their child's disability and what it represents for them. This is not distinctive to the child, but more about the fear of being different and the fear of something that they are not used to and, therefore, cannot perceive themselves as managing. The child who is different forces this fear and personal vulnerability into the foreground.

A young mother confided that when she embarked on her first pregnancy she was hoping to give birth to a daughter who would play volleyball "just like me, and be my lifetime friend and companion." Instead, she had given birth to a girl with a severe developmental disability. Although this in itself was a trauma, her biography provides a complicating context: She had grown up with a sister who had a disability. Throughout her childhood and adolescence she had become particularly aware of the public response to disabilities. Perceiving the life ahead for both herself and her daughter as "intolerable," she described her fear of her child's muscular contortions. All that she could see in her child was the condition and its consequences. Her situation was complicated by a strong attachment to ideal models of parenthood. Anxiously, she asks whether the counselor thought that she loved her child.

THE FEAR OF DREADED EVENTS

The type of mindset generated from the reputation of some diseases or experiences represents an obstinate hurdle to traveling one's own experience. Individuals sometimes just live in fear of what may happen. The young mother introduced previously does not know how her own life and that of her child are going to turn out. Neither does the father mentioned previously know that a group of boys will taunt his daughter. Perhaps things will have changed regarding such bullying; individuals may become better educated than they were in his childhood. In the days following diagnosis, little had yet actually unfolded. Nevertheless, these parents were thinking far into the future—"my child will never be married"—and similar life markers were toppling. The propensity for fear to take over is understandable. Receiving a diagnosis associated with a dreaded event simultaneously moves a montage of present and future scenarios that have been learned from childhood forward. Counterweighing such memories sometimes is a challenging task.

Cancer, AIDS, multiple sclerosis, Huntington's disease, Down syndrome, spina bifida, and cerebral palsy are just a few of those conditions that have dreaded properties. It is not surprising that their reputation might cause an individual to be frozen in fear and unable to actually process the information offered by professionals that follows such a diagnosis. For some, there is no middle ground; the reputation supersedes any personal information to the contrary. For others, the reputation prevents them from acknowledging what has happened to them. Often, they run from the reputation rather than the condition itself. In our practice, we have come across people who, 2 years postdiagnosis, continue to avoid affiliating with any aspect of their disease and remain unable to speak its name: "That C word," they say instead.

Escape from threat is difficult, however. Individuals have very little control over the information they receive. The media and social interaction frequently threaten to pierce personal defenses and further overwhelm and unbalance the individual. Randomly, numerous people remark on stories they have heard: There is someone they know with a similar condition. Television intrudes into the living room with prognoses about individuals with certain conditions. Newspapers, magazines, and the like herald tales of individual plights. Notice the flavor of the words and themes associated with serious conditions. An adversary such as cancer is portrayed as a formidable opponent; the battle or fight is on, and the individual is regarded as undertaking a "brave fight against great odds." Not surprisingly, when friends or other people are informed about such conditions, the predominant reaction is fear. It is interesting to view the following sequence: A 45-year-old dentist received early confirmation of a neurological syndrome so forbidding that she found it virtually impossible to say the words. She asked, "Who can I talk to? The friends I tell show me their fear. They look at me differently. Their fear makes me more frightened." Perceiving the way they treat her differently, she tried to downplay what she had by reassuring them that it's "no big deal." This felt strange to her, however: "After all it's me who has it."

Mixing with colleagues at work, she feared that they would recognize subtle changes in her speech and ask her about her health. She believed that they, too, would find out and treat her differently: "Why wouldn't they know—they should be able to put it all together," she thought. When someone caught her off guard with a random remark about how tired she appeared, she pictured them as getting closer to her true predicament. She stated that she actually had to leave the room when advertisements about her particular condition appeared on the television—they brought to mind looming thoughts about her possible future. She vacillated between wanting to curl up in a corner and wanting to run away.

> "WHO CAN I TALK TO? THE FRIENDS I TELL SHOW ME THEIR FEAR. THEY LOOK AT ME DIFFERENTLY. THEIR FEAR MAKES ME MORE FRIGHTENED."

Knowing and Dealing with the Future

To be forced to face the possibility of a protracted, degenerative, or terminal disease is a daunting and incredible task. Modern technology has enabled individuals to "know" intrinsic aspects of their future. Individuals "see" the outcome of multiple sclerosis on their television sets. They take in extraordinary amounts of information about genetic possibilities. Watching their parents, they now understand the link—their parents' physical conditions may very well be theirs. They know the tell-tale signs of early disease, and they are warned about how to reduce these personal statistical liabilities. Not surprisingly, much of the fear surrounding increased ability to predict the future of one's health has itself in part generated the revolution in exercise and healthy lifestyles. People want to believe that they can control the future.

In situations of cancer, the individual is bundled out of diagnosis with a host of statistics relating to their probability of survival. A table tennis match in an individual's mind begins between "shoulds" and "what ifs." "You'd be an idiot if you didn't do chemotherapy—what sort of person would take the risk?" "You'd go to a naturopath, Traditional Chinese Medicine practitioner—whatever, if you were smart!" And finally, if you did not beat cancer: "You did not try enough cures."

There will also be the person who has grown up daring threats just like the kindergartner who was acclaimed for his daring to jump on sidewalk cracks. Links back into childhood lead him to believe that he can outsmart or outrun threats, that personal resources are enough. In the face of personal adversity he determines, "I'll beat this on my own, just like every other time."

The realistic fear and anxiety that surround knowing one's future, possibly involving threat, pain, and death, were not dealt with in Freud's day. Medical technology was not sophisticated and people's futures were still foretold in crystal balls. With today's technology, an individual can see his or her tumor, know its "aggressiveness," its "lethality," the time it will take to grow and become terminal. To integrate such a future demands an extraordinary psychological feat. Individuals are warned to monitor the progression of their diseases, to carry out continuing surveillance and counter the threat. The fact that, at the same time, they live with realistic fear often is downplayed. When individuals bring up their fear, focus quickly shifts to the "challenge" and the "brave fight." The same situation often surrounds impending death. The mere mention of death can bring up a swift counterargument: "Don't give up. It's never too late."

SUMMARY

This chapter, based on observation and reputation, has focused on the fear surrounding dreaded events. The occurrence of some such event activates these fears. This activation of fears is nonvolitional. That is, individuals do not "choose" the thoughts or images that come into the forefront of their thinking. They have been set well in place early in an individual's development. Linking back to the early formation and importance of groups, it is emphasized that the fear of dreaded events and the fear of being ostracized from the group are inextricable.

Apart from the fear of becoming different, this chapter has introduced the realistic anxiety and fear that individuals have when their possible future is foretold. Simultaneously, a sequence of psychological threats are set in motion; various degrees of self-identity, self-esteem, and psychological equilibrium are at risk. For individuals in these circumstances feel as if they are between two worlds—a frightening state that is described in more detail in Section IV. In essence, it involves a struggle to achieve a balance between the identity with which an individual is familiar and the emerging "new world."

Before turning to the extremely complicated task of adapting to such an all-pervasive threat, particular attention is given to the dread relating to a less overt threat. From the discussion of identity development in Section II, it is evident that individuals become attached to certain aspects of themselves—how they would like to be. What if expectations, dreams, and hopes are unmet? In the following chapter the focus is on identity and the private reputation of dreaded events.

A 40-YEAR-OLD MAN FEARS LOSING CONTROL OVER HIS IDEAL BODY IMAGE: "I HAVE TO GO EVERY MORNING TO THE GYM. EVEN MISSING ONE DAY WOULD WORRY ME; WELL, ACTUALLY, I GUESS I WOULD BE FRIGHTENED THAT IT WOULD GET THE BETTER OF ME, BECOME A HABIT. I KNOW MY FRIENDS, THEY WOULD JUMP ON IT, SEE IT AS A SIGN THAT I WAS BUCKLING AND I WOULD RETURN TO BEING OVERWEIGHT."

CHAPTER 9

DREADED EVENTS

Private Reputation

This chapter turns attention to the private reputation of dreaded events. Getting a divorce, having a miscarriage, being overweight, or not making the swim team are examples of events that may assume a private reputation for individuals. Likewise, such events can elicit fear. For some individuals, these events represent dreaded possibilities; principally, the individual consciously or unconsciously anticipates an overwhelming threat to his or her identity when confronted with a variation from what represents an *ideal self*. The individual cannot tolerate a self or an existence that is a departure from the version of self to which he or she is attached. Hence, fear has become the driving force for the man who feels he must rigidly adhere to a gym routine in order to retain his ideal self-image.

Although all life events have potentially powerful consequences for one's sense of self, it is only by considering the part certain roles play in an individual's identity that an understanding can be reached about why some events hold particular dread. Individuals are virtually programmed to certain scripts; personal loss is defined as discrepancies with such scripts. Enmeshed and synonymous with identity, it is difficult for individuals to relinquish these scripts without compromising their identities. As Section II of this book highlights, theorists concerned with development point to socioemotional contexts and how identity develops (Erikson, 1965) and to early caregiving behavior and the role of attachment in personality development (Bowlby, 1988). These contexts provide the bedrock for the development of secure individuals; in addition, the function of certain roles in identity formation can be tracked through individuals' development.

Fear of Being Alone and the Need for a Protector

Identity development proceeds in stages (Erikson, 1965; Rutter & Rutter, 1993), and in fits and starts. It is a peculiarly delicate process open to many vagaries typically involving slow transformations. Over the course of identity development, ideally an individual gains a sense of who he or she is, has volition, and feels that he or she can more or less survive as an individual. Section II of this book has shown that this aspect of development can be precarious, as in the 17-year-old boy's case in Chapter 4. This adolescent's separation and individuation from his mother did not take place and his identity formation was somewhat sabotaged.

For individuals with such incomplete identity formation, attachment to a significant other can remain integral to their survival. Faced with events such as separation and divorce, such individuals may not be able to perceive survival without a partner. These individuals remain trapped by their fear of not being able to survive on their own. They may feel that they need people, activities, or things to shield them or protect them in the world. Drugs and alcohol can take on the roles of protector, particularly in providing a sense of security. In adolescence, the 15-year-old finds a brave self when he or she drinks alcohol: instant transformation! With the awkwardness dissolved, now the teenager can leave the corner of the party room and approach strangers. Now he or she can move about and dance, free of self-consciousness. The stares of the party-goers, many of whom are friends at school, have been defused and have become blurry. The 15-year-old has actually been freed of the fear of them.

For other individuals, the dreaded event might also be one that causes them to face the world without a protector. Protectors might include siblings. For instance, in one case of sisters, an older sister had become the protector in a family where physical abuse was always a threat. The younger sister spent her childhood following her sister around. Although this was first done to secure safety, later it became her habit: "It's just what I did—I became her shadow." In the end, this young girl virtually became a clone, dressing and acting just like the older sister. At school, her relationships with friends followed similar patterns; she was a shadow to all her friends. In her marriage, she came face-to-face with her dreaded event when her husband left her. For the first time in her life she had no one to "protect" her. This young woman could no longer operate in a slipstream with others and just drift.

FALSE REPUTATIONS AS DREADED EVENTS

Attachment to notions of self do not happen by accident. As outlined in Section II, an individual's perceived attention or acclamation from parents and significant caregivers in the early years begins an identity formation that is later mixed with acclamation or attention from significant others and the societal ideals to which we have attributed value. Alternately, a person can become almost robotically aligned with what one's family of origin may have belittled or denigrated. Here are the same derivations of elitism, sexism, racism, and the like. Either an individual dreads that he or she may become what has been systematically belittled or denigrated throughout one's family life or, conversely, one dreads that he or she would be forced to *align* with the values and attitudes of his or her family.

These alignments are not immutable. What in youth was a determined effort to debunk the family's beliefs and attitudes might exert a sort of latent, underground pressure later on. Thus, in midlife, a 55-year-old entrepreneur had started to feel conflict in his feelings for his wife. The crux of his conflict lay in his learned attitude to his wife's early work as a dancer in a nightclub. This man's father had labeled such women as "whores"; "You are not marrying your kind," he had told his son. At times when his wife and he quarreled, this man found himself aligning with his father's belief.

Gaining and Losing a Reputation

The development of—and attachment to—versions of self is complex. Over time, a relationship unfolds wherein certain roles, skills, and attributes become enmeshed with identity and linked with self-esteem. In the end, it makes up an individual's notion of what he or she considers "me" or what makes "me" feel special. Aspects of this are touched on in the discussion of dreams in Section II. Should an individual be forced to relinquish an aspect of self to which he or she has become singularly attached, identity and self-esteem may be simultaneously threatened. Consider a child who from an early age is singularly pursuing sports or special skill-based activities (e.g., ballet, gymnastics, music). When the child reaches adolescence or early adulthood, she may feel threatened if she has to relinquish this activity because it has become inseparable from her notion of self.

Further dimensions of this concept exist, as well. Routines of training and practicing often psychologically underpin a feeling of safety and security. Ironically, for some individuals free time creates a feeling of anxiety, although they no longer need to follow the demands of an external clock or timetable such as that associated with a 9 to 5 job.

Routines, "On-Buttons," and Security The safe harbor that routines often offer is not unique to early development. Days move into years, and an individual slowly integrates a work identity. Commanding competence, respect, and a ready-made group of companions, this version of self has the potential to become particularly powerful. Over time, an individual's time clock becomes synchronized with the routines and structures of the workplace—almost like an internal driver. For many people this taken-for-granted security provided by the time clock allows them to perform optimally. In less-guided environments, people are more likely to flounder, particularly if they do not set up their own personal routines or timetables. For example, much of the anxiety and depression frequently experienced by women becoming first-time stay-at-home mothers might be attributed to the fall-away of the markers and routines provided by the workplace. This is similarly the case with an individual's transition from secondary school to a university. So, for many individuals, work identity is psychologically benevolent. Often for the first time in their lives people's roles and responsibilities, their charter—"this is what you *do*"—is clear, and individuals can function without the emotional knots that characterize relationships with partners and family members.

As the manager of an engineering industry, a middle-age man frequently hands out his personalized business card. He believes this role represents him, guarantees automatic respect, and creates and shields his credibility. The very routines of his work provide security, and the responsibility vested in the position provides purpose. There are no questions surrounding what to *do*. Financial rewards are only the icing on this cake. Trusting that he is indispensable, that his company feels the same way about him that he feels about it, he is understandably shocked and betrayed when he is let go; "I *was* that company. I gave them everything," he thinks to himself.

Dislodged from his routines and his positive source of information about his capabilities, depression, at the very least, should theoretically follow this man's loss of position. Not only have the external feedback and support for his view of himself been pulled out from under him, but his internal clock, which over time had become synchronized with his work routines to provides cues of what to do and when, is now redundant. Viewed in this light, parallels can easily be drawn with the separation of children from their parents. Particularly, those individuals who have spent all their adult life with one firm are unprepared to function independently of their work identity. By way of introduction, an 80-plus-year-old resident in a senior citizens' residence hands out a 30-year-old business card. There can be no doubt as to the central role work played in the lifetime of this individual. The card introduces a version of this man's self that he is proud of and that he hopes will command respect and divert attention away from how he may now fear he is perceived—as an old man. In contrast to the 80-year-old man, adolescents are in the process of trying to locate a version of themselves that feels authentic.

Designing an Identity in Adolescence

As adolescents are faced with significant physical and cognitive changes, extensive redesigning of their "selves" takes place. Teenagers study their icons and anxiously contemplate their emerging selves: A pair of sunglasses is placed meticulously, a sweater is purposely draped. A blemish might be a viewed as a major catastrophe to this delicate balance.

In the preceding chapters, much attention has been paid to the need for an internal consistency of self. Conversely, in adolescence, identity is conceptualized as being composed of a number of "false selves" (Harter, Bresnick, Bouchey, & Whitesell, 1997). That is, there is an inherent lack of internal consistency. This is extremely unsettling, for it leaves adolescents largely in the hands of others. What others say, what they think, and the comments and stares they give become amplified as a fragile sense of self keeps adolescents' ears to the ground for feedback about themselves. If one is clearly defined as being "cool" and eligible to enter the "cool group," a bit of stability has emerged to this process of becoming. Conferment by others is pivotal. Keeping and protecting membership in this group, or considering how one might be granted this eligibility, can become ongoing quests. A skill base that separates one from the pack and puts one in the limelight can be useful. The gymnast proudly notes such a skill: "I can do tricks; my friends cannot. I can take risks that they cannot."

Trauma and Identity

Harter et al. (1997) highlighted the differing self-perceptions available to adolescents. Drawing on the work of James (1890), the "conflict of different me's" is regarded as particularly salient and normative during this stage of development. Harter et al. postulated that excessive conflict in the attributes of an adolescent's self-portrait harbors a psychological risk. Although a typical adolescent's self-portrait might reflect the following anomalies: "Who am I? I seem to be all these people....I'm like this to my Mom, but with my friends I'm different," a trauma in adolescence is likely to create very disturbing anomalies. Should a traumatic event occur at this stage of development, a gradual examination of this emerging self based on a range of feedback that is psychologically tolerable is jeopardized. Feedback from others becomes unbalanced and skewed around the rapid unfolding of a dramatic role. One serious incident and one version of self can become too predominant. In an instant, an adolescent can be overdefined in relation to the event.

In secondary school, a 15-year-old whose brother had been incarcerated for rape felt as though all eyes were on him. His self-consciousness amplified whispers in the schoolyard: "He's the one whose brother was sent to prison." In fact, this adolescent felt as though it was branded on his forehead. Simultaneously, he became isolated from his peers: The common base was gone. His friends' reactions to pimples now seemed "majorly petty." He sensed that the seriousness and blackness of his internal world was not welcome in such talk of girls, parties, and sports. Not wanting to risk exclusion, he decided to hide this part of him.

This itself is a critical decision, for if this boy is to practice separating from his parents, he needs the peer group. But within the peer group, this young boy has doubts about those who have maintained a friendship: "Is it about me, or do they just feel sorry for me for having a brother like that? What do they really think?" In essence, he is asking whether the behavior of his friends is phony. Alternately, there are adolescents who will not find the focus too overwhelming; for instance, sometimes the feeling of being special and receiving attention surrounding personal tragedy, adversity, or trauma will be perceived as enticing and have advantages (albeit shortlived) for maintaining friendships.

In either case, when dreaded events occur prior to the attainment of a balanced version of self, that is, before the "false selves" merge into a unified and stronger sense of self, a dreaded event takes too much precedence. The necessary road-testing of who one *could be* is obscured by the tragedy. The young boy mentioned previously who already feels terribly different and isolated from his friends was shadowed by his reputation. Often, the proportion this dreaded event takes in the merging of selves is too dominant. An inestimable and continuing effect might be placed on this boy's further identity development (Terr, 1985). Apart from a distrust of the motives of his friends, he will have a shaken trust in the safety of the world.

Identity development proceeds in stages, and the relationship among cognitive development, the stability of the identity, and dreaded events is intricate. For children in particular, once a traumatic perception is taken in it may remain an "indigestible mental image" and part of the growing personality (Horowitz, 1986; Terr, 1985). In fact, some emotional experiences can be forced to remain enigmas. Emotional experiences that are not shared with others and made sense of tend to gain potency over time. They can become like a series of unexplored and highly defended "hotspots." While some individuals may, of their own volition, explore such life experiences at later points of their development, others may not. In old age these memories can surface because individuals no longer have the ability to distract themselves from their thoughts. Similarly, they may surface in situations of dementia when psychological defenses can no longer successfully guard painful memories (Cheston, 1998).

DISPARAGING REPUTATIONS AS DREADED EVENTS

Identity development may include accommodating a version of self that is perceived as negative. In particular, some people think others feel sorry for them. This perception seems to stem from their childhood experiences; an individual who had a limb amputated in adulthood states: "Kids who were different at school lived lives that were awful, I felt sorry for them all the time!" Having the sense that one is pitied is almost regarded as personally offensive. It certainly is not an attribute that brings esteem from others. Along these lines, these same people find talking about personal pain very difficult. In the midst of telling their story, they pull themselves up and state something such as "I hate whiners; you don't want to listen to all of this." These individuals cannot tolerate the idea that they have become the very person whom they have traditionally rejected or pitied.

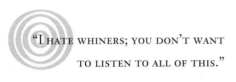

"I HATE WHINERS; YOU DON'T WANT TO LISTEN TO ALL OF THIS."

Most people find it extremely difficult to tolerate the public scrutiny that goes hand-in-hand with being or becoming different from the mainstream. Blending in and seeking attributes that are affirmed by peers is a persisting concept throughout development. Of crucial importance for individuals during adolescence (Erikson, 1965), more often than not, "blending" continues to have an influence throughout life. Disability and illness, or any event that singles a person out from mainstream society, almost guarantees that one will not blend in easily. For the wrong reasons, an individual will lose anonymity. Not surprisingly, many people are extremely threatened by being in the limelight or being stared at, particularly when it is about something that is personally perceived as negative (Goffman, 1963). Thus, the woman who describes an adolescence that involved "spending time trying to look good," and who still strives to be a member of what she describes as an "in-group," has major obstacles in the way of adapting to life with a child who has a significant disability. Following therapy, she reflects, "Now, I guess my son is forcing me out of the in-group." Until this woman's identity can surmount the threat of being aligned with disability, her son will take the blame. Recurring thoughts of what life would be without him keep her in limbo.

SUMMARY

This chapter has examined the relationship between identity formation and dreaded events. Identity slowly builds to represent a matrix of experiences of who one is (refer to Figure 4.1). A result is a perception of self to which one is attached, or alternatively a perception of self that has a level of comfort attached to it, because *it just is*. In adolescence this matrix is still forming and is precarious. In adulthood too much of the matrix may have had as its locus a particular aspect of identity. In either case, losing a certain reputation or gaining a certain reputation is dreaded. In the former (adolescence), the danger of a dreaded event becoming a characterization of an adolescent's identity has been emphasized. In the latter (adulthood), the intricate relationship identity has with routines and how they provide internal time clocks has been reexamined.

The prospect of grieving and adapting to nonfinite loss seems extremely complex and daunting. In some situations of adversity, it might almost involve weaving and virtually attaching to a new version of self. Section IV of this book explores the complexities in grieving nonfinite loss. The role of cognitive development and identity formation on the ability to grieve is explored, and attention is given to the characteristics of threat and its resulting effect on reality testing.

"THE ABYSS IS A CHASM, AN INFINITE
RIFT, IN REALITY. IF YOU BUT NOTICE IT,
IT MAY OPEN BENEATH YOU. YOU MUST
EITHER TURN AWAY FROM IT, OR FACE IT,
FAIR AND SQUARE....BUT NOW I DECIDED—
OR WAS I FORCED—TO EXPLORE A CHART-
LESS LAND BEYOND THE REACH OF ALL
CHARTS. THE LAND WHICH FACED ME
WAS NO-LAND, NOWHERE."
—SACKS, 1991, P. 78

SECTION IV

COMPLEXITIES IN GRIEVING NONFINITE LOSS

A MOTHER RELATES A CONVERSATION WITH HER

12-YEAR-OLD DAUGHTER ABOUT THE GIRL'S FATHER, WHO

HAS PARKINSON'S DISEASE. OUT OF THE BLUE, THE GIRL

WAS OVERWHELMED WITH TEARS. "I THOUGHT SHE

UNDERSTOOD THAT HE WOULD NOT RECOVER. BUT WHEN

I ASKED HER, 'WHY CRY NOW, 10 MONTHS LATER,' SHE

REPLIED, 'I HEARD WHAT YOU SAID, BUT I HAD

MY OWN THOUGHTS.'"

CHAPTER **10**

COGNITIVE DEVELOPMENT, IDENTITY FORMATION, AND GRIEFWORK

Different stages of cognitive and socioemotional development allow different understandings of what words and situations mean. Children learn and flesh out what they mean over time. How might this natural pace of learning, which constrains a child's breadth of knowledge and consequently narrows his or her interpretation of events, affect the grieving response? This chapter explores how cognitive development and identity formation, with particular reference to issues of separation, individuation, and different realities, affect individuals' abilities to conceptualize loss and tolerate the task of grieving.

This chapter's opening quote illustrates well the idea of different realities. A 40-year-old mother and her 12-year-old daughter talk about a progressive and disabling disease that the father has had for 10 months. Each has a different perspective coming from the world of adults and the world of children: two different developmental stages that guarantee two vastly different realities. The 40-year-old "knows" all about disease, but for the 12-year-old reality is only unfolding. Thus, although an adaptation process is virtually mandatory for mother, father, and daughter—all have to make certain changes to their routines—each hold their own vastly different views on the father's prognosis. These different understandings call for quite different emotional responses.

119

COGNITIVE DEVELOPMENT AS A PSYCHOLOGICAL SHIELD

Versions of reality are distinctly tied to cognitive development (Piaget, 1954). Grieving can be inhibited because a child is not able to conceptualize the irrevocability of loss (Grollman, 1967). For instance, consider the preschooler's notion of time. Her father has left for a business trip. "How many sleeps till Daddy is back?" she asks her mother. The notion of time virtually confines the child to the present. Necessarily, a child's reaction to a diagnosis of an ongoing medical condition is quite different from that of an adult who has a dimension of time and thought that allows him or her to perceive the extant meaning of a diagnosis.

The process of establishing the permanence of loss cannot depend on what is shown or said to the individual. There is a difference between being shown, being told, and seeing how it is. Stages of socioemotional and cognitive development as they interact with personal, hands-on experience directly affect the interpretation an individual makes of personal adversity. Neural system development enables perceptual and cognitive advances that gradually open up an increasingly differentiated and complex world (Harris, 1998; Piaget, 1929/1951). The boundaries of an individual's understanding incrementally gather breadth and depth. Contrast an early childhood view of the world with the world of adolescents and adults; the former might be likened to a narrow lens, the latter to a growing comprehension of the "big" picture.

This developmental criterion has vast implications for the meaning and significance that an individual is actually *able* to make of a loss, and whether an individual can actually perceive or construe an event as a loss. A mother says to her 3-year-old son: "Your father has left us. He is going to marry someone else." What meaning does the boy make of this? Days go by, and changes in the household routines persist. Daddy is no longer at the table, no longer in bed with his mother in the morning. The child can only learn over time what his mother's statement means. This learning process will be paralleled by various intensities of physical reactions related to separation. But at the same time, the child may ask on every other day: "When will Daddy be back?" "You will see him later," replies his mother. "When is *later?*" the child pleads. The word "later" offers no consolation, and for many children there will be separation anxiety. The child may at the same time be harboring an alternative sequel; that his father would never leave him and that he will return.

In the naive state of the narrow lens, socioemotional and cognitive development restrict the interpretation of life experiences. Experiences are actually being woven in as they unfold. A child, newly diagnosed with an ongoing disease, learns what the diagnosis means and weaves it into the personal model of the world that is taking form. A finely tuned knowledge base about the nuances of the condition and its limits will become part of his or her self and world. It will become familiar, but only over time. For a boy with serious asthma, for example, his experience of the world will form a far different set of knowledge structures and personal models than the child who does not have a chronic illness. By becoming familiar and entwined into the child's identity from early on, this experience can become relatively tamed through practice. This familiarity may even have its own rewards: A girl comments about her diabetes, "It's no big deal," which engenders awe from school friends who admire the fact that she can actually self-inject insulin. Ironically, it was not until she went to elementary school that she found out that "no other kid in my class has to do this."

Unwoven Trauma

Experiences that threaten large aspects of the familiar represent a potential trauma. While in childhood we have the chance to weave adverse experiences into the familiar, in adolescence there is a propensity for personal adversity to swamp the individual's identity and form a disproportionate place in the individual's emerging sense of self (Horowitz, 1978). For an adolescent who contracts cancer, for example, the majority of feedback about self all of a sudden is about the cancer. The world changes; friends "know" him as having cancer. The world talks about cancer. Unfortunately, because adolescents are extremely self-conscious at this stage of development, the feedback is amplified and it is very difficult for the adolescent to maintain a sense of self that is not intricately eclipsed by cancer (see Figure 12.1 in Chapter 12).

In adulthood, a condition that eclipses or swamps the identity has a better chance to be temporary and less damaging. The adult has over many more years established a range of different feedback about self—cancer, albeit awesome, is but one of many experiences of self. Simply put, an adult over time has had a chance to consolidate a sense of self, and overall there is an integrity and soundness to this concept: "I have a firmer idea of who I am." Conversely, the adolescent is still in the process of consolidating his or her identity.

Traumatic Information

Theorists concerned with information processing explain that information that is exceedingly novel, traumatic, or both does not fit existing patterns in individuals' memories in adulthood (Bowlby, 1980; Herman, 1992; Horowitz, 1988). In childhood, such information may not be processed at all—it is not understood. How could it be catalogued in one's system of memories if it is not named or understood? Highly charged experiences are not worked through. Instead, they become stored as part of the individual's personality (Herman, 1994; Horowitz, 1986; Terr, 1985). As life goes on, these incidents are held in check by a combination of the individual's inability to "know" what has happened to him or her and psychological defenses that trap the incidents out of conscious awareness. These incidents might be usefully construed as storing a backlog of awareness and of grieving.

These life incidents or stored memories may be retriggered through an event that has similar themes (Gloor, 1992). This phenomenon often occurs in situations of dementia (Cheston, 1998). One example would be an older woman who, institutionalized by her husband, had been sent to boarding school in her early childhood. The theme of abandonment and helplessness and its emotional response is amplified as she relives the trauma related to the childhood experience: "You must look after me," she pleads with her husband, "You've left me, just like my parents did." For older adults, long periods of being alone, without distractions, may make them relive earlier traumatic experiences they had avoided thinking about in their lives.

DEVELOPMENTAL CONTEXTS AND GRIEFWORK

The interaction between the ability to grieve and the following factors in combination—socioemotional and cognitive development, the capacity to conceptualize loss, and identity formation—has been discussed by various theorists (e.g., Bowlby, 1980; Horowitz, 1988; Raphael, 1984; Wolfenstein, 1966). These variables that make up unique realities for individuals have profound implications for grieving. Specifically, some wonder whether it is possible to process any experience outside of one's own developmental context (Harris, 1998; Sekaer, 1987). It might be useful to illustrate aspects of this point by considering the remarks of a 30-year-old woman who had come to therapy to explore issues of loss and grief. When she was a teenager, her mother died of cancer. She reflected with shame on her thoughts at the time:

> My mom got sick with cancer when I was 12. She lost her hair, got wigs, the whole thing. It went on for 3 years. She was always sick. I had to lift her on to the toilet....I wanted to stay out more than be at home. This is going to sound really bad, I know, and looking back I feel really guilty about it. But then, on and off, I actually wanted her to die. I felt really sick of her being sick.

These thoughts and feelings are inextricably tied to the developmental needs and egocentricity of adolescence. Stages in development allow the interpretation of personal adversity to gain further breadth over time. The adult stage of development permitted this 30-year-old woman to redefine the traumatic experience that she herself had in adolescence and to forgive the harshness of her thoughts at the time. A discussion of the interplay of cognitive development, identity formation, and griefwork follows.

IDENTITY FORMATION

Many theorists have considered it unlikely that children can tolerate the pain associated with the grieving process (Deutsch, 1937; Dietrich, 1989; Freud, 1960; Nagera, 1970; Sekaer, 1987; Wolfenstein, 1966). In addition, children have developmental capacities that restrict them from accurately conceptualizing loss or engaging in a mourning process (Dietrich, 1989). Along these lines, Silverman, Nickman, and Worden described a child's loss of a parent as, "seeming too difficult to contemplate" (1992, p. 497). For example, a 10-year-old boy states that he "can't think about his father being dead" (p. 497).

Although the child may be forced to adapt over time to the death of a parent, emotional adaptation to the same is far more complex (Dietrich, 1989; Silverman et al. 1992; Wolfenstein, 1966). While the child is learning day by day that his father is not coming back, a largely covert relationship with the father can commonly take form. For instance, the father might become a protector, a "guardian angel who one day will return," "whom I will meet again," "who talks to me all the time." It is evident that the immature cognitive and socioemotional development enables such a response.

In adolescence, although this fantasy or hope may be more difficult to maintain there still is an avoidance of reality testing. Specifically, Wolfenstein (1966) proposed that an anticipation of what the finality of loss—in this case, death—would mean creates overwhelming panic that actually forces a retreat from reality testing. In the avoidance of reality testing, numerous examples exist of bereaved young adolescents throwing themselves into study or sport, or deciding to be "strong, just like my mom told me to be." Both involve links that create connections with the deceased—a continuing relationship that serves an important developmental function. Symbolically, the absent parent is, in some form, kept alive and represented in the child.

Despite adult explanations about things that happen, characteristically in this stage of development adolescents will have their own thoughts on the matter. This establishment of independent ideas and opinions plays a significant part in the demarcation of the adolescents' identities from that of their parents. The result is that frequently the private convictions held by adolescents may be vastly at odds with what an adult is telling them. For the 14-year-old just diagnosed with diabetes or some type of ongoing medical condition, a wait-and-see approach often emerges. More often the case than not, the passing of time provides proof of what the doctor or parents said. In fits and starts, reality seeps through this approach and the stand cannot always be upheld. Even if the 14-year-old states adamantly: "It will go away," inside she is slowly learning the converse—that diabetes remains.

Griefwork is about reality testing, and it can be seen that reality for varying stages of development is a complex, personal affair. From the outside looking in, not much might be seen to be happening for this 14-year-old girl. But in reality, an emotionally arduous battle is taking place between her own thoughts, hopes, and wishes and what is actually shaping up. The battle becomes overwhelming when reality continually threatens the viability of the stand she has taken. Naturally, there is an emotional buildup behind defending this stance against individuals who persistently tell her the illness is not going to go away. Naive beliefs, wishes, and hopes made possible because of her stage of development meet a brick wall—the knowledge base that composes "adult reality," the seemingly endless replies of adults who might know better: "No, it won't get better." "No, you won't get better." Adolescents' responses to such common-sense comments may surprise others. Recounted the mother of the girl with diabetes: "There was no way of predicting it—she got upset out of nowhere. I had just said one thing about her condition—one thing. How she might have to consider changing her diet to avoid some complication of diabetes down the road—and she lost it."

> "THERE WAS NO WAY OF TELLING IT—SHE GOT UPSET OUT OF NOWHERE. I HAD JUST SAID ONE THING ABOUT HER CONDITION—ONE THING. HOW SHE MIGHT HAVE TO CONSIDER CHANGING HER DIET TO AVOID SOME COMPLICATION OF DIABETES DOWN THE ROAD— AND SHE LOST IT."

What seemed to come out of the blue had actually been gathering momentum, however. The dynamic between reality testing and protection of an independent view creates a buildup of emotions. The conflict between the stand taken and the reality that is emerging exerts considerable psychological pressure. On some days the reality forces the floodgate of strong and dark emotions to open. With the pressure expelled, the 14-year-old may now return to her independent stand. Time goes by, perhaps a day, a week—the floodgate closes—tightly shut, if possible.

This is griefwork for this 14-year-old girl. A forced realization of her reality as it emerges parallels her development. Intellectual adaptation is how she learns what her diagnosis means: Her own picture of what "is" is slowly being modified to meet what she is being told. Only in adulthood will it become closer to dovetailing with her parents' view. Meantime, her emotional responses may be sporadic and represent a buildup of things not turning out how she had wished or hoped. This personal stand actually doubles as a distracter from the immensity of meaning that some diagnoses or events hold. The stand is made more feasible as this stage of development, which unlike the adult stage of development, does not cultivate long-term forecasts—the future is "way out there." Distanced from future versions of how things may be, reality as it is is easier to protect from further threat.

The Unshielded Individual

The ability to juggle ways to feel safe against a background of dreaded events is a constant imperative for individuals. In childhood we look to parents or other trusted adults for messages about safety. As was explored in Chapter 4, a certain amount of naiveté about the world and the strength behind the parent's assurances allows the child to gather up steam and push into the opportunities that the world offers without too much fear. However, the child starts to question the veracity of these assurances in adolescence. Simultaneously, certain long-held assumptions about safety are stripped away. The individual is left with him- or herself and, it is hoped, a trusted peer group that can close this enormous gap.

Ideally, the learning environment with the family has equipped adolescents for this shift in their psychological world. Optimally, by this time of their lives, their experiences have provided them with feedback that the world can be trusted and that they can survive in it, emotionally and physically. In fact, finding out that one can cope, can survive threats, is the underpinning of the development of resilience and a central positive affirmation of self. This piece of self-knowledge, a vital psychological bedrock, has vast implications for an individual's ability to grieve.

The process of griefwork demands a face-to-face encounter with one's loss and the depth of emotions that this encounter forces. However, it is ironic that just as this psychological strength is being demanded, the crisis itself plummets an adult into a relapse of childlike fears and reactions. Figure 10.1 illustrates this paradox. Drawn by a 50-year-old woman undergoing chemotherapy for an aggressive case of cancer, she reflected on the part her feelings of childhood were playing in her present personal crisis: "This is me, this is how I feel, helpless as a child—anything but a 50-year-old mother of four!" The same triggering of childlike states can be recognized in the 60-year-old woman, in remission from breast cancer, who nervously questioned whether she was "tempting

Figure 10.1.   Crisis-induced relapse of adult into a childlike state as drawn by a 50-year-old woman.

fate" and risking recurrence if she made a will. Intellectually, this woman knew that a will is a sensible course to follow, but a childlike superstition threatened her. In this childlike state, emotional messages extrapolated from childhood threatened to dominate.

The self-knowledge that one can survive in the first place is integral to an assessment that one can survive in the absence of something or someone. Picture the 17-year-old boy in Chapter 4 who could not leave his mother to go on a boat trip. What were his chances of facing the loss of his mother—or facing personal loss without his mother? Clearly, the child who has made headway in separating from his parents and who has experienced the ability to survive without them is in far better shape than the child who has not psychologically separated. What proof have these children that they can survive the loss?

According to Wolfenstein, if the giving up of the child–parent relationship in adolescence has not been accomplished, then "the adult remains unable to accomplish the work of mourning in response to loss" (1966, p. 117). Why is this so? Essentially, an individual senses an incapacity to deal with the implications of the loss, which is so great that it actually is perceived to threaten his or her own survival. "What will happen to me? I am not strong enough to get through this," are common beseeching statements. Mounting emotions revolve around issues of loneliness, abandonment, and helplessness; the outcome can be excruciating panic. The incapacity centers around the inability to recognize that one can survive in the absence of another or in the absence of an aspect of self. Instead of incrementally integrating the loss and incrementally expressing the emotion connected with the loss, the individual overdefends and keeps the loss at arm's length. Thus, separation—individuation as a key task of identity formation—is integral to the ability to face loss and grief.

In situations of personal adversity, this predicament may be amplified. Even a man long separated from his mother who died more than 40 years ago finds himself yearning for her. This may be the first time that the actual loss of his mother has been felt so powerfully. An older woman struggles with painful rheumatoid arthritis. She pleads for a poor stand-in for her own mother: "I want to be looked after in the hospital."

SUMMARY

Loss is constantly being reworked in terms of the past, present, and future. The emotional component of griefwork is intricately tied to the socioemotional development of the individual, and the intellectual component of grieving seems contingent on his or her cognitive development. Applying this notion to children, one can speculate whether their stage of cognitive and socioemotional development allows them to fully conceptualize loss. Some question whether individuals who have not separated from adult figures can fathom the depths of their loss for griefwork to proceed. In focusing on the developmentally related separation of adolescence, identity formation must not be disregarded as a crucial factor in the ability to grieve. The stage and strength of identity formation become of utmost significance when loss jeopardizes aspects of identity. This issue is not confined to adolescence. Identity formation plays a central role in determining the ability to grieve in adulthood.

Another major area of complexity in grieving nonfinite loss has to do with its actual manifestation. Is the diagnosis crystal clear? Is there room for hope of recovery? These concerns about refutable or irrefutable threats are addressed in Chapter 11.

A 50-YEAR-OLD MAN WITH A DEGENERATIVE
DISEASE REFLECTS, "LOOK, TO TELL YOU THE
TRUTH, I'M UNCONVINCED WITH WHAT THE
NEUROLOGIST SAID.... I'VE HAD ONE BOUT,
BUT 10 YEARS HAVE GONE BY AND SURE,
THERE ARE SIGNS, BUT THEY ARE SO VAGUE."

CHAPTER **11**

CHARACTERISTICS AND IMPACT OF THREAT

What happens to griefwork when loss is open to changing interpretations? A threat has occurred, but its aftermath has not yet become exposed. It is apparent that for many reasons a threat can be clear or unclear. Contact with significant others and situations in the environment can either accentuate or camouflage a loss. The loss can be camouflaged by an individual's stage of development. For instance, a grasp of the significance of the threat may be beyond the individual's cognitive ability. This applies, in particular, to children, adolescents, and individuals with intellectual disabilities. As well, psychological maneuvers play a vital role in defending against realities that might otherwise overwhelm personal coping capacities. In terms of the nature of the threat, aspects of griefwork may be realistically suspended. Following an examination of what might constitute clear and unclear threat, the implications for griefwork are discussed.

TYPES OF THREAT

What is a clear threat? One example is when indisputable injuries are sustained, such as the loss of a limb in a serious automobile accident. An example of an unclear threat may be a brain injury with mild personality and physical damage. In many situations of unclear threat, what is experienced or perceived does not consistently support and confirm what a person has been told in a diagnosis; the threat may be disputable. In some situations, there is a mixture of the two. For instance, diagnosis produces initial dread, but physical symptomatology does not initially support diagnosis (e.g., some types of cancer); or physical symptomatology is sporadic or dormant for long periods of time (e.g., rheumatoid arthritis, multiple sclerosis). For example, a 40-year-old woman with a degenerative condition has had 10 years between symptoms. At this point in her life, she cannot conceive of having to use a wheelchair: "In some moments, I actually find myself wondering if the diagnosis was correct!"

The vacillations inherent in early dementia or Alzheimer's disease are open to similar questions and doubts. There often are perceptual paradoxes that create dissonance for the caregiver. For example, a man's spouse with dementia may have periods during which her behavior appears so typical that the man questions the diagnosis itself: "Looking at her last night at the table, it was as though she was her old self."

Apart from the vagaries of a disease trajectory itself, differing perspectives emerge, with family members using their own knowledge base, cognitive ability, and emotional concerns to personally assess a situation.

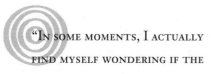

"IN SOME MOMENTS, I ACTUALLY FIND MYSELF WONDERING IF THE DIAGNOSIS WAS CORRECT!"

After 8 months, an older man speaks of his wife: "The neurologist was right; she has Alzheimer's. I saw it quite clearly today. She will not recover." The 14-year-old granddaughter says the same but 16 months later than her grandfather did, and she is more open to the option of recovery: "Who knows?" she says. The 50-year-old son, himself a doctor, has no such naive or wishful thinking. He knows there is no recovery. He is adept at seeing the discrepancies between who his mother was and how the disease is now affecting her. There is, however, still room for the contemplation of hope that occasionally tempts him to focus on what remains the same in her.

While expanding further on the concepts of clear and unclear threats, this chapter introduces the concept of "tally boards" to accentuate the features that contextualize personal information processing. Each individual will have a certain checklist of ticks and crosses before he or she concedes that change has taken place, that a diagnosis is indeed correct, or that a child is not developing typically.

Clear Threat

When the threat is clear, a relentless set of ticks mount up on the personal tally board. Loss, damage, and diagnosis are virtually impossible to dispute. The discovery of unwelcome news instantly threatens the loss of a version of self. Instead of being able to pace one's self-learning in this new world, the individual has been forced to acknowledge the *certain* potency of the threat. In these situations, it will practically be impossible to moderate the information about the loss. Particularly, it may be difficult to extricate oneself from overwhelming information and to pull away from the diagnosis and reclaim one's own personal experience of the situation. At the same time, even though the potency has been established, the meaning that the individual makes of the threat will not correspond with the definition that any other individual makes of the same set of circumstances.

A father responded to a neurologist's diagnosis about his young daughter's condition: "After he told me about my child's problem in detail, he showed me pictures of the disability's accompanying facial disfigurement—how my daughter would look when she was 10, 20, 40.... I could no longer recognize Danielle. She was lost in this syndrome or whatever. Danielle was no longer my daughter. She was *one of them*." The father had seen these features—but only as isolated individual concerns. Without medical specialist knowledge, the somewhat different features did not in themselves constitute a major threat. He had not actually consolidated them into an atypical "syndrome" per se. When he put them all together into a syndrome and drew out future contexts of how the syndrome would emerge, the neurologist created a major threat. Instantly, the daughter's features are seen in a different light; the father actually feels the loss of the child that he had prior to diagnosis.

The clarity of the threat makes it difficult, without breaking from reality, to maintain techniques that limit the threat. Yet, individuals do try. In the case of Danielle, her father started to avoid going home after work. What followed was almost a situation of phobic avoidance of his daughter. Simply put, not only did the delivery of the diagnosis eclipse the father's perception of his young child, but the description of the syndrome itself traumatized him. An outcome for this parent was a dislocation of the attachment bond. The potential for a diagnosis to eclipse a parent's perception in this way is possibly greater in early childhood when the parent holds a yet-unfledged personal knowledge base of his or her child.

Unclear Threat

An unclear threat arises when the threat cannot be consistently confirmed as a fact. When the veracity of diagnosis can be questioned, it is psychologically enticing to do so. A father of a 4-year-old boy diagnosed with a mild developmental delay stated, "I'm not prepared to accept any diagnosis as yet. One time, the neurologist said himself that John may grow out of it. Since then, he's suggested a number of possibilities. So, I have decided that I don't have to go along with any of it. He'll grow out of it."

Not surprising, individuals want to escape this portending nightmare, and the tendency will be to search for ways out. Information and perceptual cues that support this escape and relieve the anxiety will be sought. In this case, comparisons and contrasts in the environment may support an individual's disregard of either the "fact" or the "permanence" of loss. A friendly neighbor decides to buoy the hopes of a young mother whose child's speech is delayed. She recounts the story of her sister's child who did not talk until he was 4 years old.

Reality testing is taking place, but the veracity of the information that is being offered is questionable. At the same time, however, it is alluring, and if an individual chooses, reality testing—and grieving—can be suspended. The impending loss can be put on hold. Perhaps the doctor's visit is considered hasty, and it is cancelled. In this case, the unclear characteristics of the threat collude with an innate resistance to threatening the status quo, one's comfort zone. A lack of action may also be fostered by the entrenched, learned connotations that surround appealing for help or special attention. For some individuals, there is an innate fear that one might be making a big deal, or fuss, out of the situation. Sometimes there also is an innate disbelief around the idea of serious personal misfortune itself: "...as if this would be serious!" The permutations involving unclear threat and learned resistance are boundless.

A certain consistency of information is required before one's definition of the situation can be challenged, as is a certain momentum of information. The greater the incongruity among the individual's subjective perception of the event and the diagnosis or information received, the easier to sustain an interpretation that nothing has changed. A man told about his wife's cancer had replied, "But she looks all right. She looks just the same." Eventually, he conceded with the correctness of the diagnosis, but it was done only over time and using his personal criteria.

The checklist of crosses are also held in abeyance by the parents of a child with suspected autism spectrum disorder. Characteristics of autism in 2- to 3-year-old children often may be seen as falling within the typical range of obsessive or controlling behavior exhibited by children of that age group. The information from the social environment supports a tenacious view that all is okay. Interactions that may expose incongruities with this interpretation may be avoided or managed (see Goffman, 1963; Voysey, 1970, 1975). Many parents, especially fathers, are not often exposed to contrasts with typically developing children, and a certain view of their child remains unchallenged. Protected from making crosses on their tally boards, a perception of reality becomes way out of kilter with that of the spouse, who may frequently be faced with obvious discrepancies between their child and other children. In some scenarios, a person may defensively reduce social and certain professional interactions that threaten the ability to avoid the fact of loss.

Individuals who have not been exposed to situations that assist them to define the loss realistically are protected from making crosses. A useful example here is the individual who has left the hospital after sustaining an injury; the extent of the injury and its effect on the quality of life become clearer on return to home and social environment. Another is a situation in which a parent of an 18-month-old child with a mild developmental delay has not had opportunities to observe her child with groups of children acting in an age-appropriate way. In these situations, the lack of contrasts and comparisons restrict the definition process.

IMPLICATIONS FOR GRIEFWORK

According to sociologists (e.g., Goffman, 1959), an individual's identity is created and validated in the social arena. It is in this social arena that contrasts and discrepancies can be gleaned and the individual's personal construction of what has happened to him or her is forming or consolidating. In adolescence, the potency of the social arena is easily observed. An individual's process of "becoming" involves keeping an ear to the ground, listening for feedback, paying minute finicky attention to who is looking, and studying one's appearance and how it is coming together. Following a significant threat to adult identity, a similar process is set in motion: keeping an ear to the ground, listening, looking, and positioning. The social arena has an integral place in the construction of what has happened. What is the same; what is different? Do others perceive this as temporary? Can they see the change? What might they be thinking?

The psychological complexity of the process of acknowledging even seemingly indisputable objective facts has been demonstrated by the work of Davis (1963; people who had polio), Roskies (1972; people with characteristics associated with thalidomide exposure), and Fitzgerald (1970; people's reaction to blindness). In Section II, the process of identity building as a slow, incremental process of consolidation was introduced. A similarly gradual process operates as changes take place in identity. This dismantling of self involves highly personal features. It involves information building to a point in which changes gather momentum, when the threat and its magnitude gain inevitable clarity. The precise point at which the information gathers momentum and topples individuals will obviously vary. Some individuals are like the woman with cancer described in Chapter 5, clinging to the last bastions of self—in her case, a stiletto-heeled shoe.

A distinction between the impact on griefwork of clear and unclear threat is essential. In the former (i.e., clear threat), the salience of the threat itself indisputably changes an individual's reality. Consider the situation of the parents of children born with severe physical anomalies, almost a total contradiction of what was expected. In an instant, the parents are practically overexposed to their present and future. It is extremely difficult, if not impossible, for these parents to contain or minimize the emerging reality. Understandably, in these types of situations, the individual is overwhelmed.

In the latter (i.e., unclear threat), however, present reality can undergo minimal change. Threats to the future can be considered later. In this case, the characteristics of the threat are revealed slowly, with the identity slowly absorbing them rather than being eclipsed by them. A more tolerable pace of reality testing, one that is incremental, is possible. In some situations, such as those described in this chapter's introductory quotes from the 50-year-old man, the individual can actually be underexposed. There is not enough consistent information to support the fact that the disease is real. Doubt enters, and alternative futures are entertained. The characteristics of the threat, the facts surrounding the loss, the emerging reality, the psychological maneuvers, and griefwork are outlined in Table 11.1. A determination of these variables, namely, the representation of reality and the perceived threat for an individual, constitutes a first step in the application of the therapeutic approach taken in this text.

Unclear threat has significant and crucial effects on the grieving process. For grieving to proceed, the irrevocability of the loss needs to be established. Theoretically, without the establishment of this fact, the individual will remain in a state of separation anxiety. He or she will stay susceptible to seeking solutions, finding cures, and attending to information that might end the nightmare. Some individuals will be totally preoccupied with possibilities to avert the permanence of their loss. This is a little bit like a loved one being lost at sea, missing, or unaccounted for or like children whose cognitive development limits their understanding of reality. Without a finale, without proof that it is impossible, an individual is vulnerable to refute the fact of loss or the permanence of the loss and seek solutions.

Cognitive Development and the Significance of Threat

As discussed in Chapter 10, actual perceptions of the magnitude of threat can be protected by an individual's stage of development or cognitive ability. Cognitive limitations and circumscribed knowledge bases surrounding a particular scenario can restrict the child or adolescent from conceptualizing the relentlessness of the threat or the part a chronic ill-

Table 11.1. Characteristics of threat and its implications for identity and griefwork

Characteristic of threat	Fact of loss	Reality and implications for identity	Maneuvers	Griefwork
Clear	Irrefutable (e.g., serious physical injury with salient consistent change or damage)	Emerging reality (incorporates present and future) is potentially overwhelming—makes it difficult to preserve identity—amplifies fear, anxiety.	Psychological maneuvers are required to defend against realities and consequences of loss and to provide sense of control.	Reality testing can be self-sabotaged; intellectual and emotional components of griefwork suspended. Parts of intellectual component of griefwork will be forced because of changed conditions.
Unclear	Refutable: Disease or disability is sporadic, dormant, not salient (e.g., early stage of Alzheimer's disease, mild stroke, early stage of cancer), or loss can be revoked (e.g., divorce, separation). Alternatively, cognitive and socioemotional stage of development masks reality.	Emerging reality can be suspended and self-paced; identity can be preserved. Fear and anxiety may be contained.	Resistance to fact or permanence of loss is encouraged; sense of control may be protected. Threat may be unclear because stage of cognitive development provides defenses against conceptualization of threat (e.g., preformal operations), and stage of socioemotional development forces defense against full conceptualization of threat (e.g., pre-separation and identity formation).	Reality testing is compromised. Intellectual component of griefwork parallels emerging reality. Emotional component of griefwork is suspended or may be self-paced in tolerable amounts.

135

ness will play over time (Flavell, Miller, & Miller, 1993). Crosses are held
in abeyance by the 12-year-old. When her father had a stroke, a deluge of
information about its aftermath was given to her. Unaffected at the time, it
was almost 8 months later when the girl dissolved into strong emotions.
"But I told you all about it," her mother said. She replied, "I had my own
ideas about it. He was going to recover. It would go away. I have been
praying for him." This 12-year-old actually has learned the relentless deterioration that often follows a stroke. She has had to forego some of her
wishful thinking, which essentially emerges from her naiveté. This is not
to say that she will not return to her original position, at least temporarily.
However, as time passes, this position will become increasingly tenuous.

Naiveté surrounds all diseases in childhood. What do the words
arthritis or *untreatable* mean to a 9-year-old? Fantasy, wishes, and beliefs
of personal invulnerability characterize childhood, with the latter (albeit
with degrees of tentativeness) culminating in adolescence (Dietrich, 1989;
Shabad, 1989). It is very important to consider that an individual who receives a first serious threat in childhood actually only "learns" its meaning
over time. Thus, an 11-year-old girl, newly diagnosed with a blood disease, sees her returning visits to the doctor as a possibility for being told
that the disease has gone away: "Each night I pray to Granddad. When
my blood count improves, I know he is making it go away."

Obviously, children do not form comprehensive knowledge struc-
tures surrounding chronic illnesses. Nevertheless, their knowledge of the
characteristics of illness will become more sophisticated over time.
Simultaneously, it will be woven and
included into a self-schema. The
"EACH NIGHT I PRAY TO   significance of the initial threat will
GRANDDAD. WHEN MY BLOOD   only be realized in retrospect as
                         griefwork extends into adulthood. A
COUNT IMPROVES, I KNOW HE IS   balance between the hope for res-
MAKING IT GO AWAY."   toration and the self-assessment of
                         the ability to make emerging threat
and one's future meaningful and tenable is an ever-present dynamic in
grieving nonfinite loss for children, adolescents, and adults.

A Fine Balance   The place of hope, regardless of whether it is realistic, resembles the place psychologically friendly dreams play in an individual's development. That is, amid the chaos created by change, even
ill-founded hope provides a certain order and direction that undergirds
individuals as they test reality. The difficulties in negotiating emerging reality (a concept also explored by Elliott, Witty, Herrick, & Hoffman,
1991) are inherent in the vacillating realities of nonfinite loss. For
instance, for the childless woman, her perceptual set might be unconsciously and consciously directed toward information surrounding fertility,

surrogate mothering, and the like. The adopted person, or the husband separated from his wife, may be left in a state of uncertainty, constantly open to being teased by possibilities of and opportunities for realizing dreams, hopes, and expectations—the reunion, if you like. In fact, without the possibility of completion, without a definitive, nonnegotiable "end," it is extremely difficult to stifle the energy that is directed at the possibilities to restore "what should have been" or to attain "what should have been." In a very real way, and somewhat ironically, repeated efforts to restore or recover even the routines of therapy reinstate, if only temporarily, a perception of control. Irrespective of the unrealistic nature of the goals, such efforts might be likened to a survival strategy.

Negotiating an emerging reality and grieving such a reality is necessarily problematic. The cognitive task of grieving involves the restoring of self-organization and schemata to an acceptable accord with postloss reality (Horowitz, 1983). This means consciously bringing up memories and expectations to which the individual is attached, reviewing them, realizing that they cannot be attained, becoming resigned to the fact that expectations must change, and relinquishing them. It is a finely balanced process, for in this reorganization and reconstruction the individual must not lose his or her sense of self. The individual often constructs a hope or fantasy of restoration or rehabilitation that protects the self. This process, unique to each individual, depends on many factors including those of a developmental, psychological, social, and spiritual nature. Naturally, as expectations or dreams are intricate and precious attachments, a great deal of emotion is involved in relinquishing them. In their place, an individual is required to set about constructing a set of expectations that fit the changed state and the new version of reality.

SUMMARY

A clear relationship exists between perceived threat and the ability to check out the emerging reality. The emerging reality can actually sabotage or compromise the task of reality testing. In the case of a clear threat, individuals are frequently frightened of reality testing; in cases of an unclear threat, it is apparent that in some cases reality may be particularly difficult to assess. In these situations, greater emphasis necessarily is placed on the role of psychological maneuvers in limiting and managing information.

Reality testing is a challenging task. It is not surprising that if there is any way around it, individuals will find it, even to the point of employing strategies of extreme avoidance. The thought of who one might become can be a threat that is too horrible to contemplate. Importantly, difficulties encountered in testing reality may have as much to do with the complicated and nonfinite nature of the loss as they do with the personality of the individual. Inevitably, there is a strong relationship between the characteristics of the threat and the corresponding griefwork. How does an individual grieve a loss that might be considered a shifting entity? The following chapter outlines the complexities involved in this process.

AN 18-YEAR-OLD WITH A DEGENERATIVE ILL-
NESS RECALLS, "WHEN MY MOTHER USED TO
TELL ME THINGS ABOUT MY ILLNESS, SOME-
TIMES I WOULD NOD BUT UNDERNEATH THE
TABLE I WOULD CROSS MY FINGERS. SOME-
TIMES IT FEELS JUST LIKE THAT WITH THE
DOCTOR... ON ONE LEVEL I HEAR EVERY-
THING, AND I NOD. ON ANOTHER LEVEL, I
GUESS I STILL HAVE MY FINGERS CROSSED...
I'LL JUST WAIT AND SEE. SOME DAYS I ACTU-
ALLY FEEL QUITE OKAY. "

CHAPTER **12**

GRIEVING
A CHAMELEON

Having indicated in the previous chapters the role of psychological maneuvers in the face of unclear threat, we introduce a number of individuals experiencing varying types of nonfinite loss. What might characterize their
grieving response? What might complicate their grieving response? How
does an individual "grieve a chameleon?" We begin this chapter by exposing the chameleon-like characteristics of various situations of nonfinite loss.

The young woman described in the opening quote of this chapter
has had clear signs that she has a degenerative disease, but on some days
she feels normal enough to entertain a doubt about the veracity of the
doctor's words. *She will have to wait and see.* Another woman, Catherine,
has had a stroke involving such extensive physical changes that she has
been abruptly cut off from the self with which she was familiar. She will
not totally recover—*she will have to wait and see the full extent of change and
who she will become.* For both individuals the loss is unfinished, a continuing threat that evolves and transforms, sometimes dormant, at other times
clearly revealed.

LOSS AS A CHAMELEON

Changeability, inconstancy, unstable equilibrium, vacillation, fluctuation: These
are words that can aptly describe the changing definitions and interpretations of a traumatic event or episode. Such chameleon-like characteristics

result from continuing interaction with many and varied sources. The initial loss occurrence is likely to become episodic in its impact. Against a background of sometimes horrendous change, in cases of chronic disability and disease individuals will receive periodic diagnostic information from medical personnel (Davis, 1963). Extemporaneous comparisons and contrasts perceived in the social environment (Bruce & Schultz, 1992; Bruce, Schultz, & Smyrnios, 1996; Bruce, Schultz, Smyrnios, & Schultz, 1994) accentuate or temper such information. Vulnerable to numerous interpretations, the meaning of an original loss regularly shifts (McHugh, 1968) and may be compounded over time.

This process is particularly apparent in cases of congenital or acquired disabilities in which the sequence of the disability or illness parallels the sequence of typical development. For instance, neurological damage acquired in childhood has its own manifestations, with epilepsy sometimes presenting in adolescence. The anxiety and fear embedded in these transient "wait and see" situations are evident in the following vignettes.

VIGNETTE 1: NEGOTIATING REALITY

Prior to her stroke, when Catherine wanted to get up and go out, a series of finely tuned muscle movements enabled her to follow through with her intention. She had little conscious awareness of the sequence of thoughts and physical movements that led to this action. Following her stroke, that sequence was blocked. Catherine wanted to get up and go out, but this time the intention could not be carried out. In such instances an individual's instinctive acts, volition, or "on-buttons" are thwarted and the routine has lost its sequence. An enormous change such as this throws an individual off course and leads to varying degrees of internal and external disorganization. Catherine's experience enables an examination of a common background context for individuals who are grieving. Individuals often are in a completely disorganized state—they are addled by the number of physical functions that no longer operate automatically.

Gone, also, are aspects of self. Individuals in this predicament are way out of their comfort zone. In a state of emotional disequilibrium, Catherine was forced to rework how she operated in her world and to adapt to what was emerging in her new world. The cognitive task of confronting what has been lost represents an extremely complicated and ongoing challenge. As described in the previous chapter, this task involves an intricate psychological adaptation that has been termed *griefwork*. Not surprisingly, this task is complicated by the tendency for individuals to hold on to the past and wish for what might have been.

To better understand the task of griefwork it is useful to extract two components: the intellectual and the emotional. They often are lumped together, but it is clear that the intellectual component often precedes the emotional aspect of griefwork. In Catherine's case, she must first mount some form of intellectual adaptation. She is forced to rework the personal models of her world, some of which at this point are patently redundant. For instance, showering involves a set of specific new learning skills.

Catherine's emotional adaptation attached to relinquishing her independence is a separate issue, although equally as problematic. The emotional component may be held in abeyance: Catherine may hold tightly to a number of personal wishes and fantasies that protect her from the emotional gloom of her current situation. Furthermore, she may hold the threat of the emerging reality at a distance. It is helpful to draw on the concept of the personal tally board introduced in Chapter 11. How many ticks and crosses appear on Catherine's personal tally board before her conviction of the reality of the situation with which she is faced reaches a certain momentum? What sort of personal experiences, prognoses, and feedback will hasten this conviction? What wishes and fantasies will mute the reality? When and will she be able to relinquish them?

For the individual, this process involves vacillating between a hope for restoration of health and assessing one's ability to mount a challenge to this debilitating condition. Catherine's personal assessment stems from childhood messages and her experiences of withstanding personal adversity. How has she always looked at the world? Did the messages she learned about the world in her development teach her that it was eminently able to be taken on and tackled? Did the personal messages she learned about herself engender the thought that she indeed *could* conquer her fears? If restoration of Catherine's health is not possible and she remains severely incapacitated, these same internalized messages from childhood will inform her ability to make meaning out of her limitations.

VIGNETTE 2: GRIEVING AN EVOLVING REALITY

Dagmar, a 60-year-old woman, had institutionalized her son Martin when he was 2 years old. At the time he was diagnosed as having severe cerebral palsy and mental retardation, and she was informed that her son would not walk or talk. In the words of the neurologist, "Martin will be a vegetable." Twelve years later, a physical therapist informed her that things might have been different: "If I had been exercising your son, he would have walked." One day, two residential care workers supported and walked Martin in front of her. Having never seen her son in an upright position, Dagmar watched her son's walking with amazement. They sat him on a couch opposite her and closed the door. After several minutes, the cushions on the couch fell away and Martin collapsed. Dagmar reflected to her therapist, "You know, I was relieved that he fell. Can you believe that? I am his mother and I was relieved that he could not really have walked. I could not have lived with my guilt, if he had been able to walk." As this mother's story shows, reality keeps on presenting different versions. Individuals must constantly rework, or realign, their internal expectations with a shifting reality. These tasks, all with variable degrees of threat, are met with a good deal of psychological resistance; the individual's innate wish is to hold on to the world as it "should be." Against this background, the loss itself may involve inherent contradictions over time.

Considering the characteristics of dreaded events, particularly the shifting definition over time and notions of refutability and revocability, it becomes clear that getting expectations to fit an emerging new reality is complicated. It is conceivable that in order to preserve identity in the face of personal experience of a dreaded event there is some survival value in constructing a somewhat sterilized version of reality or flirting with notions of hope for recovery and the like.

VIGNETTE 3: CONFRONTING DREADED EVENTS

Doris, a 50-year-old woman who has been in remission from cancer for 3 years, spent a day worrying about a woman she has read about in a women's magazine: "She had what I had—she only lived for 3 years." Doris was having trouble discerning her own experience from that of this woman; in response, her therapist asked her if this woman's story was relevant to her own situation.

Like an uninvited image in a crystal ball, the features of dreaded events can forecast an imagined future that automatically threatens one's version of self. The individual cannot tolerate the enormity of the impending loss and fears for survival of him- or herself. Instantly, the preservation of identity becomes difficult. Overexposed to the potential threat, the individual perceives it to be *too* dangerous to test reality: "I dare not fathom this loss; I cannot safely fathom its depths." Some aspects of griefwork may actually represent a threat to psychological well-being. Who could realistically contemplate the physical changes attached to a diagnosis of multiple sclerosis, motor neuron disease, or cancer without it gravely challenging one's emotional well-being and attachment to life?

"I DARE NOT FATHOM THIS LOSS; I CANNOT SAFELY FATHOM ITS DEPTHS."

As is evident in Doris's situation, individuals rarely have the scientific or medical knowledge to accurately discriminate and interpret their own experience. The attributions surrounding dreaded events dominate. They provide a template that filters the perception and interpretation of elements of their emerging world. Inevitably, an individual who is learning exactly what has been lost (i.e., what the diagnosis or the event means) will be exposed to a lot of personally irrelevant stories before he or she can objectively discard them.

Figure 12.1 schematically depicts the process of integrating a dreaded event. Although overly simplistic, the relationship between the two circles: "Who I am" and "Who I may become" represents the process over time. Individuals can be eclipsed by the dreaded event, almost totally absorbed by it. Others may keep the dreaded event at arm's length, almost as a separate reality and identity. A good adaptive outcome represents a melding of the two circles. By mastering their fear of who they may become, individuals absorb the dreaded event; neither one nor the other circle, they become a composite of both life experiences. Remarkable though it may seem, in a multitude of instances individuals who have mastered their fear of a dreaded event can become, in a sense, proud of the part it plays in their personality and identity. No longer estimated as a psychological threat, it provides a certain proof about an individual's innate characteristics of resilience. It is an outcome of this nature that enables the loss of "who I was" to be somewhat placated.

VIGNETTE 4: GRIEVING
AND THE LOSS OF IDENTITY

For Erika, a female architect who has a child with paraplegia, pushing the wheelchair in public involved a threat to her own identity. Erika could not endure the stares; looks that she pronounced as "pity" were precursors to her angry refusal of any offered help with her daughter's wheelchair. This middle-age mother spoke of a wish to protect herself from individuals who might regard her "just as a mother of a child with a disability." She wished she could wear a name tag stating clearly, "I am an architect."

Aspects of one's self that are held as integral become very apparent when life circumstances threaten their viability. For this mother, the image of her child in a wheelchair threatens her version of self as a competent, successful businesswoman. For those individuals who experience trauma with resulting irrevocable changes to their selves and world, obviously large chunks of one's identity are at risk. Losing limbs or mobility, or realizing your partner cannot accept you as changed, results in a number of social roles that define an individual as suddenly redundant.

Consumed by images of the person he or she may become, an individual may be forced to avoid reality testing. When this happens, only bits and pieces of griefwork take place. Certain individuals may be able to let go of some of their expectations about themselves in the world, but

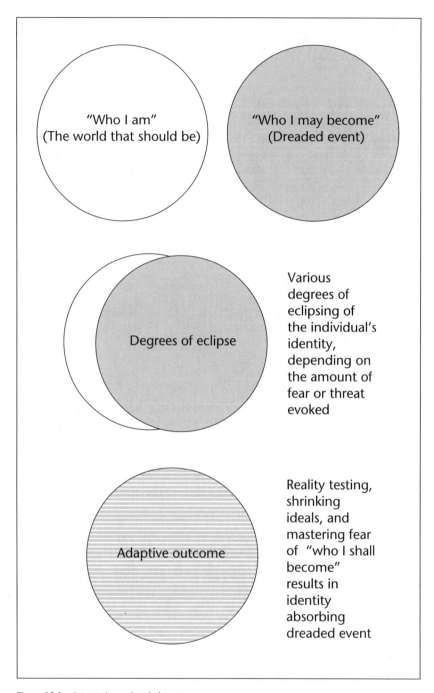

Figure 12.1.   Integrating a dreaded event.

not others. In some instances, actual griefwork surrounding the essence and gravity of the loss cannot be, and never is, confronted. An executive tests positive for HIV under a pseudonym and refuses to tell his friends or colleagues of the diagnosis is one such example. He exclaims to his partner, "My colleagues will consider me dead if they find out I am HIV positive." Eventually he runs his business from his bed, his customers still unaware of his medical condition. Along the same lines, a woman who had cancer continued almost obsessively to take care of her husband. Terribly upset about her condition, her husband did not understand his wife's reaction: "It's as though nothing has happened for her." To cope, she clung desperately to the daily routines of domestic life.

"MY COLLEAGUES WILL CONSIDER ME DEAD IF THEY FIND OUT I AM HIV POSITIVE."

In these situations, both of these people were able to salvage the appearance that nothing had changed. It was possible to exercise a certain amount of impression management; that is, they were able to present what they wanted and needed to present to others.

For individuals who have more obtrusive problems, the disguise of the personal impact or damage is not possible. To salvage the old version of self, some may choose to become reclusive and cut off contact with all people who knew them as they were before: "I would not want anyone who knew me before to see me now"; hence, the mutual dismay felt by a patient in a rehabilitation unit and an old high school friend—a hospital volunteer—who is assisting her. The volunteer finds her old friend unrecognizable apart from her name at the head of her bed. For the young woman who has been disfigured, the encounter is excruciatingly painful—she feels overwhelmed by the exposure.

VIGNETTE 5: RETHINKING THE FAMILIAR

Gerard, a 20-year-old laborer who had seriously damaged his right hand, illustrates how the aftermath of a negative event provokes individuals into rethinking the familiar—what they have always taken for granted about themselves and the world (Leick & Davidsen-Nielsen, 1991). Never before had Gerard actually considered this right hand of his. "Out of action," however, and separated from his workplace, the extraordinary value of his hand became amplified. A physiotherapist led him to a discovery of the muscles, tendons, and nerves that provide its fine capacities. "Man, this hand, I just don't believe how it operates." In therapy, he talked about the exercises that were slowly restoring his hand: "See this movement in my hand? It's getting stronger. Slowly but surely I'm feeling it. I'm looking after it." Essentially, he had begun to feel a love and deference for a hand that he had not focused on before, simply because it had been taken for granted.

Gerard's hand will heal. His hope for recovery will be answered. He is able to anticipate a return to his old world; he will not be forced to create and build an attachment to a world without his hand. He will take with him a changed sensibility about the notion of keeping safe, however. His accident will be translated to a general vigilance about safety. This young man had not actually considered or *seen* the need for being cautious before. For him it was "just something adults were talking about all the time!" He cannot understand the change in himself: "*Me* thinking about saving people? Telling my friends to put seat belts on? We just used to fool around, never used to wear them—now I do it first thing!" While this is a short-term personal crisis, he has been forced to encounter identity assumptions that were previously unquestioned.

Figure 12.2 illustrates what happens to self-identity (A) when that identity is under threat. The endangered aspects of one's taken-for-granted world (B) become objectified for scrutiny for the first time. Between two worlds, the individual's equilibrium is thrown out of balance. It is understandable that amid this disequilibrium of often extreme anxiety, the endangered aspects of self-identity stand out like lifeboats, ways back to feeling okay or at one with one's self. With the threat of

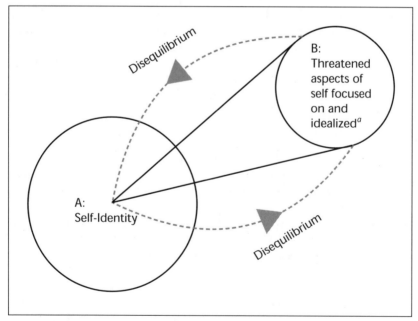

Figure 12.2.   The disequilibrium created by threat. ([a] In instances that threaten large aspects of self, B may be almost equivalent to A in size, with the disequilibrium extreme.)

loss, the attachment to the threatened aspect becomes intensified, in most cases idealized.

From this process emerges a paradox. In the process of losing a part of ourselves, whether it be a body part or a person with whom we have had a close association, we often for the first time actually *see* what it has been to us, the significance it has played in our world. Under this spotlight, the loss can sometimes be heightened. Ironically, attachment to what has been lost may be intensified and relinquishment of what was is made all the more difficult. To make matters worse, the individual is often plagued by dreams centering on the lost body part or person (Sacks, 1991); the dream ends with the individual finding that his waking life is the nightmare.

SUMMARY

Through these vignettes, this chapter has explored the conceptualization of the world that begins its formation with the threat of a negative event—dreaded, significant, or both—with particular reference to nonfinite loss and griefwork. The process of learning what the emerging world will be like is paced by the learning situations and information that the individual acquires. It also is tempered by the individual's need to limit the threat perceived to be inherent in the event. In summary, a grieving process related to nonfinite loss is complicated by the intricate relationship among an individual's innate need to protect a particular version of self and the world, the perception of the threat to that version of self, and the characteristics of the threat. As part of this process, individuals are faced with numerous challenges. They are asked to try to construe their own future as it is pitted against the reputation of dreaded events, to manage the chronic nature of their grief, to sustain hope, to make goals, and to retain some sense of control in life. Given the uncertainty and continuing threat that often characterize nonfinite loss, these are onerous tasks.

How does the therapist adequately portray to the client the general flow of adaptation which, ideally, parallels the grieving response? Despite the individuality and complexity of griefwork, it is possible to identify commonalties in the experience of grieving nonfinite loss. While working closely with many clients, we have discovered many cycles and themes. These are described in the following chapter.

"In grief, nothing 'stays put.' One keeps on emerging from a phase, but it always recurs. Round and round. Everything repeats. Am I going in circles, or dare I hope I am on a spiral?...But if a spiral, am I going up or down it?"

—Lewis, 1961, p. 46

CHAPTER 13

CHARACTERISTIC CYCLES OF NONFINITE GRIEF

Considering the variety of reactions to nonfinite loss and grief described in Chapter 12, it seems almost ludicrous to try to discriminate a set of universal stages or cycles that might characterize the grieving process for nonfinite loss. But on examination, in the midst of major ebbs, a general flow of adaptation can be deciphered. There are identifiable commonalities within a myriad of individual differences. As is evident in Chapter 10's opening quote by Oliver Sacks or in Catherine's story in Chapter 12, aspects of adaptations are often forced. The emotional component of this adaptation often has lagged way behind. This is not surprising because the painful emotions that surround such losses are threatening. In this chapter, we attempt to elucidate a cyclical pattern of themes that might represent the process of adapting to nonfinite loss. We begin by reiterating the basic elements and features of this process.

THE PROCESS OF ADAPTING

As outlined in Section I, grieving involves the reworking of personal models of the world that become redundant following significant loss and change. It is an adaptive process with dual components: the intellectual and the emotional. From the preceding sections it is evident how integral these personal models are to a sense of control, a sense of well-being or balance, and a sense of "who one is." These models align with what may be termed a *comfort zone*. They include a plethora of taken-for-granted nuances and an assembly of ways in which individuals come to deal with the world. Loss and change threaten comfort zones.

Section II of this book elaborates on the development of an enmeshed relationship among expectations, ideals, and the notion of self-identity. Attention is given to the physiological equilibrium woven into individual personalities as they develop and the creation of sometimes quite fragile comfort zones. Recall the adolescent boy who needs his sunglasses placed "just so" on his head. What emerges is an intricate connection between self (i.e., "who I am") and both physiological and psychological balance. In the physiological sense this might translate into a feeling of being "in sync" with one's inner metabolism; in the psychological sense, it might surface as a feeling of being "in control." With his new haircut, the adolescent boy does not feel in sync and lacks a feeling of control. Thus, he avoids meeting his girlfriend's parents. This seemingly insignificant incident creates a significant disturbance for the boy, and provides a clue to the gravity of reaction that may accompany traumatic loss.

Becoming estranged from one's taken-for-granted self can equate with a frightening sensation of being out of balance. As has been shown, there are extreme variations in examples of estrangements from old versions of self, from the loss of sunglasses to the loss of a limb. Confronted with a self that is seen as damaged, the individual grapples with losing the esteem of others and of his or her self-esteem (e.g., the fear of becoming like Michael, the little boy described in Section II).

In this process of adapting, individuals are caught between two worlds but cling desperately to the first world, the one that they are accustomed to navigating. For people with significant disabilities, the world as they knew it can no longer operate automatically. Large parts of normal routines and patterns of activity have become impossible and are proving to be redundant. It is no longer appropriate to plan or to follow prior goals, some of which might have been an individual's guiding maps for years.

Against the background of these sociological and psychological contexts it is possible to extrapolate a grieving process of cycles with key themes. The cycles characterize the recurrent nature of themes and the recurrent mood states as continuing features of grieving nonfinite loss. The lability of the cycles is affected not only by the ongoing representations of the loss over time but also by the propensity for a fluctuation of ego states. The issues amplified in situations of nonfinite loss predominantly involve a needs-based dependency on adult figures, parents, spouses, or caregivers. Maintaining an adult ego state is frequently too difficult because nonfinite loss accentuates fears of abandonment, isolation, loneliness, safety, and survival and prompts assessments of whether one is still loved. Child versions of self can quickly be evoked and the cycles of grieving instantly affected.

The following vignette of Frank illustrates the general flow of adaptation. A geological analogy that follows Frank's story is used to capture the essence of nonfinite loss. Although Frank's cycles relate to a situation of serious injury that has left him a paraplegic, they can be translated to any situation of personal adversity that continues to evolve, that is, *it is incomplete in its initial presentation.* There are common themes; irrespective of the type of nonfinite loss—overt or covert—anxiety, fear, and relentlessness are connecting features.

Frank is a paraplegic, a condition resulting from a car accident when he was 22 years old. At first, a focused goal of fitness assisted him in creating a new identity and adapting to his injury. At that age, his fitness matched his goal; it all fit together okay. Whether Frank actually was able to work through the emotional component of his grieving is questionable; it is probable, given the traumatic nature of his accident, that he was suffering from posttraumatic stress disorder, a condition likely to stand in the way of the emotional component of grieving. When we met him at the age of 40, his ability to sustain physical fitness was waning. He was face-to-face with limitations again. He had become a father and was finding particularly painful his inability to perform his role with his children in ways he had idealized.

Not surprising, his dreams were about playing football and tennis with his kids. As on the first occasion when we had met, Frank again protested: "Why me? What did I do to deserve this?" Momentarily, Frank was forced back into a state of protest and wanting to fix his life; not only was he railing against his inability to reverse the accident and reclaim part of himself but also against all of the bad luck in his life. The original crisis was again reviewed with respect to its effect in the present. Current "Why me's" merged with past "Why me's," including those from before his injury, right back to childhood.

Nonfinite loss is about the interaction between time and the meaning and significance of loss. As in Frank's case, shifting time frames cast different perspectives. For instance, the divorce of an individual's parents that occurs in his or her childhood often becomes more attached with meaning in retrospect; at the time, there were apparent bonuses— trips to amusement parks and so forth. However, as we grow older, contexts provide greater depth of understanding of where incidents fit into life pictures. Similarly, although chronic illness and disability are about changing physical states, they themselves happen against normal sequences of developmental change in the life cycle. In combination, they are perceived and judged differently because of an individual's stage of development.

Given this background dynamic, capturing and describing the essence of nonfinite loss and the griefwork it impels is difficult. Systematic stage-like approaches to griefwork seem naive. They show no respect for the changes over time. The following analogy provides imagery that respects an underlying movement toward adaptation but also heeds the continued attacks on the identity that include the original threat.

When there is a tremor or earthquake, plates of the earth's crust shift and layers of earth collapse. The ground ruptures and threatens to give way. Without getting into the complexities and intricacies of this process, over time a foundation is restored. But it is a permanently changed version of stability; we cannot rely on it as we did before. We are suspicious of further tremors. The reformation of the substrate that provides the foundation for the layers of earth resting on it, however, is built around an intrinsic fault line. The fault line might be likened to a condition that creates a continuing vulnerability to the havoc of weather, time, and so forth. For the person enduring nonfinite loss, the initial tragedy (i.e., earthquake) brings a loss and in its aftermath leaves a susceptibility (i.e., fault line) to shifting time frames that cast different perspectives.

Applying this geological analogy to Frank's case, it would seem that the intrinsic fault line, camouflaged earlier, has been disturbed by the vicissitudes of his age and by the ideals that come to the forefront of his mind because of his changed role as a father. Therapy with Frank is about griefwork related to the changing effects of the original crisis. Nevertheless, he is probably on far firmer ground now than when he was 22. Frank does not have to start all over again. Frank's earlier adaptation can serve as a type of inoculation against a replay of the extremities of the original shock.

Before we elaborate on the cycles that we believe to be somewhat characteristic of grieving nonfinite loss, it is important to highlight the place of anxiety, fear, and relentlessness in the experience of nonfinite loss. Despite age and stage of development, the dilemma facing an individual and his or her caregivers and family is adaptation to more-often-than-not continued threat and uncertainty within themselves—perhaps the hardest thing for the psyche to tolerate. In fact, varying intensities of disbelief, anxiety, and fear parallel, but also restrict, the griefwork of nonfinite loss.

Anxiety, Fear, and Relentlessness

The very questions that arise out of anxiety about illness and injury in childhood cannot be vetoed. Answers to such questions that a child anxiously asks his father or mother (e.g., "Will it go away?" "Will it get better?" "Will I be all right?") change from "You'll be fine" to "No, it will not go away; you may not get better." The notion that things cannot be fixed represents a strange mix of amazement and desperation for many people, particularly for those who have no life experience of an ongoing medical condition or disease. The inconceivability is demonstrated in statements such as "I can't believe that something can't be done!" It also is about the relentlessness of the threat; the individual exclaims, "But there's no end to this. It's just going to go on and on! If I knew it was going to stop it would be different."

The relentless nature of nonfinite loss may account for a flirtatious relationship that sometimes develops with the possibility of death, or in the caregiver's case, of leaving. The contemplation of either can provide a vision of relief to a seemingly endless threat. Paradoxically, these contemplations, or even fantasies of recovery (Rochlin, 1965), offer a strange psychological support to keep going. "If I can see an end point, some relief, I can rally," says the father of a child with schizophrenia. The notions of cure, recovery, rehabilitation, restorative surgery, regaining abilities through strenuous physical exercise, and the like all represent the opening of an important psychological door. A comment made by a bereaved 84-year-old mother illustrates this point: "I can only go on living *because* I know I will see my son soon. Had this happened when I was younger, I could not have survived it." Basically, this approach attempts to reduce the relentlessness of the loss.

PREDOMINATE CYCLES OF GRIEFWORK

The proposition of endless threat, continued anxiety and fear, and the often insidious presence of emotional learning in childhood provides a consistent thread in grieving nonfinite loss. Tables 13.1–13.5 introduce five cycles of griefwork. The concept of ever-evolving cycles and recurring states of mind provides scope not only for shifting time frames but also for the nonlinear and individual natures of the grieving process. It accommodates the sometimes obscure and unclear nature of the emerging reality. Deference is given to the idiosyncratic developmental course of chronic illness and disability that takes place quite apart from the changes within ordinary life development. These life circumstances have their own broad terrain, paths that are prescribed by what the course of illness or the course of the disease takes over time.

"I CAN ONLY GO ON LIVING BECAUSE I KNOW I WILL SEE MY SON SOON. HAD THIS HAPPENED WHEN I WAS YOUNGER, I COULD NOT HAVE SURVIVED IT."

Each of the five tables details the keywords, characteristics, signs of resistance and hope, reworking of schemata, social implications, typical comments, and possible problematic outcomes. Invariably, and regardless of the nature of their tragedy, the people we meet in practice initially proclaim, "We will not accept this. This is unacceptable!" With this emphasis in mind, the following cycles are about adaptation rather than acceptance.

Cycle 1: Themes of Shock

"This is unreal. This can't be happening!" The emotions of Cycle 1 (see Table 13.1) express the disruption of a taken-for-granted reality that has simultaneously affected our internal balance and sense of control. However, although we know we are under some extreme threat, the process of becoming convinced of the actualities of this reality and its emotional content lags. The physical concomitants reflect the threat, with cycles of hunger, sleep, and metabolic systems affected. Concentration and memory are similarly impaired. The psychological state, however, may be likened to depersonalization or a detachment from reality. Picture the paralyzed state in which you find an animal rendered helpless by a bright light in a dark forest. The individual is internally paralyzed from large portions of independent thought: instructions, patterns, and routines that are physically possible mask the extent of this damage to control. Typically, this mask is convincing, and people unknowing and not wanting to think otherwise comment on how well the person experiencing the loss is doing!

Consider a report from a doctor who had given a diagnosis to a mother and father concerning their son. The news was not promising. In fact, the doctor had told them that their child had a degenerative condition in which they would see his ability to walk and talk deteriorate over a 10-year period. Ultimately, the condition would lead to his death. During the difficult delivery of this information, both parents sat erect and listened with transfixed expressions to the future that was forecasted for their son. Even after the news, they thanked the doctor, passed some pleasantries, paid the bill, and drove home. Not surprising, the perception of the doctor was that they had "handled it well." In fact, the routines masked an indubitable trauma.

Cycle 2: Themes of Protest/Demand

"Why did this happen? I don't believe this! There must be a way out of this mess!" The idea of an individual lost in a maze is a useful analogy in Cycle 2. Numbness and shock may begin to dissipate, but it is "early days." Disbelief, which may be sustained for extended periods of time

Table 13.1.   Cycle I: Themes of shock

Some key characteristics	Psychological maneuvers required to survive threat			Social implications	Typical comment	Problematic outcomes
	Resistance	Hope	Reworking of schemata			
Shock forces an anaesthetized state.	What is happening is screened as though a foreign reality.	Immobilized by fear, anxiety.	Emerging reality not owned.	Psychological isolation as membership in familiar groups is threatened (loneliness with or without social contact): "I feel different from them."	"This is unreal."	Traumatic response (posttraumatic stress disorder)
Numbness, shock, disbelief.	Anaesthetized state provides avoidance.	Glimpses of hope that there has been some mistake.	Existence is robotic—everyday routines or action by rote give impression of control.	"They have no idea what I am going through."	"I don't believe that this is happening."	Dreaded event is so traumatic and/or threatens core aspects of self so much that it forces individual to avoid implications totally.
Breakthrough waves of anxiety and fear as disorganization contributes to a sense of impending loss of control. Underlying mood of sadness.		"It is a bad dream and it will go away."			"It feels as though I'm someone else."	Individual feels so overwhelmed as to wish for death or to contemplate suicide: "I don't see much point in going on."
Detachment from reality.						"At this point I don't care whether I live or die."
Depersonalization as major disruption to internal and external patterns; out of balance; physiological concomitants (e.g., cardiovascular, endocrine, immunologic).						If physical effects involve intense pain or core parts of identity, a similar response is likely.
Disturbance of sleep, eating, concentration, memory, and decision-making (i.e., concentration).						
Breakthrough of predominate anxiety, fear, and sadness.						

because of the lack of clarity of the situation, continues. This disbelief involves a need to account for why it happened (e.g., "I've never done anything to hurt anyone else, so why does this happen to me?"). With identity under threat, an interplay between hope and resistance is crucial. The individual attempts to minimize the threat by resisting the acknowledgment of the possible consequences of the threat. The underlying fear of the consequences intensifies the psychological work that is directed to staying the same—not changing. All of this requires avoidance, which is quite healthy and adaptive up to a point, but it may become phobic. Specifically, the fear of "who I might become" can be almost overwhelming.

If the threat is relentless and hope is continually stifled, individuals feel helpless to control any part of the situation. This outcome might be predicted from the statement made by a young mother of a child with a disability: "When is all of this going to stop? They tell me there's something wrong with her metabolism, then they tell me that she's not going to continue growing properly, then the speech-language pathologist tells me she won't be able to talk properly, and the kindergarten teacher says that she might not be able to enter mainstream school. I can't see any point in going on. It's just one blow after another."

The psychological situation in Cycle 2 (see Table 13.2) often is further complicated by a sense of dependency that restricts a sense of control. When this occurs, an individual automatically reverts to childhood versions of self and yearns for unconditional care from parent figures. As Tony Moore, in his acute and moving personal account of recovery from extensive injuries sustained in a car accident, wrote,

> I am not ashamed to admit that at the time of the accident, at the age of 44, when the destruction and devastation of the injuries combined to produce an overwhelming emotional rubble, I missed my mother. Her own mental frailty prevented her from providing me with the cradling comfort of my childhood. I lay in the hospital bed hoping for some mystical earth mother to visit and nourish me. I needed someone of strength and stability whose gentleness I could trust and in whose comforts my awful inadequacies would be tolerated. (1991, p. 36)

In fact, it is this battered physical and psychological state that returns an individual to a sense of dependence on others.

Cycle 3: Themes of Defiance

"I can fix it." In Cycle 3, the background, as before, is one of anxiety, fear, and sadness; with the physiological symptoms continuing, although abating marginally. There may also be some energy for defiance, however: "I can fix this by recovering, rehabilitating, reuniting with my partner." The fact

Table 13.2. Cycle 2: Themes of protest/demand

Some key characteristics	Psychological maneuvers required to survive threat			Social implications	Typical comment	Problematic outcomes
	Resistance	Hope	Reworking of schemata			
Anaesthetized state abating as threat continues and emerges as real.	Psychological maneuvers required to retain sense of control and safety.	Endeavor to construe information so as to reduce threat.	In limbo between two worlds and beginning to objectify aspects of loss. Sense of detachment from old self with no attachment to emerging reality.	Psychological and social isolation from mainstream and fear of "who I will become."	"Who am I?" / "Who will I become?"	Identity crisis as separated from core aspects of identity. / Avoidance becomes phobic as intrusions about possible future scenarios overwhelm.
Diminishing numbness and disbelief.	Search for meaning: "Why?"	Hope as a necessary degree of avoidance to preserve identity that is under increasing threat.		Intrusions representative of "who I may become."	"Why should I have to take " this?	
Beginnings of protest, agitation, restlessness.	Resistance to the real consequences of loss: "It cannot be as bad as this!"		Modification of expectations/ schemas not yet accepted as necessary; work is directed to not changing the world—disorganization.		"What did I do to deserve this?" / "How bad can it get?"	Continued threat creates helplessness: cannot control or fix; leads to depression: "What is the point of going on? There's always something else wrong."
Episodic breakthroughs of fear, anxiety, anger associated with loss of control and safety.	Avoidance of information that hinders resistance.		Short-term routines forced to change.		"I don't believe this."	
Underlying sadness.						
Continued depersonalization and detachment as disruption to internal and external patterns continues; out of balance, physiological concomitants persist.						
Psychological maneuvers are required to retain sense of control and safety.						

157

of the threat may be acknowledged, but its permanence is psychologically refuted (see Table 13.3). The situation may be likened to a state of separation anxiety, with intermittent bouts of protest. Despite the protests, however, the emerging reality is forcing the modification of day-to-day and short-term expectations. Long-term forecasts of the future must still be held at arm's length. Although this is adaptive and limits the damage to the identity, for some people an obsessive and desperate search for a cure is intensified. This behavior represents their adaptation. Between two worlds, aligned with neither, a sense of isolation is amplified.

Cycle 4: Themes of Resignation and Despair

"I cannot fix this; I cannot return to where I was." With a sense of protests unheard, and aspects of self and versions of the world seemingly irrevocable, an atmosphere of resignation and helplessness distinguishes Cycle 4 from earlier cycles (see Table 13.4). Extinction of anxious, searching behavior may have taken place; an individual acknowledges that total recovery or reversal may not be possible. A more adult version of self might become restored and available at this point. Although parts of the enormity of the loss are fathomed, some threats cannot be safely understood and will remain at arm's length.

An elaborate adaptive process is taking form. For the identity to survive, connections with new versions of the world have to be made. To reduce the size of the threat, the outcome for self has to be regarded as psychologically feasible. This is a complex juggling task, for during this process, we consciously and subconsciously wish that the trauma had not happened and know that what is emerging is a poor second best. Thus, reality testing comes in fits and starts. We must encourage and entertain positive outcomes and reduce the importance of what we were. Yet there must be a linking thread. A complicated reworking of core expectations begins. In fact, it is questionable whether we ever truly relinquish expectations to which we are attached. In order to survive, we modify them or express them in different ways. If we are to conserve an ability to look forward to the future, we avoid modifying all of our expectations.

Cycle 5: Themes of Integration

"I guess something has come out of all this—I feel a sense of balance." Cycle 5 (see Table 13.5) represents a merging and integration of old and new versions of the self: "Remarkably, this comes together, and I can be both; I can be me and I can have cancer—I'm not one or the other."

This is schematically depicted in Figure 12.1 in Chapter 12. Invariably, there also has been an abstraction of some meaning from what

Table 13.3. Cycle 3: Themes of defiance

Some key characteristics	Psychological maneuvers required to survive threat			Social implications	Typical comment	Problematic outcomes
	Resistance	Hope	Reworking of schemata			
Anxiety, fear, sadness as substrate.	Resistance to permanence of threat.	Hope for recovery fuels a directed search.	In two worlds with a view to not accepting long-term consequences or aspects of change.	Psychological and social isolation from mainstream: "They don't understand."	"There will be some cure—I can recover."	Overavoidance of experiencing who "they" are prevents reality testing and amplifies isolation.
Yearning, searching, frustration, anger.	Efforts to continue as though nothing has happened.	Avoidance of information that threatens aim to fix.	Forced to modify short-term expectations.	Refusal to become "one of them" (e.g., a person with a disability; a divorced woman) on a permanent basis: "I'm not one of them."	"I will be able to return to work; it'll be okay."	Obsessive reaction: Identity is unidimensional—part of identity that is threatened is idealized.
Diminishing disbelief.						
Depersonalization and detachment in varying degrees.	Preoccupation with recovery, with episodes of possibility that situation may not be able to be fixed.	Selection of information that supports hope.	Triggers of world that should have been and contrasts and comparisons with emerging reality force review of expectations and schemas.			Perception that no other aspects of identity are valuable.
Physiological concomitants continue in varying degrees of intensity.			Physical triggers (e.g., pain, amputation) force review of schemas.			

159

Table 13.4. Cycle 4: Themes of resignation and despair

Some key characteristics	Psychological maneuvers required to survive threat			Social implications	Typical comment	Problematic outcomes
	Resistance	Hope	Reworking of schemata			
Anxiety, fear, sadness, and intermittent sense of disbelief as substrate: "I would never have imagined that my life would have turned out like this!"	Resistance threatened as permanence of illness/ disease cannot be refuted.	Hope for a recovery as both unconscious and conscious wishes are able to be stimulated by news of cures (e.g., technical, religious, spiritual).	Significance of loss is limited—connection with new versions of world established.	Isolation from mainstream; experience forces a desensitization to "them."	"I would never have appreciated life this way, if this had not happened. Now I make the most of each day."	Characteristics of loss threaten identity: cannot contemplate such a life— overavoidance (obsessive about overcoming or things not changing) or suicidal thoughts.
Helplessness, anger, depression, and despair as individual cannot control outcome.			Meaning of new reality is translated by way of goals or heightened pros of outcome for self—"new me" is built up to reduce size of loss.		"This was something that was meant to be—it was meant to happen for a purpose."	Cannot shrink world or self that might have been (i.e., world or self remains idealized).
Forced habituation to emerging reality and beginnings of physiological balance.		Hope as a technique for survival reduces fear, anxiety, and breaks down size of threat.	New reality is made tolerable. Beginning attachment to new self and reality.			Cannot translate meaning to new version of self and world.
			Possibilities for surviving the trauma emerge, and active grieving takes place.			
			Vacillation between "who I was," and "who I could have been" and idealization of these versions of self with the version of self that is emerging.			

Forced revisions of
expectations, schemas;
safety and predictability
begin to be restored.
Revising of expectations
cannot be prospective.

Changes connected with
the loss continue, and the
need to preserve certain
aspects of identity makes
it difficult to relinquish
some expectations fully.

Sense of control emerges.

Table 13.5. Cycle 5: Themes of integration

Some key characteristics	Psychological maneuvers required to survive threat			Social implications	Typical comment	Problematic outcomes
	Resistance	Hope	Reworking of schemata			
Substrate of anxiety, fear, and sadness as uncertainty and threat continue. Sense of disbelief. Retriggering active grieving states (e.g., yearning). Fragile balance achieved between physiological and psychological states.	Forced to resign to permanence of loss: more intellectual than emotional acceptance.	Hope translated to vague notions and wishes of recovery—existential meanings—possibilities of recovery in afterlife—(potential for susceptibility to news of cures remains).	Significance of loss is acknowledged but is balanced by amplifying connection to special attributes that are gained. That is, a meaningful connection is made with new self and version of world (e.g., becoming a world-class Paralympian). Learning of emerging reality forces expectations to be continually revised. Grieving continues affected by internal and external triggers of the world and self that was and "should have been" (waves of protest, sadness, and despair).	A member of both groups, with self an integration of both, neither drowned by or fearful of "them."	"I value what I have become—I was very shallow before all this happened." "I could have done without cancer to learn about my strengths but I guess that is one thing that has come out of it."	Continued threat with no room for control creates depression. Inability to create meaning in new reality. Unable to identify with "them."

162

has happened: "I will help others" or "I have found a new value in life, in nature." This is not to say that the reality is accepted. There will be a continuing relationship with hope, albeit vague. As mentioned previously, perhaps it is because individuals can entertain notions of cure and recon-ciliation as part of their inner world that they do adapt to a future.

"I CAN BE BOTH; I CAN BE ME AND I CAN HAVE CANCER—I'M NOT ONE OR THE OTHER.".

Reworking expectations is a somewhat strategic exercise, and it will never be perfect. Learning of the emerging reality forces internal-ized expectations to be continually revised. Thus, ongoing griefwork is a phenomenon of nonfinite loss. Grieving may be intensified by exter-nal triggers, but it also can be influenced by internal states cultivated by dreams or subconscious thoughts. The substrate of anxiety, fear, and sadness remains, but these emotions are linked to triggers representing realistic threats to psychological equilibrium. Physiological sensations associated with a perception of threat are simultaneously experienced.

THE CYCLICAL NATURE OF NONFINITE LOSS

Whereas the five tables indicate possible patterns in the adaptation pro-cess, Figure 13.1 demonstrates the fluidity of the cycles over time. There is an inescapable feeling of being unsettled and of incomplete-ness in grieving nonfinite loss. The cycles are not linear, have no end-point, and are prone to recycling again and again. Individuals may reach an adaptive relationship with the original threat, but further threats, the effects of age, and stressors over time can force them to revisit cycles of protest, defiance, and despair. The yearning and searching for cures, remedies, and reconciliations—although dissipating in intensity over time—are likely to still be subject to reactivation, much of which will be nonvolitional. Even when a major loss has occurred, there may be con-tinued efforts to reclaim, or preserve, parts of the old self. The fear of "who I might become" creates a continuing anxiety state. This state might be likened to a type of separation anxiety. As emphasized in Tables 13.1–13.5, varying intensity of anxiety and fear might be consid-ered characteristic features of nonfinite loss. Inevitably, anxiety and fear states are amplified in situations in which symptoms or signs herald fur-ther threats (e.g., the lead-up to and day of periodical cancer checks).

In Figure 13.1, we are careful to include the part that childhood schemata play in nonfinite loss. Frequent returns to feelings of depen-dency are inevitable. Outbursts of anger, bitterness, and sadness pre-dictably erupt when such childhood schemata become too dominant. In particular, beliefs about the self, about the schemata of the world that

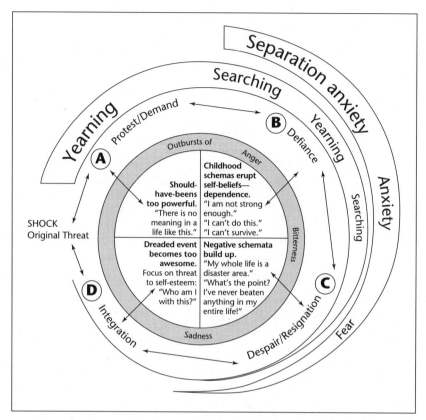

Figure 13.1.   Cyclic themes of nonfinite loss. Outer circles represent continuous fluctuations of anxiety and fear, yearning and searching. (*Key:* A = Protest reactivated in response to threat. May wax and wane. B = Defiance may not follow as a sequence or be typical. C = Despair will be intermittent. D = Integration represents a constant consolidation of changes (discrepancies with the world that should have been). Inner circle depicts fragile patterns of thought (schemata) learned in childhood, which frequently erupt. Shaded areas relate to the emotions that the thought patterns can evoke. Arrows depict a dynamic relationship between themes and schemata learned in childhood.

should have been, and of dreaded events are isolated. They represent an underlying dialogue in the individual's relationship with loss. The individual may periodically, particularly when tired or stressed, slip into thinking how the world should have been and protest, "Enough is enough!" Alternatively, the sense of being abandoned and of no longer being "protected" from feared events takes over intermittently, if only temporarily and for shorter periods of time. Relapses of this nature are familiar to those who are grieving nonfinite loss and may sabotage the ability to grieve. In an individual's process of adaptation, childhood versions of self might be considered an adversary to be acknowledged and challenged.

SUMMARY

Shock, protest/demand, defiance, despair/resignation, and integration are cyclic themes triggered by varying presentations of the losses experienced in adversity. Although each of these themes may be revisited, generally the underlying thrust is toward a sense of integration. Fear, anxiety, searching, and yearning are typical recurrent themes of varying intensity. Therapeutic principles for facilitating and managing the grieving of nonfinite loss are presented in Section V with eight case studies that illustrate the translation of theory into practice.

SECTION V

PRINCIPLES AND CLINICAL APPLICATIONS

CHAPTER **14**

THE DEVELOPMENT OF INDIVIDUALS AS STRATEGISTS

This chapter presents an overview of the clinical applications that are described throughout Section V. It addresses issues of direct relevance to the practice of a psychoeducational approach to grieving nonfinite loss, including the philosophical orientation, basic premises, goals, aims and objectives, processes, strategies, tasks, and other special considerations in facilitating an adaptive outcome for individuals grieving nonfinite loss.

PHILOSOPHICAL ORIENTATION

The philosophy underlying the therapeutic approach advanced in this book is commitment to 1) a psychoeducational method whereby the therapist is constantly coaching and educating the individual; 2) a partnership between therapist and individual that fosters mutuality and co-operation in achieving predetermined goals; 3) a respectful, supportive, and encouraging environment that gives attention to the affective, behavioral, and cognitive components of the individual's experience of loss and grief; 4) a robust regard for the uniqueness of each individual; 5) a deference for the nature, magnitude, and intensity of personal loss; and finally, 6) self-empowerment of the individual. This orientation is based on several premises.

Underlying Premises

Both broad and situation-specific premises undergird a therapist's approach to helping individuals deal with nonfinite loss and grief.

Broad Premises   In facilitating the individual's grieving of nonfinite loss, the therapist operates on the basis of the following three premises:

1. Fear and anxiety are fundamental to the human condition. Personal experiences in early development, the feedback of significant others, and an underlying disposition mold an individual's unique relationship to fear and anxiety.
2. An individual has an innate need to sense his or her identity as a continuum with meaning and purpose. This engenders a sense of control. Ideally, on reaching adulthood individuals have a sense that they can survive without their parents. Personal experience through early development (e.g., the feedback from significant others, transactions with the environment) and an underlying disposition culminate in producing a soundness of this sense of self and predict whether it will hold up in the face of personal adversity.
3. By its nature, a loss that is nonfinite presents in various intensities throughout a lifetime. The grieving process will involve cyclical themes of yearning and searching; protest/demand, defiance, despair/resignation, and integration; as well as anger, bitterness, and sadness. These cycles will be interspersed with childhood schemata that momentarily generate strong themes of dependency, fears of abandonment, and internalized messages from childhood.

Specific Premises   A number of specific premises related to the grieving of nonfinite loss serve as prompts and reminders to the therapist. In establishing and maintaining a supportive partnership with the individual, the therapist must not lose sight of the following:

- The difficulty individuals have in pacing reality
- The innate resistance to change
- The part that fears and ideals play in exacerbating the experience and grieving of loss
- The enormous threat that nonfinite loss can pose to the integrity of self-identity
- The intricate effect that childhood learning has on the ability to legitimize a personal loss and give one's self permission to grieve
- The need to restore homeostasis and control in order to achieve positive attitudinal and behavioral change
- The need to give deference to socioemotional and cognitive aspects of stages of development as they relate to these six premises just described

The psychoeducational approach that is founded on these premises and the stated philosophical orientation requires amplification in terms of stages, goals, and interactive processes.

THE PSYCHOEDUCATIONAL APPROACH

The psychoeducational approach to facilitating the grieving of nonfinite loss follows the general stages customarily used in individual-centered counseling environments. These stages include the initial relationship and rapport-building tasks; the exploration and clarification of the individual's situation; the establishment of goals for, and the fostering of, a partnership in the work being jointly undertaken; the facilitating of action; and ongoing monitoring and evaluation of progress. This general framework and the skills required are taken as givens in the present context in which the focus is on clinical applications to the grieving of nonfinite loss. The following work between therapist and individual illustrates the specialized nature of nonfinite grief therapy.

The collaborative tasks undertaken include initial and ongoing assessment of the individual's situation, clear statement of the overall goal of therapy, initiation and pursuit of parallel and interactive processes (to be discussed in detail later in this chapter), close attention to the full complexity of the grieving process, focus on constructive feedback, positive self-talk, and the devising of self-prescriptive strategies.

Initial and Ongoing Assessment

From the traditional therapeutic perspective, it is often assumed that the individual absorbs the full implications of a loss at a particular point in time. In contrast, we have argued that awareness of the implications of loss is far more complex and is contingent on several factors including time and the information it reveals progressively and periodically about the distressing event or episode; stage of development and identity formation; the individual's need and ability to defend against the threatening nature of the information stemming from past and present sources; and, finally, the interaction among these variables. The task of critically assessing these factors is crucial to the steps taken and decisions made in working toward the main goal of therapy.

Goal of Therapy and Indicators of Achievement

The overall goal of therapy is for individuals to achieve a sense of mastery over their grief—an adaptation—that encompasses the preservation of identity; the reinstatement of control over emotions, cognitions, and behavior; and attachment to the emerging reality.

Indications that this goal has been or is being achieved are to be found in the effective management of grief through self-prescriptive strategies and an adaptation, however incomplete, to the new and emerging reality. The processes embarked on demand ongoing facilitation and education. As these interactive and parallel processes are worked through, the complexities of grieving nonfinite loss become apparent to the individual. This knowledge base acts as a motivator and challenges individuals to reach outcomes related to homeostasis, balance, and equilibrium.

Interactive Processes

Four parallel processes are strategic elements in the psychoeducational approach. They address directly the goal of therapy through control of information flow; emotional expression, legitimization, and memorializing; paced reality testing; and abstraction of meaning. The reader is referred back to Figure 3.3 for an overview of these strategic elements. In combination, they translate into specific objectives for the therapist, namely, to assist individuals in the following:

- Exerting management over the "information flow" evoked from *both* internal biographical review and from external sources
- Reality testing of integral and cherished ideals
- Desensitizing themselves to their dreaded event
- Continuing to express their grief and memorialize their loss
- Abstracting meaning with regard to the life-changing circumstances

Sensitively selecting, weaving, and timing these objectives is essential.

Figure 14.1 illustrates the innate difficulties of an identity in jeopardy and how the therapist facilitates the individual's process of negotiating the emerging reality. Providing a graphic illustration of the dynamics at work within an individual during therapy, the braces emphasize the nonsequential scrutinizing, juggling, and pulling in of the three primary developmental and biographical contexts: the world that is dreaded (fears), the world that should have been (ideals), and messages learned about self (self-talk). Providing the subject matter for the negotiating of reality, each context requires formulation and reformulation. The ultimate aim and outcome, as displayed in Figure 14.1, is the negotiating of the emerging reality and the expression of grief at tolerable levels. This negotiation is expedited through the four interactive and parallel processes under discussion. Its explication occupies much of the remainder of this chapter. Prior to that, the processes that include the control of information flow; the emotional expression, legitimization, and memorializing of grief; the pacing of reality testing; and the abstraction of meaning are described.

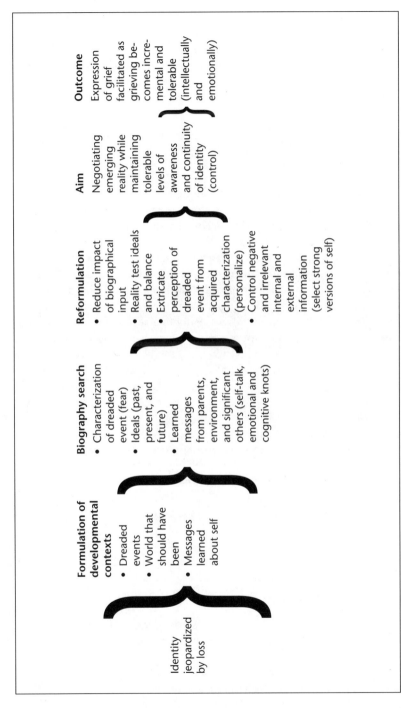

Figure 14.1. Negotiating emerging reality within biographical and developmental contexts.

Control of Information Flow   Therapy aims to assist individuals in developing a sense of mastery over their personal plight. This begins with controlling the flow of incoming information. Ideally, individuals need to establish an incremental flow that assists them in absorbing the information gradually rather than being overwhelmed or eclipsed by it. Coincidentally, the identity of the individual is preserved. It might be conceptualized as the creation of a type of "holding bay."

The triangle in Figure 14.2 depicts this optimal situation. Segments of information taken in bit by bit secure the crucial feedback and realization that individuals can survive what is being asked of them. Individuals do not have to master it all at once. Their reality can be explored piecemeal—as long as it *is* being explored. The self-feedback: "I can" and "I will survive" are the building blocks that allow individuals to continue to explore the changes in their world. Gradually, the broadening takes place. Obviously, the appropriate selection of what an individual *can do* is crucial.

In many situations of loss, a gradual processing of information is not feasible: The magnitude and the rate of the flow of information mean that information processing is overloaded. This can occur inadvertently: Uninvited or invited information may be presented through a variety of external sources. Alternatively, in an instinctive search for answers, individuals find themselves attempting to decipher vast amounts of material. Either way, instead of being able to incrementally absorb the aftermath of a diagnosis, individuals are bombarded with a very complex task, namely, absorbing information that simultaneously threatens and jeopardizes their identity. Returning to the analogy introduced in Chapter 12, the wealth of information eclipses an individual's identity and renders him or her helpless. It is unquestionable that such situations may produce posttraumatic stress disorder, a condition listed by the American Psychiatric Association

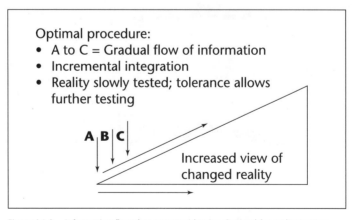

Figure 14.2.   Information flow that protects identity: Optimal for reality testing.

(1994) in the *Diagnostic and Statistical Manual of Mental Disorders, Fourth Edition,* as requiring intense psychotherapy. An essential derivative of this condition, according to Horowitz (1979), lies in the bombardment of an individual with internal and external information that does not match his or her version of self or the world.

Parents of very young children who have a chronic disability are constantly offered images of what the future may hold. Often, these parents do not have the knowledge base to discriminate among various pieces of information; it is all deemed as relevant. The parent who is determined to take an optimistic stance is taxed; despite a variety of possible scenarios, often the worst image prevails. The therapist's task becomes a type of working backwards—how to break this mass of traumatic images into sizeable bits that the individual can master and include? This task is schematically shown in Figure 14.3. The oval represents the traumatic images—a culmination of past biographical material, present, and future images. Together, the therapist and individual aim to decipher and reformulate this material in such a way as to facilitate an optimal rate of information processing.

Therapists may want to warn individuals against creating any extra demands or putting themselves into any situation that is novel and amplifies the chaos. The client should be encouraged to scrutinize the amount of new information or situations to which they are exposed. The goal of the therapist is to work toward the individual's being able to self-prescribe a response to his or her perceived levels of internal and external imbalance. Both with regard to the short-term and long-term

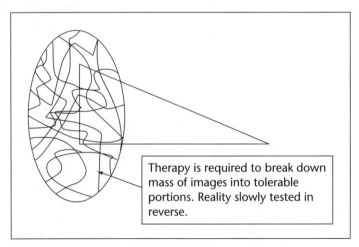

Therapy is required to break down mass of images into tolerable portions. Reality slowly tested in reverse.

Figure 14.3.   Information flow that threatens identity: Magnitude and rate of information flow is too great.

vicissitudes of nonfinite loss, individuals are steered toward moderating, as much as is feasible, their own internal balance.

Similarly, in an attempt to decrease anxiety or panic, individual and therapist work together to devise self-prescriptive strategies to ward off these attacks and recognize signals. When does the anxiety or panic occur? What are the triggers? What do these triggers symbolize? It is important that the therapist convey the idea that the anxiety and panic are expressions of imbalance, an upheaval of one's comfort zone, a fear of the unknown that will diminish over time, particularly if control is exerted over information flow.

Emotional Expression, Legitimization, and Memorialization

When a feeling is not named or is wrongly named, an individual's feelings are dismissed and confused. Often, the feelings become submerged. This is quite often the case with individuals experiencing nonfinite losses. They have not had the opportunity or help to name their feelings accurately. Instead, a range of superficial feelings are expressed that remain incongruent with the depth of the emotions that are actually being felt. For instance, a father of a child with a serious degenerative condition called his feelings "disappointment." It was only after therapy in a group of parents in similar circumstances that he felt permitted to choose the words "gaping wound" to describe the pain he felt both for his child and for himself.

For individuals to master situations of personal adversity, it is critical that their loss is legitimized and that they be given permission to grieve. Individuals experiencing nonfinite loss, however, are frequently reticent to call their feelings *grief*. Therapy is directed to exposing and examining the place of previously learned messages in the present experience. Individuals are encouraged to label their experience realistically and to begin paying respect to their emotional pain.

"PEOPLE HAVE IT WORSE THAN I DO; I SHOULDN'T COMPLAIN. IT'S REALLY NOTHING."

When publicly recognized social sanctions provide shared definitions for what has happened, loss and grief are legitimized. Nonfinite loss rarely has such public sanction. It is apparent that this environment leads to the individuals themselves sometimes hiding their emotional pain and doubting the veracity of their feelings. When individuals experience dissonance in validating their own emotions, there are echoes of messages from childhood: "People have it worse than I do; I shouldn't complain. It's really nothing."

Alternatively, when an individual's life has become a series of operations and personal crises, the loss can become personally played down and seldom talked about at length. Why? Frequently, individuals actually fear being "pitied" or fear being excluded because they have what might be construed as bad luck. An associated connotation is that they might not be esteemed by others any longer. This connotation underpins the common judgment that other people would not want to "be burdened with their lot."

Disenfranchised by the public (Doka, 1989) and now by themselves, many individuals experiencing a personal tragedy cannot find an avenue to share their grief. Often, the feelings are left to seep out. A woman whose husband has a degenerative disease made this comment: "I don't even like myself anymore. When a woman tells me that something has happened to her husband, I say to myself: 'Now you'll know how I feel.' That sounds dreadful—but all along no one has really understood what *I* lost when Fred came down with Parkinson's."

The magnitude of the loss personally perceived must in some form or fashion be revealed and expressed. The loss needs to have a place bestowed in the individual's personal story; it requires memorialization. Individuals must be given permission to communicate, through any medium they choose, their grief and their inconsolability. The idea of inconsolability is important. Notions of acceptance and the resolving of grief are antithetical to the continuing nature of the loss. In fact, the very idea that individuals will "accept" their loss simultaneously minimizes the integral place the loss has taken in their lives. Finding a symbol to memorialize loss and grief often is expressed by way of strong proclaiming statements such as: "I do not have to accept this loss. It is unacceptable!" A refusal to contemplate plastic surgery to conceal scars is another method of memorialization.

> "WHEN A WOMAN TELLS ME THAT SOMETHING HAS HAPPENED TO HER HUSBAND, I SAY TO MYSELF: 'NOW YOU'LL KNOW HOW I FEEL.'"

In an effort to relieve the tension revolving around the notion of acceptance and respecting the part it may play as a symbol of protest, therapy shifts focus to the goal of adaptation. Individuals are taught about the buildup of emotional intensity that is created when grief is not expressed. The therapist advises the individual on ways to reduce this bottleneck; there is a continuing need to talk openly about disappointment, sadness, anger, and fear. Individuals are challenged to present their grief to their spouse and friends and to teach their friends what they will need from them. Being able to talk freely about hopes, fears, and pain immediately diminishes the power of loss—the lump of almost congealed pain is broken into smaller, more emotionally manageable bits. For a person who has held back the fear of mentioning his or her pain for 20 years or so, the comfort of being able to talk about it freely is a revelation: "I am just not frightened any more. I'm not scared to talk about what happened to me!"

The need to cry is presented as a way of restoring a certain amount of balance back into an individual's system. Yet often, especially for males, crying is difficult to do. Crying is sometimes easier if it is done by way of empathizing with others, or when it is stimulated by moving words or tunes in musical pieces. Borrowing a sad videotape or listening to music that evokes sad and pensive thoughts are methods that respect emotional pain that will require regular ventilation. In this approach, individuals are taught to connect with their loss and grief, and to recognize its central place in their lives.

Pacing of Reality Testing For reality testing to proceed accurately so that new versions of reality can be assimilated, individuals need to bring the reality of loss into their awareness as much as possible. Ideally, the information is brought into awareness at a tolerable pace, allowing the grieving process to be sporadic with time on and time off. This rhythm allows the emotions to be distributed and protects the individual from becoming overwhelmed by the emotional nature of the task. Basically, it becomes a desensitization of raw feelings.

In situations that involve dreaded events, this pace is often way out of one's control; instead of being slowly desensitized, the individual can become sensitized. There are further complications. As circumstances surrounding loss are subject to change over time (e.g., chronic disease, disability, infertility, divorce), the task of revision is ongoing; by the minute, day, year, a consolidation of pictures, thoughts, and meaning is being compiled. As emphasized throughout this book, however, the compilation process often is made more difficult because of the chameleon-like characteristics of the threat and the loss. The basic human need to categorize information is impeded.

The often insidious onset of multiple sclerosis, rheumatoid arthritis, and early dementia are specific examples. What is reality? In one instant a man with dementia is lost in his childhood reality, the 1920s. In the next instant he talks to his wife of the recent state election. Moved among time frames, his wife is forced to grapple with her wish for him to recover. "Is he pretending when he does that business of thinking it's 1920?" she asks. A woman's stroke permanently affects her ability to contribute to household chores. Although it is apparent that on some level her husband has understood the neurologist's conclusion, of widespread physical damage, he periodically protests, "Why can't she take her plate to the sink? Why can't she help me?"

Throughout this book, numerous illustrations are provided to support the argument that the process of realization is particularly complicated (Haan, 1977; Snyder, 1989). Irrespective of the way one learns about the loss, because of the individual's need to reduce the overwhelming nature of the loss, its content and its possible ramifications will be tempered. Limiting negative information and reducing awareness to tolerable levels is recognized as an integral part of this process. Individuals are encouraged to pace the reality that they absorb, that is, to pace their griefwork. This, in itself, may be described as an adaptive process.

Abstraction of Meaning   If an individual finds the ability to turn around and face the threat, rather than being bombarded and therefore running from it, a changed perception of the threat begins to form. Namely, an individual begins to exert control over the management of the devastation. Meaning and the potential for purpose in the future are being gently pursued; not so much as a forcing away of defenses, but a slow unfolding of possibilities. A harbor for the identity is established as the individual gradually absorbs what has changed in self and worldview. As the individual is being desensitized to the fears that have been associated with dreaded models of the world, and the power of cherished ideals is being reduced, a continuity in identity is being restored or accentuated. Yet, amid this restored connection there are aspects of self that are irrevocably changed.

What meaning might be abstracted from this life-changing circumstance? What can the collaboration between therapist and individual find to enable the individual to forge a beginning attachment to aspects of his or her changed self and world? A type of trapeze needs to be established. This aspect of therapy requires a great deal of intuition in relation to the individual's private relationship with hope. In some instances, an attachment to the emerging reality and the consideration of meaning is based on a private conviction that it will only be necessary in the short term. A delicate balance is apparent. Attention is shifted to tracing the individual's narrative. In numerous conversations the therapist aims to expose the ways an individual has changed *and has stayed the same.* The therapist's ability to listen and isolate themes that might abstract meaning in the changed self is vital. Because individuals have lost confidence in themselves, supplying constant summary and feedback is particularly important. Optimally, through devising ways of broadening the feedback individuals receive from their environment they will be challenged to consider the various meanings their changed world may have. This will inevitably arouse existential questioning: "Why me?" "This is not fair!" "Life makes no sense." "What does it all mean?"

The psychoeducational approach works on locating individuals within the extensive range of life's traumatic experiences. In the middle of life's misfortunes, the "why me?" may slowly become depersonalized. Shifting away from a feeling of persecution, there comes a realization that "it is less about me than it is about life." It becomes part of a self-healing path, if only in the sense of an adaptation to a new version of self and the world.

SPECIAL CONSIDERATIONS IN NEGOTIATING REALITY

Returning to the negotiation of reality, attention is directed to the biographical and developmental contexts illustrated in Figure 14.1: What is meant by formulation and reformulation? How is this accomplished? The formulation is based on an extensive biography search that seeks to position the place that ideals have taken in an individual's identity, the place that fear and dread have taken in his or her development, and the type of emotional messages that have been learned from interactions with parents and peer groups. Therapy aims to enable the individual to reformulate the part these contexts play in his or her personal crisis by reducing their potency. These tasks and the development of self-prescriptive strategies warrant consideration.

Formulation and Control of Dreaded Events

Individuals need to be able to tell the therapist who they are frightened of becoming. As was explored in Section II, much of the response to personal adversity has been established in an individual's early childhood experiences. Learned messages about disease, disability, and the fear of becoming "unesteemed" by others, or excluded from groups, amplify the loss and the difficulty in grieving. The development of the fears and their relationship to an individual's identity need to be explored. What characterizes the individuals' views of what has happened to them? What does it mean?

First, who have they perceived (or do they now perceive) themselves as becoming? The therapist "returns" with the individual to his or her kindergarten, primary, and secondary school environments. Together they might unearth memories of occasions when the person was singled out, ostracized. There might be memories of an individual, a classmate who was bullied, and whom, perhaps, the client bullied. Who were the individuals who were not esteemed? Perhaps the individual him- or herself has been subjected to being excluded from the mainstream before. The therapist directs the client to characterize dreaded events. What are the pictures that form with certain words or phrases, such as *Parkinson's disease, Hodgkin's disease, adoption, divorce, disability*? The biography search aims to broaden the individual's understanding of the derivatives of this fear and the place this learning takes in the present crisis.

Reducing the Potency of the Characterization of Dreaded Events Working with the individual, the acquired characterization of dreaded events can be identified. Now the characterization can be objectified as a learning tool that requires critical examination. It can be scrutinized by therapist and individual. It may be symbolized as the enemy. This is particularly effective because the objectification actually offers an opportunity to separate thoughts and images from their immersion *within* the individual.

How accurate are the characterizations? What are they based on—and do they accurately portray the situation? Are they skewed? Several features of an individual's thinking must be challenged. For instance, is it a fear of what other people think, a childhood fear, or an adult fear? Does the fear hold up if one examines it through adult eyes? From where does it emanate? What experience can the individual recount? For example, in the case of someone who has had a limb amputated, it may be the fear of being stared at. For an individual recently separated it may be the feeling of never having been really accepted in adolescence. Individuals are taught to objectively and scientifically consider and assess their fear.

Carefully considered new information can be constructively introduced to begin a desensitization of the fear that surrounds the dreaded event and the normalization process. Examples of well-known and admired people who have become disabled or even children who have endured the same misfortune serve to foster alternative views to the often heavily stigmatized versions created in childhood. Are these people still admired even though they have ongoing medical conditions? Biographies, film, and text also are useful. The therapist is endeavoring to produce more flexibility in the individual's traditional way of thinking. A challenge is mounted, and a more balanced picture of the individual's situation emerges. Guiding and consolidating this new picture is a subtle process involving timely selection of the part that each new bit of information might play. If it can be offered sensitively without the individual constructing a defensive stance, it may be internalized and considered. It is almost like rearranging jigsaw pieces.

Reformulation: Establishing Control over Dreaded Events   The triggers related to the individual's fears should be traced and clearly identified. Both internal (e.g., memories, moods, physical sensations) and external (e.g., images in the environment) triggers should be explored. What things, people, or places create fears in the individual? Where do they take the individual in terms of his or her train of thought? What things does the individual read or see in the environment that encourage this line of thinking? Next, the triggers should be listed. It is useful to continue drawing these triggers out. Tackling them one by one, the individual may be asked to rate the degree of potency of each trigger and the degree of distress that it evokes. It is helpful to use a scoring base of 1 to 10, with a score of 1 used to denote minimal distress and a score of 10 used to denote maximum distress. This feedback will give the individual a clear idea of some of the noxious stimuli that are exerting psychological pressure on him or her. The table also will provide a picture of what images are coming from the past and how they are clouding the present situation.

Once identified, the individual can be coached to try to master these fears. What might some such triggers be? A young mother with a 2-year-old boy with cerebral palsy found herself frightened of the children with the same condition whom she routinely saw in the waiting rooms of neurologists. She was given the task of overcoming aspects of this fear. Together, she and the therapist set this task as a goal; she was to talk with one of these children in the waiting room.

Of course, the timing and designs of tasks are very important. However, there is no limit to the amount of times a task can be broken down as long as the individual is receiving positive feedback about the *possibility* of mastery. Information equally as disturbing as these triggers can be controlled. After identifying information that *can* be controlled, an individual can be taught skills of threat estimation and distraction: If you read this magazine article, what are the likely outcomes? Can you discriminate between your experience and the person who is the subject of the article? Will it be too scary? What amount of information from others will be psychologically friendly? How much of your future can you realistically handle at this point? When individuals realize that they are able to become selective about what information they can tolerate at certain times, they will begin to discover a sense of control. From here on in, a certain amount of information control has been established and the individual has begun to manage and, therefore, reduce the perceived threat.

At a later stage, it is not inconceivable that individuals themselves will be able to control some of the information that they will receive from doctors. For instance, if a person has an ongoing medical condition, he or she could be coached to ask the doctors for easier-to-manage pieces of information rather than great amounts of information that might come up in the future. The notion of asking doctors to deliver information differently becomes particularly important for parents of children with chronic conditions or children who are facing surgery. Sometimes diagnostic information and the procedures for surgical operations are inappropriately shared with children. Too much fear results!

Formulation and Control of the World that Should Have Been

Individuals need to tell the therapist who they were; they need to relate their fear of losing aspects of this identity. In facilitating the individuals' biographical search of the place of ideals in their identity, individuals must be protected from being overwhelmed and flooded by biographical memories that amplify their current state of crisis and disorganization.

Weekly therapy sessions provide some intrinsic structure and containment of the sense of chaos. In this environment, consistent, therapeutic feedback provides validation of intense emotional feelings of loss and isolation and clarifies thought sequences while at the same time connections and continuities in identity are drawn out. The individual is encouraged to affirm who he or she is and to talk about and around aspects of loss. Because thoughts and emotions are expressed on a regular basis, information processing is eased and the individual's sensation of being overwhelmed emotionally is considerably reduced. In this therapeutic environment, which essentially is aimed at preserving the integrity of the identity, supporting the individual's relationship to hope is vital.

The ideals that make up "the world that should have been" need to lose their potency. However, the prospect of facing up to a new self and a new reality is terrifying—so much so that the individual prefers, and is sometimes forced, to remain in limbo rather than move into uncharted terrain. The therapist aims to try and guide the pace that the individual takes in reviewing and relinquishing ideals. Attention and deference to the emotional pain intrinsic to this process legitimates the individual's feelings of grief and gives permission for continuing ventilation of emotion. Ideally, the outcome is that the expression of emotions is shared and emotions remain fluid.

Reducing the Potency of the World that Should Have Been A therapist's primary goal is to reduce the dominance of ideals and expectations in how individuals perceive themselves. This is seldom an easy task, but threads can be extracted and ideals can be shrunk. Sometimes the ideals can be exposed as not being authentic to the individual; perhaps they represent a need to please a father or mother, impress a sibling or a group of friends? Perhaps the ideal of "perfection" reflected a parent's fear of differences in other people? Other times, ideals and expectations may be recognized as a vestige from one's childhood or adolescence. Ideals and expectations can be held onto but represented differently in a person's life. There are various ways of fulfilling a fathering role, a relationship with a sport, a need to be the best.

The therapist searches for ways to reduce the inflexibility of previously held ideals and expectations and their potency. By introducing a different slant, connections between old and new versions of self begin. What does the emerging world offer? Does it have the potential to allow extraction of some meaning? Does it provide an opportunity to demonstrate a formerly dormant part of self such as resilience, competence, bravery, commitment to rights? Can this be extracted from the individual's biography?

Engaging in activities, joining groups of people who have themselves experienced adversity and lost ideals, indeed, placing one's self in as many situations as possible keeps the mind working with alternatives. The mind is entertained with possibilities, openings: How do other people put their lives together again after personal adversity? Could I do that? Although this exposure is vital, however, it is difficult to monitor. The content of the information and the pacing of its rate and magnitude remain crucial to positive and realistic feedback.

Reformulation: Establishing Control over the World that Should Have Been Individuals are encouraged once again to identify the triggers that return them to comparisons and contrasts with symbols of the world that should have been. The therapist should explain to his or her client why this tendency recurs. Apart from describing this context as almost hardwired into one's memory sequences, it might be useful to draw on a more symbolic analogy. For instance, sometimes of their own volition and sometimes not consciously, individuals need to find a form for their loss. The recently separated individual taking a walk in the park finds him- or herself drawn to looking only at couples. Why? The couples reflect what the individual yearns for, show him or her what has been lost. Similarly, the child who has gone to live in a foster home finds himself staring at what he perceives to have lost—perhaps a "happy family."

Such comparisons trigger a different state of mind. Circular or ruminating thoughts reflecting the "world that should have been" dominate. Grief is experienced. Instantly the mind returns to the whys. It is like an unsolvable problem. This cogitating is made all the more difficult because often the individual's thoughts are hampered by negative themes from childhood. What has happened in the present is not a discrete entity; it is enmeshed with the way the individual has learned to look at the world, his or her place in it, and what has happened before. Unfortunately, the negative mood state forces the resurfacing of memories that represent the same mood state. An amplification of the negative mood is simultaneous and inevitable.

Again, if it is technically explained, the process becomes intelligible. Furthermore, it might feasibly be explained as a purposeful exercise. For instance, the process denotes the significance of the loss, desensitizes raw feelings, and diminishes pain over time. For some individuals, however, the process becomes overwhelming and the raw feelings are not incrementally worked through. Instead, the individual might avoid any painful reminders of what he or she has lost.

The therapist warns the individual of the dangers of overavoiding painful reminders. He or she is taught that the brain actually needs to test reality in order to adjust its knowledge structures. If an individual stays away from reminders there is the potential to experience greater psychological stress when a trigger is next encountered. Together, therapist and individual can devise a program to slowly expose triggers that are being avoided. The devising of a table of triggers with the rating of potency and degree of difficulty can serve as a worksheet for the individual. At the same time, a certain amount of avoidance is deemed necessary in order to prevent an overwhelming amount of information. Individuals who are being overwhelmed by thoughts and emotions connected with the world that should have been need assistance with the management of these intrusions. A dose-on, dose-off approach (Horowitz, 1986), using a range of thought-management and complex task-based activities, is recommended to the individual. The techniques are aimed at reestablishing control over information flow. Individuals do not need to be at the mercy of these intrusions.

Formulation and Reformulation of Messages Learned About Self

The potential to shift into childlike versions of self is always present in situations of loss. Amplifying dependency, the situations evoke versions of self that often sabotage a self-evaluation or feeling that one can cope. The therapist works to steer the individual away from helpless and dependent versions of self to facilitate the emergence of the most competent version of self possible. Initially, the individual is educated about the propensity for states of tiredness, hunger, anger, and information bombardment to overwhelm coping capacities. Individuals are advised to monitor these states.

  Reducing the Potency of Messages Learned About Self   The therapist begins a search for messages in the individual's childhood and beyond that have been internalized. The search is likely to find some messages from parents or significant others that the individual perceived as true assessments of his or her strength, endurance, bravery, and so forth: "You can do it!" a father or mother might have been known to say. "I've never seen you shirk a challenge," perhaps from a coach or teacher. It is also useful to trace the negative messages. Often, these negative messages are cursory comments made by teachers. Such comments gather potency because of a child's cognitive and socioemotional stage of development and the resulting inability to assess the veracity or intention of the remark.

"I'VE NEVER SEEN YOU SHIRK A CHALLENGE."

Condemnation and negative labels retain a great deal of force unless they become scrutinized from an adult perspective. These memories need to be critically analyzed.

  The search should also track the key challenging experiences for the individual. Times when one had to recover from personal adversity or make an individual stand are particularly useful. In all individuals there will be some incident. Even in the biography of a shy child, surviving being bullied or enduring situations of unpleasantness on one's own provides important feedback about endurance. Being excluded, being the last one to be picked as a member of a team at school, enduring the trauma of parental divorce, recovering from an illness, being shifted from school to school, or getting over a fear of the dark are the sorts of experiences worth uncovering. Once located, individuals are encouraged to assess the impact of these challenges on their character; for example, attributes of resilience and the ability to endure strong and uncomfortable emotions (e.g., fear, anxiety, anger). Accentuation of such events and the things they say about a person provide crucial feedback. They can mount a challenge to feelings of helplessness and dependency.

Reformulation: Establishing Control over Messages About Self
The individual is made aware of the triggers that force out weaker versions of self. It is useful to conjure up as vividly as possible the idea of a stronger and weaker version of self, that is, an adult and a child within the individual. This might be done pictorially on a chalkboard or by way of photographs of the individual as a child. The therapist might ask the individual to critically evaluate what a child's view of the world offers the present situation in which he or she is in. The adult version of the individual can then be pitted against the child version of the individual; individuals are then challenged to critically assess the fears that they have learned about being different. What do they perceive other people to be thinking about them? What does this mean? Are they legitimate conclusions? As Sections II and III illustrate, it is the child who originally develops idealized versions of the world and fear of people who are different. So what if the individual is an adult now? Evoked, this child-version of self can still create feelings of dependency and weakness; it is an adversary to adaptation.

The therapist works with the individual to expose an intimate knowledge of what makes the individual slip into a child-state. What experiences return an individual to feelings of helplessness? How can this process be circumvented? What might individuals need to do in order to protect themselves? The therapist teaches the individual to evaluate what situations may need to be managed.

A biographical search seeks to establish what individuals' experiences of loss have been in their past. Did their parents allow them to express grief? How did the individuals' mothers, fathers, or siblings handle emotional expression in the family? What was the culture surrounding emotional expression? What messages did the individuals learn about attention and illness? Were the individuals' illnesses, emotions, or physical feelings validated in childhood? These emotional and cognitive knots need to be exposed to individuals for the part they play in the present experience of personal adversity and the ability to grieve. For instance, is their fear of pity, or of being seen as attention-seekers, standing in the way of showing and validating their grief to themselves and others?

One area remains to be explored for particular comment here, namely, self-prescriptive strategies. Underpinning the tasks of therapy are the broad techniques of constant coaching and educating to assist the individual in understanding the difficulties integral to grieving nonfinite loss. The ultimate goal is that individuals will become sufficiently educated to achieve a sense of mastery characterized by self-prescriptive strategies to deal with their griefwork.

Self-Prescriptive Strategies

The outcome of a successful therapist–client relationship is the realization by the individual that he or she can manage his or her world. In most instances of personal adversity, a lifelong task of managing varying amounts of grief is imposed. An ongoing task of "best adaptation" is called for. The therapist aims to teach a self-prescriptive method. First, teaching about personal approaches to balancing avoidance behaviors and intrusive thoughts is required. Individuals learn to read the signs that indicate that they have been overexposed, or overwhelmed, by prospects of the future. Time-on and time-off techniques are important, and the therapist teaches individuals these distraction techniques and how to create time off.

Some individuals are able to get a rest from thinking through their work. Often, however, the distraction is for too long and individuals experience a flooding of emotions when they leave the containment offered by these strong structures. This flooding of emotions represents the bottling up of emotions and thoughts that have been put on hold. Individuals should monitor the amounts of distraction they have; too much and the individual is not being provided with the opportunity to master his or her personal crisis.

If individuals do not work outside the home, or have no task demands to meet, they often are left at the mercy of thoughts that can flood them. A feeling of being out of control becomes more imminent. Individuals are introduced to the need to restore a certain amount of psychological relief through some form of structured activity of doing. Activities that provide some relief or "off-time" might include crosswords, jigsaw puzzles, or an ongoing sculpture project. These activities might be structured to provide a sense of routine or they may be used as a response to a buildup of emotional tension or panic. Either way, *knowing what to do* when emotional buildup occurs provides a sense of control and offers containment. Rote activities temper the emotional tension and can be preferable to just sitting with emotionally intense thoughts, particularly when expression of the feelings would be too alarming. Similarly, walking diminishes the sense of being emotionally overwhelmed that frequently accompanies thoughts and feelings.

Individuals need to know these things. The therapist strives to inculcate in individuals the need to develop a relationship with their emotions, to understand and control the dynamics, rather than have the emotions rule them. The important point is that when intense emotions crash in, the individual must *do* something: walk with these feelings, talk to the feelings, talk about the feelings, write them out. By legitimizing them, and expressing them, the individual sets up a different relationship with them. The warning signals for a buildup of emotions should be identified. What could be the lead-up to feeling out of control? Is there a pattern? Can the buildup be charted and monitored?

There will be numerous occasions when the personal experiences of individuals present aspects of their new world that will be psychologically confronting. They will demand to be processed. Individuals should be taught methods of debriefing such as writing or talking, if not to a significant other, then to themselves. Informed that their adaptation depends to a large extent on a gradual confrontation with exposure to aspects of their loss, individuals can be encouraged to use the optimal flow triangle (see Figure 14.2) to note and interpret what is impeding a tolerable approach to the process of including change. Observed closely, an individual's unique patterns will be revealed and a delicate balance will become apparent. Individuals can become acutely aware of what they can process or deal with and what, at different times, they cannot. Even the nature and content of personal dreams or nightmares can reflect imbalance and a feeling of being unsettled. Individuals train themselves to respond appropriately: "What can I handle now?"

SUMMARY

Chapter 14 concentrates on key elements in the development of individuals as strategists. Chapter 15 builds on these clinical applications with an outline of principles for facilitating the grieving of nonfinite loss and achieving the goals of therapy. A narrative style is adopted in the case studies contained in Chapter 16. Examples are given of how, in situations of nonfinite loss, individuals are encouraged to expose the magnitude of their loss; examine the potency of ideals and dreaded events; and focus on the preservation of identity, relationships, and their ability to safely re-explore their world.

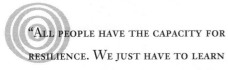

"ALL PEOPLE HAVE THE CAPACITY FOR
RESILIENCE. WE JUST HAVE TO LEARN
TO DRAW IT OUT AND TO SUPPORT THEM."

—GROTBERG, 1999, P. 3

CHAPTER **15**

PRINCIPLES FOR FACILITATING THE GRIEVING PROCESS

Psychological stress is brought on by certain critical factors, including loss of control, loss of predictability, loss of outlets for frustration, and a perception of things worsening (Sapolsky, 1992, p. 296). These factors are characteristically presented when a person experiences nonfinite loss. All play havoc, to a greater or lesser degree, with an individual's adaptation to changed versions of self and reality and the ability to grieve: "How much change can my 'self' and my 'world' safely include?"

The three primary objectives of therapy are to 1) preserve identity, 2) restore control, and 3) facilitate adaptive reality testing and grieving. Underlying these objectives are psychoeducational principles that have been described in more depth at various points throughout the text. They are summarized in this chapter under six major headings that mark shifts in the focus of therapy over time:

1. The expression of grief commensurate with the perception of the magnitude of the loss
2. The preservation of identity
3. The reinstatement of control
4. The potency of recurring ideals
5. The potency of dreaded events
6. The need to attach meaning to the emerging reality

ATTENDING TO THE EXPRESSION
OF GRIEF COMMENSURATE WITH THE
PERCEPTION OF THE MAGNITUDE OF THE LOSS

Principle 1:   *Therapy is directed toward establishing a therapeutic rela-*
tionship that provides an individual with attachment to someone else that
is secure and unconditional, from which the individual can re explore him-
or herself and the world.

Attachment relationships that are secure and unconditional provide
bases from which optimal development may proceed. Often, these relationships are unavailable after a significant loss; hence, the therapeutic
relationship-building becomes crucial. Attachments change following
severe disruption to a sense of self. Often, in one's increased sense of dependence on significant others, relationships produce internal and external conflict. When an individual's self-esteem is affected and his or her
sense of control is limited he or she feels insecure: "Does my spouse still
love me the way I am?" "Am I a burden?" The personal magnitude of
loss often makes it seem inconceivable that anyone, even the caregiver,
could actually understand the loss: "It's all right for him. He doesn't
know what it's like not to have your health."

Principle 2:   *Therapy is directed toward creating a therapeutic alliance*
that defers to the loss and facilitates the expression of pain, anger, and grief
as it manifests periodically over time.

The grief in bereavement is respected and socially acknowledged. That is,
it is symbolized, ritualized, and memorialized. In situations of nonfinite
loss, often the fact and permanence of the loss are camouflaged. When affected individuals are frightened by what might be the magnitude of the
loss and how others might see them, they themselves often collude with
society and friends; they try to camouflage the loss. Others run a complex
relationship between trying to show their pain and not appearing to complain unduly. Regardless of whether they expose it, however, enormous
pain exists. In the end, individuals often harbor their pain until it becomes almost a part of themselves, held inside almost belligerently as a
punishment to others. With friends or others, the unexpressed pain hinders social interaction: "I listen to what they are complaining about and
I'm thinking all the time, 'I'd like to tell you about my life because what
you've been through is nothing compared with what I am going
through.'" As a corollary to this, the individual fears that should the loss
be exposed, it will be minimized. The upshot is that the loss is not adequately memorialized and the emotional pain is never adequately expressed. Ironically, the individual is angry because deference has not been
given to the pain, but fear of experiencing one's self as an object of pity

hinders this process. As the loss is cumulative over time, a buildup of strong emotions is inevitable. Creating a fluidity with, and an avenue for, these emotions is critical to maintaining healthy relationships.

Principle 3: Therapy is directed to affirming that grief and complicated feelings such as ambivalence, apathy, detachment, and guilt are normal and that separation anxiety from preloss versions of the self and world will recur.

The process of grieving is complicated when the source of one's grief remains: a beloved spouse with dementia, a child with chronic disability or illness, or a father who has separated from the family. Equally, in a strange way, this can apply to grieving aspects of self. That is, the individual does not want to admit to a rejection of the changed version of self. Attachment to the emerging self and the world may wax and wane. Specifically, how does one grieve when that grief is a powerful symbol of dissatisfaction with what is? The contexts surrounding nonfinite loss create a complex tangle of emotions. Frequently, caregivers protest: "My spouse brings out everything that I dislike in myself. Sometimes I want out. I am actually frightened to seek respite. It might make it too easy to walk away. But then I feel guilty. I feel I must try harder to make it up to her. I do love her."

ATTENDING TO THE PRESERVATION OF IDENTITY

Principle 4: Therapy is directed to preserving the integrity of an individual's identity by creating connections among past, present, and future contexts.

Versions of self and the world find their formation in childhood. Some life events threaten large portions of self. They can result in overwhelming feelings of having lost one's self (i.e., "Who am I, now that I have...?"). When people experience this sense of drowning in the dreaded event they need to find a lifeline: a thread among past, present, and future concerns to be extricated from their life stories. Some individuals try to "locate" themselves. Unable to feel herself in the present, an older adult who has had a stroke returns to old letters from her father and jewelry from her late brother. One card from her father reads: "I love you. See you soon. Dad." As she looks at these keepsakes, she says: "I like looking at these, they remind me of how much I have been loved."

"MY SPOUSE BRINGS OUT EVERY-THING THAT I DISLIKE IN MYSELF. SOMETIMES I WANT OUT."

A mother of a child with disabilities feels she has lost her identity in her child's disability. She comes to counseling because she feels she cannot be herself when she is with her child. She protests, "I'm not just a parent of a child with disabilities; I'm an accountant, my husband is a successful banker; we have a great lifestyle. We've been very successful, but people aren't seeing *me!*" A young girl in her late teens—a once-heralded athlete who can no longer compete—protests: "Who am I if I'm no longer a hurdler?"

ATTENDING TO THE REINSTATEMENT OF CONTROL

Principle 5:   *Therapy is directed to restoring control through education and self-prescriptive strategies that tackle extreme states of anxiety.*

When life events threaten major postulates or schemata that an individual uses to make sense of the world they represent significant threats to an individual's sense of identity. When integral aspects of the identity are threatened it is conceivable that individuals might perceive themselves as completely alienated from the self and the world they previously took for granted. Simultaneously, the individual's sense of balance is threatened. There will be degrees of internal chaos with anxiety, fear, and physical concomitants (see Tables 13.1–13.5). This disorganization results in a sense of impending loss of control simultaneously evoking themes of helplessness and childhood versions of self. In this unregulated state, individuals immediately focus on other people—those who might restore a sense of safety and balance. In some respects this often is why attachment relationships are so difficult to relinquish; they regulate our internal balance. The following statement illustrates this feeling of being out of kilter:

> I wake up in the middle of the night. I immediately feel a terrible sense of unease—not just with my thoughts, but my whole body feels as though it's running fast. The glands in my throat throb as though I'm about to sob. I actually feel panicky—a feeling of desperation. I sit up, extremely agitated.... I can't get back to where I was before, when everything was okay. I desperately want some reassurance. I want to be told everything will be all right. I have a terrible aching need for my mother.

Principle 6:   *Therapy is directed to balancing perceptions of self as well as of self-talk (i.e., messages we tell ourselves) to help reinstate an individual's adult versions of self.*

A present life crisis is never viewed in isolation from earlier biography. Current "Why me's?" inevitably become connected with past "Why me's?" Several key beliefs learned in childhood automatically become key themes in grieving. In childhood we learn about rewards and punishment. That is, if we have been bad, bad things happen, and vice versa. We also learn that things can be fixed. Much of the grieving surrounding nonfinite loss involves the search for what was done to deserve this fate and a search for how to fix things. Importantly, we also have relationships with our caregivers that either provide us with strong or weak versions of self. Biographical experience can accumulate around negative themes of self and mastery in the world. Self-talk such as "I've never beaten anything before, so why now?" emerges. This theme may be amplified by images an individual has of him- or herself as weak and ineffectual (e.g., "I am not strong enough. I have never stood up for myself"). Nonfinite loss is synonymous with a feeling of an inability to control or fix things and images of dependency, abandonment, helplessness, and so forth. As a result, individuals experiencing nonfinite loss and grief are repeatedly forced back into childhood versions of themselves.

Principle 7: *Therapy is directed toward creating an environment that shifts attention from acceptance to adaptation.*

Proclamations abound: "We will not accept this. It is unacceptable for my child to have an illness such as this." The therapeutic approach moves toward an adaptation that is a dynamic process—never settled once and for all. That is, whereas adaptation represents a delicate balancing process, the balance remains precarious. Although the individual may never return to the naive shock represented in the initial cycle, the emotional states and cognitive themes of the other cycles are likely to return repeatedly. There are numerous psychosocial stressors to be navigated. Amid all of this, the wish to "fix" or be fixed persists. Even after 12 years of paralysis, for example, an individual might momentarily consider the "fixing" powers of a faith healer, or the relevance of a scientific discovery.

Principle 8: *Therapy is directed toward creating resilience, specifically, in fostering skills that control anxiety, fear, and the perception of unremitting emotional pain.*

Despite one's age and stage of development, the dilemma facing individuals, their caregivers, and family is how to adapt to often continual threat and uncertainty. Disbelief, anxiety, and fear in varying degrees of intensity parallel the griefwork of nonfinite loss. Projecting one's self into a future that promises no emotional relief represents a formidable reality. The difficulty in restoring and stabilizing a sense of control and predictability leads an individual to experience recurring or ongoing physiological imbalance, potentially with no end in sight. For some individuals, the future has the potential to continue to be psychologically overwhelming.

ATTENDING TO THE POTENCY OF RECURRING IDEALS

Principle 9:   Therapy is directed to reducing the potency of ideals as benchmarks and the part they play in amplifying the perception of the loss.

The grieving process involves the reworking of expectations. Deeply embedded over time, these expectations consist of ideal versions of self and the world and represent an automatic thought process. Unlike in situations of bereavement, however, these ideals are not usually subjected to adequate reality testing. They must be reality tested and balanced, so that they do not become too powerful. A father of a son recently injured in an accident indicates the potency of ideals: "If my son had not had this horrific thing happen to him, we would have been fishing together. That scene of me and him together fishing is so strong in my mind, it's painful. After 4 years, I keep returning to it. It's almost like an obsession! Why do I keep doing this to myself?"

Principle 10:   Therapy is directed to teaching strategies that respect but reduce the potency of acute and recurrent periods of nonfinite loss.

Typically, the interplay between what is and what should be causes a buildup of disappointment and frustration. Due to his or her inability to restore self and world to the ideal version, an individual has a recurring feeling of helplessness. Coupled with life stressors over time, particular events actually return individuals to an overwhelming sense of not being able to control their lives. The resulting dependence evokes childhood beliefs. Thus, a mother of a 12-year-old child who has a congenital disability protests: "I had everything under control but now she has developed epilepsy. It's too much. Why should she—why should I—have to take any more? We don't deserve this. Life would have been perfect without Jean."

"IT'S TOO MUCH. WHY SHOULD SHE—WHY SHOULD I—HAVE TO TAKE ANY MORE?"

ATTENDING TO THE POTENCY OF DREADED EVENTS

Principle 11:   Therapy is directed to the desensitization to, and balancing of, the characterizations of dreaded events.

Grieving involves letting go of aspects of old versions of self. This process is hindered by what individuals fear they will become. The schemata of dreaded events are critical to this process. Such schemata begin forming in childhood. The fear and horror of becoming "one of them," the loss of being esteemed by others, and the loss of self-esteem are integral features of this schemata. It is important to note that the perceived outcomes of "becoming a nobody" after being an athlete, a performer, or the like may also be seen as the realization of dreaded events.

Principle 12:   Therapy is directed to the reduction of overwhelmed states by controlling the reality testing process.

The process of grieving ideally involves reality testing in tolerable amounts. As dreaded events have such powerful reputations, the individual cannot always negotiate the emerging reality at a pace that is psychologically healthy. An outcome is overavoidance, bombardment of intrusions, or both. Compounded by the propensity for the present experience to bring up memories of similar instances from one's past, negative states of mind become amplified (Gloor, 1992). One's perceptions become skewed toward increasing feelings of being overwhelmed (Alford & Beck, 1997).

ATTENDING TO THE NEED TO ATTACH MEANING TO THE EMERGING REALITY

Principle 13:   Therapy is directed at helping an individual create a relationship with hope that—in whatever form—engenders an attachment to a changed version of life.

In order to psychologically survive threats, a symbol of hope for recovery needs to be established. Hope, a resistance to accepting the fact or permanence of loss and all its consequences, is a survival mechanism. For some people, this relationship with hope is drawn out. Considering the magnitude of some people's loss, it may be the only reason survival actually takes place. Hope is about the preservation of identity.

Principle 14:   Therapy is directed at protecting an individual's identity through the abstraction and translation of meaning to the emerging reality.

The grieving process in bereavement involves a type of reconciliation process. Critically, the individual must try to establish a picture of self as surviving the threat of being left without the loved one. If the individual can reflect on times when he or she has been fine without this person, particularly in times when he or she was upset, the loss does not feel quite so overwhelming. In situations of nonfinite loss, this process is complex. To denigrate or minimize aspects of self, particularly intact health, is implausible. Grieving is immediately compromised. To admit the magnitude of this loss forces the individual to stare in the face of a threatening loss. Individuals often are forced to construct meaning from their circumstances. A resilient young adolescent with a physical disability shows how this meaning might be construed: "There was this boy who had a disability. He was an angel in this show on television. He was sent to make people understand what it felt like to be different....that was his job. I know it sounds dumb, but I sometimes wonder whether I am here to do the same sort of thing. I sometimes wonder whether I am an angel."

SUMMARY

This chapter outlines 14 principles for therapy. These principles represent a culmination of the perspectives introduced in this book. Although this chapter does not elaborate on the nuances of the therapeutic and psychoeducational techniques, the eight case studies in Chapter 16 demonstrate a general direction that techniques might take. As a proviso, any change or transition in life has the potential to trigger nonfinite loss and evoke a grieving response. It is impossible to refer to all situations of nonfinite loss. The knowledge base as it has been introduced and discussed in this book provides readers with scope to transpose the psychoeducational approach onto circumstances of nonfinite loss that particularly interest them.

CHAPTER **16**

CASE STUDIES IN NONFINITE LOSS

The therapeutic techniques described in this chapter apply when an attachment relationship between therapist and individual has been formed, providing a secure and unconditional base from which the individual can recreate him- or herself. It is from this secure vantage point that the critical timing and selection of particular client tasks can be introduced. Individuals will need to hold on to their old version of self and reality. This clinging is almost a mark of deference to the depth of their loss and pain. Desperately frightened of letting go, some people may circle or hold on to their old selves for extended periods of time. Although this behavior is most markedly perceptible in bereavement as a result of a death, it is worth becoming sensitive to the time that people need to continue this behavior. By giving an individual permission to continue circling or holding on to an old version of self, the therapist conveys the message that the depth and significance of the individual's loss has been recognized. Simultaneously, the individual's anxiety over having to relinquish a loss is reduced. In fact, being able to continue to expose emotional pain can symbolically represent a memorialization of the loss. Many of the clues associated with the need to cling will hark back to the earliest developmental tasks (i.e., separating in infancy and adolescence). Thus, this need will surround the fear and anxiety about being alone—surviving in the absence of a caregiver or protector.

The following eight case studies are presented to demonstrate the interweaving of techniques described in Chapter 15. Designed specifically to focus on selected aspects of therapy, they are by no means reflective of the entire therapy process. Introduced first is Maria, a 40-year-old teacher whose experience of being in a serious motorcycle accident when she was 18 years old still haunts her. Case Study 2 relates to Jenny and the difficulties she is having finding her own identity and grieving her 5-year-old daughter's disability. Case Study 3 presents Leah's need to develop maturity to help her deal with cancer. Case Study 4 details fairly unsuccessful therapy with Nam, a 40-year-old man who has recently had both legs amputated. Case Study 5 looks at how Allan, an adolescent, copes with chronic illness; Allan's parents need to acquire much knowledge to guide his adaptation. Bob and Jean, a married couple, are introduced in Case Study 6. Bob has Alzheimer's disease. In this case, we center attention on Jean's role of caregiver. Lorna's experience of cognitive disability caused by cerebral vascular disease forms the focus of Case Study 7. Jason, an adolescent who has been in a wheelchair all of his life, is the subject of Case Study 8. Now 16 years old, he is grieving for the world that might have been.

CASE STUDY 1: MARIA AND THE NEED TO MEMORIALIZE LOSS

Therapeutic Focus: Encouraging the Individual to Expose the Magnitude of Emotions

Maria is a 40-year-old, successful secretary. Her story illustrates how loss can become nonfinite through grief that has gone unrecognized. It also shows the importance of ritual and memorialization. Maria began therapy because she could not listen to sad songs. Some time into the first session Maria spoke about an accident she had had when she was 18 years old: "Do you think it is connected?" she asked. Her description of the accident was matter of fact; however, as she and the therapist talked it became apparent that this was anything but the case—she had almost been killed.

Maria revealed that after the accident she had undergone a year-long period of rehabilitation in which she experienced loneliness and estrangement from her friends. During this time, Maria's family told her two things. First, they told her how lucky she was to be alive, creating the impression that "she should be grateful"; second, they focused on her efforts to recover. This dual focus excluded Maria's emotions; she became a "survivor." She had locked away her grief over a totally disrupted young life when she was 18. In fact, Maria had been systematically disowning her own grief for 22 years.

Maria the "survivor" had become so powerful that an expression of sadness might expose the phoniness of this version of self. Her intellectual adaptation had displaced the emotional component of griefwork. Perhaps deep down she knew her loss had been dismissed. Certainly she seemed angry at her parents for going overseas during her recovery period. But she put on an impressive front to meet her own and what she perceived to be others' expectations of herself. Listening to sad songs had brought her perilously close to her sadness and threatened her defenses.

Maria's case directs attention to the importance of attending to the expression of grief. Ideally and theoretically, the therapist must aim to encourage Maria to give her loss and emotions form—to the *extent* that Maria feels she has done it justice. Maria's task will be made easier if other people express a shared definition of the depth of her loss and legitimacy of her strong emotions. Significant people in Maria's life need to be given this opportunity. This process is not feasible in all cases; nevertheless, the individual needs permission to recognize the importance of attempting it.

Maria's lack of emotional adaptation can be gauged, not only by her presenting problem but also by the absence of a fluidity in her relationship with her pain. One useful measure of emotional adaptation is how easily individuals are able to share their loss and its impact on their lives. A middle ground exists that indicates that individuals do not feel threatened by how others will see them if they expose this version of self. Maria could not do this. She had identified too strongly with being a survivor. Loss in adolescence can have extreme effects on the formation of identity and one's presentation of self. Often there is either an overidentification with being a victim or, conversely, an overidentification with being a survivor.

If there has not been adequate discharge or outpouring of emotion, individuals will avoid triggers that reduce their ability to control their emotions. Hence, Maria avoided "sad songs." She harbored bitterness and resentment *because* the loss had not been paid deference to or memorialized. In social interaction, such individuals often say one thing and feel another. For example, when someone listens to friends talk of their sadness over not purchasing a house, for example, he or she might say, "That's too bad," but secretly think of this as "nothing compared with what I've been through." Some individuals voice their secret relief that something bad has happened to their friends: "Now you'll know what I felt!" All of this seriously affects social interaction. Keeping this emotional pain of self private amounts to the development of keeping a big secret. For some adolescents, it becomes a weapon: "My Mom knows something is wrong. She keeps on asking me but I'm not going to tell her." In such a case, the therapist aims to facilitate the individual's expression of emotions. This process may be arduous because the individual may feel easily overwhelmed. For Maria, her defenses had become so well-entrenched that she was estranged from her feelings. Initially, Maria was slowly supported to revisit the scene of the motorcycle accident: "What actually happened back then?" "How do you envisage it?" "What must it have been like?" "What changed?" "What did you lose?" Often, because so many years have transpired, the individual has a great deal of difficulty in locating his or her feelings.

This respect for the loss and encouragement to touch and feel the pain can be interwoven throughout therapy: "Tell me how tough it has been." "Who were you and what had you planned?" "What has it been like for you?" In an effort to return to those feelings, Maria was encouraged to watch movies that depict themes relative to her situation.

Following the lead of her parents, Maria had dismissed the loss involved in the accident. This had become her habit and it was extremely difficult to help Maria to do otherwise. Not surprisingly, all of Maria's friends had taken her lead. Exposing these connections, Maria gradually realized that her disappointment in her friends' reactions was largely misplaced; she had, to some extent, set the rules.

Maria began to understand her parents' response. In all likelihood, because they felt overwhelmed by their grief for Maria, her parents had made efforts to minimize its impact. At the same time, Maria realized that their reaction, although originally misinterpreted, had hurt her. Maria revealed that a large part of her emotional responses were in reaction to that pain. Identifying a need to "see" her parents' grief, Maria organized a visit to the accident scene with her parents.

From this foundation, it was important that Maria begin to rework her own rules regarding how this loss would now be handled. With the encouragement of the therapist, Maria began to give her loss the important place it should take in her life. She began telling her parents and friends about her feelings, her losses, and her grief: As a result, Maria began to develop a fluid relationship with this trauma that had occurred in her adolescence.

Considerations for Therapy

Individuals should be educated about the need to continually monitor the occasions when they intentionally or unintentionally fail to acknowledge the loss experience in their lives and their need to express their grief. The individual can be taught a series of self-checks: "Am I only sharing half my self with my friends?" "Do I feel a buildup of frustration?" "Have I spent a difficult week watching others do things I would once have been able to?" "Do I feel isolated from my friends and lonely?" "Am I acknowledging my sadness?" "Have I had any outbursts of anger, bitterness, or sadness?" "What does this tell me about my emotional state at present?" Techniques may include a series of rituals that legitimize the individual's struggle and survival. These rituals may be self-prescribed and seen as a way to memorialize and link life's narrative.

CASE STUDY 2: JENNY AND THE NEED TO LET GO OF THE TOOTH FAIRY

Therapeutic Focus: Attending to the Potency of Recurring Ideals

"Everything would have been perfect if Hilda didn't have this disability," Jenny repeatedly remarked to the therapist. Jenny, 45 years old, had a 5-year-old daughter with severe physical and intellectual disabilities. Jenny came to therapy because she was finding it increasingly difficult to be seen in public with Hilda. "If only I had had an amniocentesis—if Hilda was not here, then everything would go back to normal," she protested. Jenny's recollection of her family and childhood was that it had been "perfect." In many ways she expressed utter amazement, then, at a series of unfortunate events that seemed to have accompanied her daughter's birth: "These things just should not have happened to my family—I still find it hard to believe," she exclaims. "Every time I see a child of Hilda's age, I can't help going back to this fact. I find myself now and then wishing Hilda were not here. I don't really mean that, but...."

Jenny was in limbo, trapped by not being able to make some sense of why her life had turned out this way. How she might have prevented it from happening remained one of her central issues. She was finding it very difficult to believe that bad things happen to good people. Rather than accept that the world is not perfect, Jenny held tenaciously to her beliefs. She would not give up a notion of an "ideal world." Thus, Jenny had not adapted to what "was"; rather, she continued to harbor a belief that she might not *have* to adapt.

"I AM NOT JUST A MOTHER OF A CHILD WITH DISABILITIES."

Jenny's idealization of the world that should have been produced a potent yearning response. She was constantly affected by images that symbolize the world she had lost. Being seen publicly with Hilda overexposed her to the reality of her plight, while also creating considerable threat to her identity. "I am not just a mother of a child with disabilities," she stated. Tracing back to her adolescence, Jenny described a constant need to be a member of "the in-group." Her biography revealed a perhaps *too perfect* childhood. According to Jenny, only Hilda prevented her perfect world from continuing into her adulthood. She recollected that, when she was a child, she considered the lives of people in wheelchairs as "not worth having."

Ideals internalized into self-identity operate on unconscious and conscious levels. Through a therapeutic technique of directed awareness, ideals are slowly and sensitively exposed; their "ideal" character is acknowledged, critiqued, and their significance slowly "shrunk." Although ideals may not be able to coexist with changed versions of the world, they may be able to be reshaped. Expression of emotions parallels the relinquishing of aspects of these ideals.

What were Jenny's ideals? Where did they come from? Were they hers or were they her parents'? Did she choose them? Had she just accepted them naively? How central were they to her sense of an intact identity? Where did they fit into her narrative? Did they represent her childhood or her adult version of the world? Would Jenny be able to withstand the loss of her idealized version of the world?

Perhaps Jenny might give up some of her ideals if she did not perceive that she was forced to do so, and if she felt she could translate them into her changing version of the world. The therapist worked with her to engage in a biography search, which initially sought to establish the role of her ideals: past, present, and future. Jenny's awareness was directed to tracing and exploring her ideals, the taken-for-granted reality that has become enmeshed with her self-identity. The therapist searched for linking objects, that is, ways in which Jenny may be able to hold on to old versions of the world and of herself but at the same time be able to reality test her world without them. Through these linking objects, Jenny might gradually discover that she was okay without them.

How do children give up the idea of the tooth fairy? Do you remember your own relinquishment of Santa Claus and the tooth fairy? Slowly, over time, the truth may have dawned on you. Sometimes, however, you preferred to return to a belief in them because you wanted to or needed to, for whatever reason. The world was better with them. Similarly, Jenny's therapy called for a slow, systematic balancing of her perception of the world, with constant checks on her psychological need to hold on to her childhood version of the world. Over time, she and the therapist slowly worked together to increasingly differentiate between her childhood and adulthood versions of reality. Her beliefs were slowly challenged and exposed as ideals. Direct challenges by the therapist to her highly cherished ideals led her to almost belligerently hold on to them. Gentle and subtle challenges, however, although tedious, helped her loosen the hold.

For Jenny to cease perceiving Hilda as a personal threat, she had to learn to consider imperfection as universal. That is, having a child with a disability was less about Hilda than it was about the nature of life. Discussion between Jenny and her therapist centered around the randomness of misfortune in the world; no one is being punished. In fact, over a lifetime, most people end up with *something* happening to them. Jenny was asked to direct her attention to the many examples of ordinary and unfair versions of the world.

Yearning for the world that should have been, Jenny learned that she had idealized images of normality and what being just like other people offered. She feared that her friends would reject her for not being like them. As far as Jenny was concerned, all her friends were thinking that she "wished she was like them." The latter theme was recurrent in her life. Jenny's membership in the "in-group" had always been precarious. Through therapy, she became aware that Hilda had not caused this membership to fracture. The issue was about her own identity problems. She, herself, "needed" to be accepted. The therapeutic focus returned to her adolescence and the similarities with her current stage of life. Jenny was embarrassed by Hilda; Hilda damaged her identity: "I'm a successful dentist. People don't see this when I'm with Hilda." In fact, the fear of being rejected *was* Jenny's dreaded event; it began way back in her development.

In not wanting her friends to think that she wished she was like them, Jenny had not exposed her pain to her friends. Instead, she had pretended that she was not upset about Hilda, that there was no loss. In a sense, Jenny only introduced part of herself to her friends. By cutting off the part of herself that was feeling pain, she continually kept her grief inside. With this superficial level of interaction, she imagined her friends to have the life she did not. The therapist works with the client to challenge this perception. Jenny was encouraged to introduce the hidden part of her life to her friends and test whether they would accept her for herself, something that she had not been psychologically strong enough to do in adolescence.

The therapist alerted Jenny to her habitual way of thinking: Each time she saw an image of the world that should have been she was immediately drawn into a ruminating cycle. She was taught to become a critical observer and note imperfections in others and the world. She was encouraged to start mastering the images and their effect on her. Jenny began observing and listing the number of triggers to which she was responding. Each time she started ruminating on what should have been, she was to challenge herself to only think about it for 2 minutes. Thus, Jenny became her own personal trainer.

The work of grappling with Jenny's long-held view of the world and exposing its naiveté involved helping her learn to grieve. To encourage her to express her loss, the therapist gave Jenny the task to memorialize and ritualize the letting go of her childhood version of the world. To deal with the cyclic nature of her grief, she was taught what will become life-long techniques. First, the dynamics of grieving for her unmet expectations were explained. The therapist emphasized that the frustration of not meeting expectations—both conscious and unconscious—is an integral part of chronic conditions. Buildup of frustration is to be expected whenever the world that should have been becomes too potent. The tendency to slip into states of yearning, protest, defiance, or despair is typical (see Figure 13.1). Second, therapy involved training Jenny to monitor her levels of frustration. She was encouraged to read her psychological state and to recognize what she needed to help ventilate her cyclic grief: In her case, talking or writing reduced its potency.

Considerations for Therapy

Sometimes it is possible to thread a version of one's ideals into the future. If it captures the individual's passion it begins a link between the world that should have been and the world that is emerging. Therapists usually have a great deal of creativity. In Jenny's case, her perfect childhood was an ideal that Jenny felt was shattered by and lost to Hilda. This loss had caused Jenny to denigrate and devalue most aspects of Hilda's childhood. Jenny was challenged to regard her public outings with Hilda as an opportunity to create the best version of childhood possible for Hilda and to use these outings to begin exercising her role as an adult. The first day that she went out in public with Hilda in her wheelchair, she was encouraged to see it as a measure of her healing—that she was going to be "all right" as Hilda's parent.

Sometime near the end of Jenny's therapy there was a clear sign that her traumatic condition was abating, that she actually was emerging into a more adult view of herself and the world. The shift can clearly be identified when the client realizes that things are different now. For instance, the parents of a child like Hilda might begin to broaden their perception of the child apart from the disability and reflect that their own emotional state is not the central issue. The way is now open for a more balanced relationship between parent and child.

CASE STUDY 3: LEAH AND THE NEED TO CAST AN ADULT SPELL ON CANCER

Therapeutic Focus: Attending to the Potency of Dreaded Events

"Here, have a look at this." Leah handed Dorothy a leaflet. "I've been in contact with my friend, she recommends this juice concoction. It looks time consuming, lots of preparation, but it's supposed to have antioxidants and it fights cancer cells." A woman opposite them commented, "Don't believe what you hear about that one. It's a waste of time. I have a friend who tried that one; she's had a relapse." Leah felt frightened. "You don't beat cancer" was something she had learned to believe because her aunt had died from cancer when Leah was 8 years old.

Leah had met Dorothy in the waiting room of the surgeon's office. Both women had been told that they had breast cancer that same day. Six weeks later they began chemotherapy, lost their hair together, and sat side by side each day in the radiotherapy waiting room. Both women's prognosis was good. When it was all over they never saw each other again. Leah had requested this. Dorothy, up-front about her cancer, was too confrontational. Leah came to therapy to find strategies to deal with her illness.

"I guess I'm constantly frightened of it coming back," Leah reluctantly admitted in therapy. Leah went to great lengths herself to try to frighten the cancer off. In fact, she was even scared to admit she was frightened: a horrible state of affairs! Since her treatment she had begun a strict regime of exercise, diet, and relaxation. Three years later she was hypervigilant about any bodily sensation that she felt to be new or different. Immediately, she would be at the doctor's office instigating medical tests. She described 2 terrible years of monitoring, testing, and waiting for results. To add to all of this, Leah had become increasingly superstitious. She had to stay "good" or risk punishment. On leaving the first therapy session, she mentioned a pain in her side: "Should I have it checked?" she asked the therapist. The question was a good example of how childhood versions of self and childhood thinking can be triggered quickly and can take over a person's response to nonfinite loss and grief (see Figure 13.1). Leah's anxiety about whether she "was all right" had exploded; she believed she needed an authority figure—taking an adult, reassuring stand—to abate it.

Cancer creates universal fear. Even when a diagnosis is not terminal, the patient has been exposed to the fragility that underpins everyday life, a fragility that everybody instinctively wants to deny. With that in mind, therapy with Leah was directed toward creating patterns in what seemed to be a life that was at the mercy of her fear. Constantly on the alert, Leah's response had started to create habitual ways of reacting. She was becoming decreasingly tolerant of anxiety.

The aim of her therapy was to create patterns for behavior that had become too out of control. A set of statements or behaviors that represented anxiety stops were generated. Fortunately, Leah's prognosis was fairly good. Was there an iron-clad guarantee that she would die in the next 2, 5, or even 10 years? "No." What were the words of the surgeon?

Leah revealed that she had been told she had a 50% chance of living past the age of 80. The therapist described people who had survived cancer and told her that hundreds of thousands of women have survived breast cancer and are still living. Leah was asked to break her automatic thought pattern that surrounded the recurrence of cancer by replacing her negative thoughts with her surgeon's encouraging words, and by picturing one of the people her therapist had told her about. Leah researched statistics on breast cancer and wrote them on a piece of paper, which she then had laminated. This was kept in her diary for reflection.

"What if the surgeon's words are not true?" Leah asked. "What if they are?" the therapist responded. Still, Leah erred on the negative side. This could be traced back to the schemata surrounding her dreaded events. Throughout her life, Leah had had considerable personal experience with people who had died of cancer. An avid reader of magazines, Leah read almost compulsively about such people. Leah's childhood and adolescence had been characterized by many versions of herself as a victim. Her father had died when she was 4 years old, and during her childhood she had been dogged by asthma. According to Leah, the likelihood of her having cancer and dying of cancer fitted that picture. She had always been "sickly" and now she was to die early just like her father had.

These images provide useful paradoxes. Leah had actually survived two highly significant threats in her life, but at this point she was centering her attention on the fact she was a victim. Leah had, in her life, been forced to find resilience. She had survived. It was probable that neither her mother nor her family had actually interpreted her life through this lens, however.

With this idea of inner strength in mind, Leah was introduced to a side of herself that had never been paid deference to before. Leah's therapy focused on this idea of her emergence for quite a while. She was encouraged to step inside her life as a small child by looking at pictures of herself as a child and imagining her fear of asthma attacks and the world that followed her father's death. Eventually, Leah was able to identify a survival theme in her life.

Inspiring Leah to take charge became less difficult over time. She was asked to stop fueling her fear of cancer by deliberately censoring the stories she read, the television programs she watched, and the tales she heard from friends. When she sensed the topic was moving toward cancer, Leah was challenged to take control of conversations and to change the subject. This was new to Leah. Like many individuals, she was used to forgoing her needs in order to remain polite to friends or people she did not even know. Changing the subject was about respecting herself. She did not have to respond to a deluge of questions or hear a deluge of information.

Therapy was directed at reducing Leah's identification with being a victim, reducing the potency of fear surrounding her dread, and challenging her resignation to her death from cancer. Once she began to personalize her relationship with cancer and extricate it from popular notions she was able to reduce her defenses. With repeated success at control, over time, she became able to distance herself from available information about cancer. Ultimately she would be in a position to preselect information she felt psychologically able to tolerate.

Finally, therapy attended to Leah's free-floating anxiety that different sensations in her body pertained to cancer. Patterns for behavior were devised. There was much to expose and talk about: whether she would have been as alert to her body's signals prior to cancer and what would have been signals for alarm and visits to the doctor; the aging process, and how this might cloud the whole issue; and how to increase her tolerance for anxiety and work out criteria that would reestablish some control. Together, she and her therapist set criteria for panic. This involved establishing a framework that would encourage a more flexible thought process—a better decision process for action (e.g., not *all* body signals equated with cancer). Starting with the most likely and moving to the least likely reasons for bodily sensations, Leah began using a broad base to self-assess her problems: virus, diet, stress, aging. She resolved that discomfort or pain would be assessed over a period of time, rather than immediately calling for the doctor and tests. She was encouraged to seek some medical facts that doctors themselves would use in the diagnostic setting. Thus, several signposts were set up for consideration before panicking. After all, the tests Leah had had over the last 3 years had yielded negative results. Rather than have tests throughout the year, Leah decided to have a battery of tests twice a year.

"IT WAS MY FAULT, I WASN'T LOOKING AFTER MYSELF. ALL MY FRIENDS TELL ME I ASKED FOR IT."

Much of Leah's behavior resulted from superstitions of childhood. It was discovered that she had had a superstitious response to her father's death. A week prior to his death, she had broken a mirror. Had her father's death happened because of this? Discussion revealed that much of Leah's current state was about her childhood. What did she believe about her cancer? She reiterated a common approach to cancer: "It was my fault, I wasn't looking after myself. All my friends tell me I asked for it. I always have worried too much." Leah was exposed to the childhood version of thinking and the dogmatic rules with which she regulated her life: Was her thinking logical? Was this the cure for cancer—to look after yourself perfectly? Would this actually create too much tension and ameliorate aspects of her goals? Instead of making her feel safe, her rules were creating constant anxiety. She was encouraged to challenge this line of thought and challenge her adult version of self to take charge of the situation to dispel childhood superstitions—to cast an adult spell on them.

Leah was challenged to envision herself as embodying both a frightened child and a competent adult. Using this visualization, Leah was asked to use her adult self to slowly coach the child version of herself to become stronger. As an adult, Leah could command the frightened child within herself to stop fertilizing her fear. She had not caused her cancer. She could occasionally forget to take her vitamins without something bad happening. She could sometimes rest in front of the television and not go to the gym. Gradually, therapy devised the patterns, rules, and limits that would contain Leah's anxiety as best as possible.

Considerations for Therapy

Ultimately, the goal of therapy is to co-create a new version of self, one that will devise its own psychological safety. A "recipe" emerges of what one needs in order to resist the urge to constantly check one's self. A return to naiveté is impossible, but protecting one's self from childhood thoughts that run riot is possible. Certain rules evolved in adulthood can foster the restoration and retention of psychological balance. Maintaining balance is a key component of the psychology that surrounds cancer. When they are constantly waiting to be told they are "all right" by medical practitioners, people with potential relapse conditions often are repeatedly forced into helpless and dependent versions of self.

CASE STUDY 4: NAM AND THE NEED TO CAMOUFLAGE RECOVERY

Therapeutic Focus: Attending to the Preservation of Identity

"What am I looking down the barrel of, here?" Nam anxiously queried the neurologist. "Me, lose my legs? You've got to be joking." The doctor, unsure of Nam's grasp of his plight, pulled out a medical text. He showed Nam pictures of the physical outcome of the syndrome. The pictures horrified Nam. Overexposed to a dreadful fate, Nam shut off: "They weren't about me. Other people get this, not me."

Unfortunately, the diagnosis was correct and did follow the course outlined by the doctor. Later, Nam was enticed to therapy. He arrived in a wheelchair, already having had both legs amputated. Twelve months had gone by since this happened, and Nam and his wife Mylin had not uttered one word to each other about it or the future that lay ahead. The handling of the diagnosis had not offered a strand of hope.

Nam's mind was on the run—away from this dreaded event. Mylin, however, wanted her partner back. She was eager for him to recover and get back to helping her with the family chores. She also wanted him to see what *she* was going through. Nam required a therapeutic relationship that would give him permission to be initially dependent on the therapist. This permission would provide an unconditional base from which he could strengthen himself.

A degenerative disease that would eventually see him incapable of looking after himself was too big a threat for Nam. Even after the loss of one leg, it was inconceivable to Nam that a future such as this would belong to him. The bigger the threat, the more inconceivable it was. Nam needed help to break down its magnitude so he could perceive psychological survival.

The assessment of what proportion of the emerging reality a person can emotionally tolerate is really an assessment of the fragility of his or her identity given the perceived threat. Clearly, Nam's identity was under extreme threat. Desperate to represent himself and to hold on to who he had been before the disease, Nam spent most of the therapy sessions describing his life before his disease. Nam described a life of an athlete "faster, taller, and stronger than his brother" who he believed no longer saw him in the same light: "My own brother, not recognizing me!" As far as Nam was concerned, he could not recognize himself. A connecting theme between Nam's past and present was required, but at this point it was obviously too early. Nam did not want a connection. The current Nam was a blight on the person he once was. Nam's perception of males in wheelchairs was of "losers, no good to no one." His preoccupation at this point was about idealizing and memorializing who he had been.

Note the chaos inside this man. Nam rejected his body. It had let him down. But he also was frightened of his mental state and the physical concomitants of his anxiety. He sought relief from what he described as a sense and a threat of impending doom, though he refused to take medication: "I've never resorted to pills." In a strange way, taking pills represented a further threat to Nam's notion of self. The therapist saw this as an opportunity to challenge Nam's mind to take control. If he took up this challenge, an aspect of Nam's identity would be preserved.

The therapist began by trying to slowly recreate and develop a sense of control through educating Nam about the links between psychology and physiology and the idea of dealing with states of unease. The dynamics of loss, trauma, and grief and how they relate to anxiety and physiological states were represented diagrammatically. Nam was introduced to the need and the methods to restore, as much as possible, a balance between his bodily and internal states. Generally, the rule is this: The more chaos, the more requirement for routines. Thus, tight, meticulous routines were created for Nam to rest, eat, socialize, express his feelings to himself or someone else, and engage in physical therapy. Routines often are left behind when an individual leaves the hospital setting; in fact, when individuals describe that setting, they can recognize the holding environment and the safety of routines. Routines can offer a psychological trapeze. If they become rote, they themselves can provide a psychological harbor. Routines assist in getting individuals to where they feared they would end up, without that state being so intensely resisted.

The following exposition on Nam provides insight that his adaptation to becoming an amputee needed to be camouflaged initially and temporarily. When and if Nam were to adapt to his reality, he would be amazed to learn that he no longer had to fear who he had become. Nam's reality testing had to be paced—a difficult task given that he had been dropped in at the very deep end of his future—the large end of the triangle that was introduced in a previous chapter (see Figure 14.2). Before Nam could stop clinging desperately to aspects of his old self and begin expressing his grief, his interpretation of who he might become needed to be addressed. Nam had not had his perception of life in a wheelchair challenged. Nam needed to be desensitized to his fear of life in a wheelchair—the impression that he might become "a loser." In the therapist's opinion, it was vital that Nam attend a self-help group and hear people's stories of survival and experiences with wheelchairs. But timing, with respect to readiness, was equally critical. Could Nam's adaptation process withstand negative examples from a participant at a self-help group? Would a survivor's story overwhelm Nam if he could not perceive himself as having similar personal skills? Would such a story spur Nam to take up a personal challenge to model a similar adaptation?

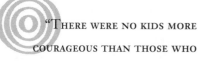

"THERE WERE NO KIDS MORE COURAGEOUS THAN THOSE WHO WERE DIFFERENT AT MY SCHOOL."

As a less-threatening strategy, the therapist decided to begin challenging Nam's view by revealing stories and presenting images of children in wheelchairs: "What do you think of children who use wheelchairs at an early age and continue on through primary school? Are they losers?" Fortunately, Nam reflected: "There were no kids more courageous than those who were different at my school"—a slight shift through reframing.

In Nam's life, the concepts of needing a wheelchair and being male seemed incongruous. What was a *male*? Here, the schemata of males had to be fleshed out. What was the model of male that Nam had learned from his childhood and his adolescence? What was his father like? What did his father teach Nam and his brother? Returning to Nam's memory of being "faster and stronger" than his brother, in therapy it was important to examine and trace how these comparisons might have become imperatives in Nam's life. Could Nam and his therapist isolate male aspects of Nam that had not been focused on previously? This was difficult. Nam repeatedly returned to idealized models of males who were seemingly "strong," never besieged by emotions. Were there such males? Psychoeducation was useful here. In therapy, Nam was introduced to the internal life of males, the emotional world of males seldom revealed in male social interaction. It would seem that Nam had not been privy to the fact that males often camouflage their fears by appearing strong—Nam had always focused on the exterior. Through these discussions, *being strong* and *being male* became more complex concepts than they had previously been for Nam. Could Nam entertain more complex, differentiated versions of *strong* for himself? Could these examples shrink the gulf Nam perceived between him and "them" (i.e., his idealized version of males)?

Nam resisted entertaining a future in which he would never be able to leave his wheelchair. Most of his psychological survival lay in his ability to master prostheses. In fact, this hope provided a psychological harbor. For, according to Nam, suicide was the alternative: "I wouldn't hesitate. It would just be as quick as that." At this point, Nam's reality testing was actually conditional on the fact that the world he was testing was temporary. Either he could interpret it as temporary through thoughts of suicide or through the hope of some sort of recovery. Was there a link that would allow him to see the beginnings of a connecting thread in his life narrative? Much of Nam's dialogue revolved around the pride of being able to survive, to take on new opportunities and dares in his life. An immigrant, he had picked up new careers and adapted in many ways. Nam was dared to take up the challenge to adapt yet again.

The therapist slowly introduced a series of gentle baits, small incremental tasks that might challenge Nam's perception of being "stared at as a loser." Would Nam deliberately shift his focus? Could the stares include admiration for a man continuing his life in such adversity? Nam was asked to look for different meanings when he was out in public. The hope was that the feedback from these cognitive and behavioral tasks might eventually accrue, and Nam's perception of himself would be forced to begin shifting. For Nam both the success of these baits and the entertainment of suicide kept him going. The challenge for Nam would be to *not* commit suicide.

Nam was lost in the trauma of prognosis. Often he would ask what the point of therapy was, given the future. His fear of the future restricted his ability to emotionally grieve for the version of his self that he had lost. The therapist encouraged him to pace his reality testing, to test what he had lost rather than predict what he would lose. Nam was challenged to stay in the present. He was reminded of Buddhist philosophy, yoga and meditation, and therapeutic strategies involving control over the mind. How might the same ire that makes Nam reject taking pills be transformed to the mind control of stopping negative thoughts? To Nam, his future represented a huge psychological hurdle. Breaking it down into smaller bits over which he could find real or perceived opportunities for control was paramount.

Optimally, Nam needed to begin to attribute his gains to his own skills and efforts. In tandem and with Nam's cooperation, it was imperative that a connection with the future be inspired. What might have meaning to Nam? He was introduced to biographies of men who used wheelchairs and had been successful, Paralympians who had become the best in their field. He was also asked about his heroes. Who had inspired him? Whom would he wish to emulate? Whose example energized him? Who or what baited him to take charge?

All of this went some way to breaking down Nam's negative versions of the world that were emerging. It also helped him engage in some vicarious grieving and emotional expression. This was all taking place while Nam held on to his dream of "beating" the prediction that he would never walk again. Therapy allowed this hope to persist. In the meantime, however, attempts to desensitize Nam to the world of wheelchairs continued. If walking failed, at least Nam would not have such a fear of the world in which he was trapped.

Considerations for Therapy

Unfortunately, Nam did not continue with therapy. Marital conflict overwhelmed him. Because they were not able to share their pain, Nam and Mylin became totally isolated from each other and their marriage virtually dissolved. Both would have bitterly stated that neither of them acknowledged the other's pain. In fact, the pain stood between them.

How much did Nam's therapy help him? Perhaps he was left with some acknowledgment of the courage he needed. Perhaps because this type of courage was asked of the children in wheelchairs whom he remembered from his childhood, it would serve as a challenge. Therapists often don't know what, or if anything, makes a difference. In some cases, understandably, people decide that life without being a certain version of themselves cannot be endured.

CASE STUDY 5: ALLAN AND
THE NEED TO TAME THE BOGEYMAN

Therapeutic Focus: Attending to
Preserving the Ability to Safely Explore the World

"I'm feeling tired," Allan noted.

"You'll be all right!" Allan's mother, Gabrielle said. Weeks went by. The complaints and lethargy exceeded the typical pattern of Allan's illnesses. Gabrielle made an appointment with the doctor. A chronic disease was confirmed by blood tests. Allan was 13 at the time. "Am I going to die? Are you telling me the truth?" he appealed to his mother. Gabrielle responded, "No, darling. You are just a 'worry wart.'" Allan found his mother's response confusing: Why shouldn't he worry? After all, he *had* gotten ill. "It had happened—so why am I called a worry wart?" So when his mother said "No," he realized there were no guarantees here; she might mean "Yes."

Just on the verge of adolescence, Allan's foundation of trust was in jeopardy. He was in the midst of learning about the fragility of safety, notions of mortality, and the randomness of awful things in the world. Danger was revealing itself in childhood, a time in life when individuals require just the opposite: namely, to believe that the world is predictable and safe.

How did Allan conceptualize his new illness? He felt different: "It's hard to explain. Out of sorts." "I don't *feel* like me," he said to his parents. Mainly, Allan had lost his ability to take the world for granted. We all like safety to be a given. So when it seems that it is not, there is immense anxiety about survival and safety. However, Allan's knowledge structures of disease were not fleshed out at this stage. He had been told that he had a disease that affected his blood. It was given a name that he had never even heard of before. He was told it would not go away. "We'll see about that!" Allan had thought. At this point, Allan was just beginning to feel there was some truth in what the doctor had said—some, at least—for it was 2 years later and the blood tests had continued.

Unlike an adult who has been exposed to diseases and their formidable reputation, Allan had not yet had this exposure. Allan could have been somewhat protected from the vagaries or "might be's" of this disease had the specialist understood that Allan was not old enough emotionally and intellectually to realize all the things this disease could do to him. The fact of the matter was that the specialist did not consider Allan's cognitive and socioemotional development or the role of fear in adolescence. The specialist dropped Allan in at the deep end: "So what we have here, Allan, is a disease that affects your blood....You must take two of these tablets each morning and night. They should leave you feeling

pretty ordinary. If you get any feelings that aren't normal to you, however, you must quickly inform me. Several organs may be adversely affected by these drugs," said the specialist. "How? I want to know." "For
how long? Or else what?" Allan anxiously asked. The specialist took his
questions literally. But Allan had had no idea that the specialist would be
talking about death. "Well, a number of things can happen...." the specialist continued. And that's when Allan had decided to have his own
thoughts on the matter. It was a stand that had been forced. But in the
background of Allan's stand was fear and anxiety.

For Allan, the specialist had gone way too far. Allan was very frightened, almost terrified. He became unsure of himself, stopped going out to
his friends' places, could not get to sleep, had terrible nightmares when
he did eventually go to sleep, and spent most of his time with his mother
and father. He began to make excuses to friends: "No, I can't sleep over,
I'm busy." Why had this happened to him? How could Allan protect
himself from his overwhelming anxiety? The anxiety had to be quelled.
Allan returned to a number of superstitious rituals he had used when he
was 8 years old. Cupboard doors had to be closed, things compulsively
straightened. He developed a habit of praying each night. "Well, if I put
my things neat like this, and if I pray I feel better. Nothing else bad will
happen," Allan thought to himself. He became very aware of what his
body felt like and had an unfillable void of anxiety that forced him to ask
his mother for repeated assurances that he was all right.

"I am frightened about what is happening to me, " Allan said. "I am
not like any of my friends. Why am I so unlucky?" He was unable to
find strength from anywhere. Over-whelmed with their fear for Allan, his mother and father had found it too difficult to conceal their own fear. Searching their faces, Allan had picked up on this: "If they're scared, things must be real bad!"

"WELL, IF I PUT MY THINGS NEAT LIKE THIS, AND IF I PRAY I FEEL BETTER. NOTHING ELSE BAD WILL HAPPEN."

Taking up on the line of the specialist, Allan's parents sat and talked
long and hard about the procedures. Occasionally, Allan's mother would
cry. Other times, Allan's father would leave the room. The potential of
the disease had become more than frightening; it was threatening his
parents. Allan was emotionally overwhelmed. It was not possible, in
Allan's stage of development, to process this life experience.

It is up to clinicians and parents to respect the child's cognitive and
socioemotional stage of development. Allan had reached a stage in which
he was forming his mature concept of self. Embarking on a key stage of
separation and individuation from his parents, Allan required strength

and confidence in his ability to survive such a separation. For this, the world has to appear safe and predictable, and parents have to remain sources of emotional strength. Allan's disease had forced him to regress to an increased dependence on his parents. Too weak to navigate the fear of the disease and simultaneously embark on finding increased independence with his friends, Allan was in a position that created extreme psychological tension.

There are ways of reducing this tension. If alcohol or drugs allowed Allan to step out of his fear and anxiety, perhaps he could then take the risks his friends took. He might feel courageous enough to leave his parents' side. An intense love relationship might provide a similar support for his identity. The alternative for many individuals is to dare the disease, or dare death, just as kindergartners will do by jumping on the cracks or lines in the sidewalk when their friends are too fearful to do so. In fact, by creating more risks some individuals simultaneously create a much-needed distraction from the anxiety related to a physical condition. So an adolescent might decide to take drugs or to steal—all distractions.

None of these potential outcomes are desirable, of course. In therapy, to prevent these negative outcomes from occurring, Allan's parents were first advised to provide a short-term psychological harbor in which he could heal his wounds and regain strength. This is like returning the individual in question to a holding environment. First, to reduce the tension, his parents were advised to tell him that he must stay home. If it became their demand, not his decision, Allan could feel protected from his own indecision regarding whether he should go out with his friends. That is, if Allan's parents forced him to stay home and take a rest, Allan was protected from the weak version of himself. Allan told his friends, "My parents won't let me come over. They want me to rest; they're being super-protective. If it was up to me I'd be there with you, but I'll just hang here to keep them happy."

Second, the therapist suggested that Allan's parents become stronger, more resolute about good outcomes and Allan's ability to take on the vagaries of the disease. This would create the possibility for Allan to identify with his parents' strength and confidence in him. Essentially, Allan had to restore his faith in his ability to be safe. Because Allan was so acutely aware of his parents' emotional turmoil, however, their transformation had to be gradual, one that Allan witnessed over weeks. If it was not an overnight change that looked phony, Allan would slowly be challenged to review the stand his parents had originally taken on his condition. Their opinion was changing. It was not the end of the world!

From this standpoint, Allan's parents were told to communicate convincing strong positive statements, as suggestive remarks now and then. No adolescent likes a deluge of parent–child communication.

Single, intermittent strong remarks drawing potent similarities between Allan and "survivors" were encouraged. These statements that did not encourage an emotionally overwhelming atmosphere would be far better received because Allan would not feel under threat. Eventually, this would culminate in a challenge to Allan's ability to take on the emotional load and a faith in his ability to adapt to it. Thus, while Allan's identity was taking form, the therapist sent strong messages about Allan's self. "How does a person become strong?" Significantly, Allan made a quizzical remark about a friend, Luke, who had a chronic illness also: "It's strange he does not seem to be as strong as me!"

Theoretically, given his stage of development, it is likely that Allan wished to know whether it was permissible for him to be scared. It is often useful to introduce a story that normalizes such a seeming incongruity. The therapist might note: "I know a boy who can be both strong and scared sometimes; no one is just strong." This assists greatly in adolescents' ability to see through the masks of peers. From Allan's perspective, namely, of being exposed to an unsafe version of the world, he found it difficult not to generalize his peers into one bag. To Allan their fearlessness was incredulous: "All of my friends seem to cope with things. They seem to be taking on their lives, almost as if they are actually daring danger."

Preserving identity is integral in this stage of development. One aspect of this is the importance of preventing the identity of the adolescent from drowning in the dreaded event. This involves a great deal of overexposure that is more often than not daunting for the adolescent. Separated from the mainstream of his peers' development, Allan had been almost branded with a difference: "I feel like it's written all over my forehead. I'm different. I'm sick!"

Allan had become increasingly alienated by the differences. At this point he was liable to overidentify with being a victim. Becoming a "whiner" would do nothing for his peer-group relations or his self-esteem, however. Keeping him in some peer group that allowed his identity to remain broad-based was critical. That is, similarities have to be brought to his attention to prevent him from separating from his peers. In Allan's case his school had a support group for children with similar challenges, which he attended. Approximately 10 children with conditions ranging from asthma to diabetes to orthopedic problems would meet together every other week. Under the guidance of a skilled leader, Allan was allowed free, unmitigated expression of gripes with the world, as well as the opportunity to regard himself as typical. In addition, because Allan also was a member of mainstream peer groups both sides of his life were being heard, legitimized, and owned.

An important balance between victim and survivor must be created. Although neither the victim nor the survivor role should be too dominant, both sides should be real. An adolescent, just like anyone else, secretly demands them to be acknowledged and respected. However, often in the parents' quest to develop the survivor, the child perceives that his parents "do not understand how hard it has been." Ironically, in adolescence the individual's stage of development demands that parents should not always be *able* to know how he or she feels. This is about the "self," its uniqueness. There is a conundrum here: Often adolescents will demarcate their separation from their parents by adopting a different stand on handling their medication, exercise, therapy, and so forth. They will begin to own their condition as an adult: "It is my stuff, not Mom's."

In Allan's situation, he was trying hard to put on a brave front because seeing his parent's reaction made him feel worse. "When my father cried, I couldn't stand it. I felt sick, as though I wanted to vomit. 'Stop crying!' I wanted to shout." So, while adolescents may have their emotional pain legitimized by seeing their parents' pain, the expression further upsets their security. In fact, in Allan's case, this vision actually weakened his ability to find safety in the world. Now, he had to be reassured that his parents would be all right.

Gabrielle was advised to curtail the information she was giving Allan. How many doctors' meetings did Allan actually have to attend? Did he require all of this knowledge? How much normality could be restored? Through therapy, Allan's reality testing began to be harnessed and paced. Having an ongoing medical condition made it possible for Allan to learn about his disease over time. Why not allow this knowledge to emerge slowly so it would enhance his psychological adaptation? Extra complications, some of which may never eventuate, were superfluous and only served to smother his development. Why tell him? Allan no longer attended reviews with doctors following tests. His parents began monitoring what information he actually required. There were no lies, just no bombardment of a reality that otherwise would have overwhelmed him. In spite of Allan's chronic condition, his health was steady unless proven otherwise. No bogeymen! Routines and patterns became less disrupted.

Allan's anxiety lessened and his confidence began, slowly, to return. Intently watching and interpreting his parents' faces and hearing their feedback further encouraged his feelings of safety. Hesitatingly, Allan asked the therapist: "Mom seems okay about all of this? Do you think she's heard it's gone away?" A careful response was required: "Well, she may be feeling that things will be okay, either way—if it has or if it hasn't." Over time, Allan probably will learn this himself, but in the short term his parents' changed demeanor translated into some needed confidence, tempered his anxiety, and provided him with some solid ground from which to rekindle his friendships.

With this background falling into place, therapy addressed some self-empowerment issues. Allan devised a schedule of goals that included his approach to his medical procedures; tablet-taking and self-administering of injections; and feelings he described as "anxiety rushes." Allan was asked to challenge himself. In his own time, he developed a personal protocol that he proudly showed to his friends. "Jeez, you're brave. I couldn't do that—ever," his friends said. The feedback was good. With the mastery of special skills, Allan began to develop a personal identity forged with the knowledge that he had overcome his fears. This generalized into a private pride in the strength he had proven to himself. Allan stated that, unlike most of his friends, he was not one of the "sheep." In addition, he was esteemed by his peers.

Still, Allan had a continuing relationship with anxiety. After each doctor's visit, and often after experiencing some side effects of his medication or some manifestations of his disease, Allan would return to his rituals. He was advised about what all of this meant, that everybody tends to revisit routines when they feel under a lot of personal threat. This was not a bad thing but might be reinterpreted as a tension-buster. To help him understand this, the therapist disclosed some similar feelings she had experienced as an adolescent. Allan believed the therapist to be strong. Knowing that the therapist had experienced stages in her life when *she* felt vulnerable and in need of support gave Allan the ability to regard fear as one ingredient in life, not a threat that had the potential to undermine his whole identity.

"THAT NIGHTMARE ABOUT THE SAND SHIFTING WHILE I AM STANDING ON IT—IT'S THERE EVERY TIME I GET A SCARE—I CAN PREDICT WHEN IT WILL HAPPEN!"

Psychoeducation helped him to understand his anxiety rushes. Allan knew that on such occasions he was emotionally taxed. He understood that sometimes he would be faced with feelings of bitterness, anger, and sadness, when his thoughts returned to what might have been. Triggers that would provoke these feelings were identified and listed; Allan would have to develop a relationship with them. For these cycles that would continually challenge his resilience, Allan would self-prescribe a number of routines. He would predict when he needed to slow down his social life; start exercising; and tighten up routines surrounding eating, sleeping, and talking or writing about his feelings. Often, nightmares would parallel times when he felt unsafe. He began writing out his dreams and seeing them as ways his anxiety was being expressed. "That nightmare about the sand shifting while I am standing on it—it's there every time I get a scare—I can predict when it will happen!" Allan also began to see the nightmares as helping him to express some of his frustration and sadness.

His response to his psychological world would become part of his life, as had his daily medication.

Considerations for Therapy

Allan's intellectual adaptation to this chronic illness will continue to take place over the years, in which he learns about the characteristics and ramifications of the disease. At some point in his cognitive development he probably will experience a major reinterpretation of the part it has played in his life. As time passes the focus on routines will probably diminish. In the meantime, the emphasis on routines has been to provide Allan with a sense that he has things to "do" when it gets too tough. The emotional aspect of griefwork will proceed in fits and starts but will culminate when he is emotionally capable of tolerating the depths of his loss. At that point, ideally he will be looking back, absorbing what his life has not been and what has been forgone and feel he has survived.

Meanwhile, in adolescence irrevocability is not a consideration. An ability to conceptualize chronicity is about *learning* that it will not go away. Adolescents can employ any number of magical thinking, superstitious beliefs, and behaviors in order to keep reality in abeyance. This ability is enhanced by their stage of cognitive and socioemotional development. When Allan was asked, "And, what do *you* think about all this?" he replied; "I've been talking to my grandpa, he's looking down on all this from heaven. He says, 'It'll be all right.'" It is apparent that the more fearful the threat, the more psychological comfort will have to be developed. So Allan's story illustrates how he is experiencing a reaction to a threat that, over time, he will come to realize will not go away—a type of prolonged separation anxiety from a typical healthy steady state. Slowly, over time, Allan will be forced to habituate to a changed state that actually has been merging with him since his diagnosis. He is on his way to realizing there are no magical tricks to recovery.

CASE STUDY 6: BOB AND JEAN AND THE NEED TO START AGAIN

Therapeutic Focus: Attending to the Preservation of a Relationship

The story of Bob and Jean is introduced with an excerpt from a letter Jean wrote to her brother-in-law, Jack.

> *Dear Jack,*
> *I apologize for this letter before I start. It's all about me. Months ago,*
> *Bob was diagnosed with Alzheimer's disease. At the time, I didn't*
> *believe it. He was forgetful, sometimes a bit spacey. We would joke*

about it. "You're going senile, you old fool. You've been hitting the whisky. It's having its effects," I would warn. But other times, early on, I'd find myself staring at him and in what was a fleeting instant, I felt he looked vague. He just wasn't the same. I couldn't put my finger on it. Only very occasionally, I would feel a bit of a panicky feel, it's difficult to put words to, but like a warning signal of trouble. It got so much worse, so much so that last month, I fell to pieces. I couldn't cope any more. I felt like screaming at Bob, and I felt constantly close to tears.

I ended up having to place Bob in a nursing home. I haven't wanted to tell you about this, Jack. I felt frightened that if I wrote about it, I would not be able to bear the pain of it. I miss him so much. Some days I spend all of my time desperately wanting to get him out of there, bring him home. Jack, I have to literally drum it into my brain that it would not be okay! It's terribly hard to resist this urge to get him back. I'm going through all of the memories in my mind. I feel like I've let him down. I should have been stronger. He's there, but he's not there. It's cruel. I wanted to live out my old age with him. It should have been different than this....

Bob had actually begun "disappearing" before Jean had noticed. Old age had made it difficult to discern what was past being a part of normal aging. Even in the neurologist's office, it felt okay. Bob and Jean were listening while the neurologist systematically addressed changes in Bob. Jean, glancing over at Bob, thought, "No—he is still Bob." The neurologist had offered hope of some good outcomes from therapy. Still, inside her head, Jean had decided to challenge the prognosis. She would save Bob.

Like many other people, Jean found the role of caregiver exceedingly difficult. Some people find their identity (albeit initially) in the caregiver role; however, Jean felt she lost her identity in this role. She felt she became almost swallowed up by Bob's demands. If Jean rested for a moment on the couch, Bob would demand a drink or something. At such times Jean would hope that Bob would register her tiredness and get it himself: "Bob, why don't you help me, just a bit?" A vague nod was all that was given back. Sometimes Jean, too tired or not feeling well, would get angry: "I'm sick and tired of this. Why don't you at least try." Bob's facial expression and demeanor would suddenly transform him into a small, frightened child. Instantly, Jean would feel guilty: "Bob has Alzheimer's disease. He is so much worse off than me. It is not his fault." Jean would then get off the couch and make Bob a cup of tea.

The potential to become overwhelmed is ever-present in ongoing caring, particularly when one is caring for a person who traditionally gave him or her care. The old patterns of the relationship surface automatically. When the therapist queried, "What about you and your needs?

Who cares for you?" Jean's unrequited need to be loved and looked after became very clear. This need to be loved found Jean searching her memories for people who had in her past provided her with a sense of being loved and cared for. "Strangely, there are moments when I find myself missing my father. He made me feel so special," Jean said. Thus, amid Jean's grief about Bob, her grief about her deceased father returned.

In Jean's case, even the intellectual component of griefwork was compromised. Jean's thoughts were all over the place: "Is Bob okay?" "Will Bob ever be able to return to what he was?" None of this could be termed denial. After a 40-year relationship, it is not difficult to understand the persistence of patterns of acting and thinking. Old patterns of her relationship with Bob, the dynamics of the relationship, were haunting Jean. In a split second Jean would find herself expecting the impossible of Bob, sometimes even blaming him for not recovering. Here, the symbiotic nature of the relationship became a problem: "I realize that he is not well, but he should at least try the exercises—for me, for us," Jean would say.

Although, over time, one could expect that Jean would be forced to habituate to the changes in Bob, the innate resistance to change that parallels griefwork made it more complicated. Jean's ingrained wish was for things to be as they were; in this case, for Bob to recover. Although she had been told of the progression of the disease, in some moments Bob seemed just like the Bob of old. Instinctively, she clung to this. Jean's difficulty in reality testing is demonstrated in her statement: "Today, Bob seemed good. I mean, he actually said things that were about now. He asked how I was, and when he did, his eyes looked at me just as they had when he was okay. In this instant, I absolutely stared at him—trying desperately to capture and fix that image in my mind, hold it, make it permanent. Yes, I did love him and he loved me. There and then I felt I wanted to take him home. In a split second he was off, talking about some incident when he was in his teens. I could make neither hide nor hair of it. He was making no sense. I could not look after him. And in some bizarre way, it was almost as though I wanted him to make no sense. It made it easier to leave. There was not so much pain about leaving."

> "HE WAS MAKING NO SENSE. I COULD NOT LOOK AFTER HIM. AND IN SOME BIZARRE WAY, IT WAS ALMOST AS THOUGH I WANTED HIM TO MAKE NO SENSE. IT MADE IT EASIER TO LEAVE. THERE WAS NOT SO MUCH PAIN ABOUT LEAVING."

With this internal conflict and the break in 40-year-old patterns and routines, it is understandable that Jean was having trouble adjusting. Her system was out of balance. Yearning for Bob, she was being cruelly teased by the versions of self that he could sometimes present. The closer he got to his old self, the greater Jean felt her attachment to him. As a corollary, Jean's need and love for him were then amplified, and she felt a great deal of ambivalence and guilt at placing him in a care facility. Actually, her reality testing was being severely compromised by her needs and wishes.

Ironically, placement in a care facility sometimes alters the dynamics between caregiver and spouse. No longer trapped in the home with relentless demands, the caregiver who is released from this duty ceases to view his or her spouse as a threat to a feeling of well-being. Simultaneously, when the frustrating and ambiguous aspects of being cared for by one's spouse end, the behavior of the person who is cared for alters; no longer is the caregiver regarded as the omnipotent adult who sometimes denies his or her wishes. Thus, just as the spouse is relinquished to care, the relationship can in some part be restored. This sardonic twist is accentuated by the tendency for separation itself to create an idealization of one's partner while also amplifying a sense of guilt in such abandonment.

Jean had come to therapy long before Bob was placed in a home. Immersed in Bob's world, his demands, day by day in their home, Jean found it difficult to isolate any positive factors. In a very real sense, Jean had become trapped in her reality—one in which she had very few transactions with the outside world. The fact was that Jean was in the middle of an extreme threat to her homeostasis. Bob's disease had made redundant a 40-year-old pattern that had aligned with Jean's sense of security. Caregiving had exposed her to things she did not like about herself; parts of this role had actually threatened her self-esteem. Bob brought things out in Jean that she did not like about herself; sometimes she felt ashamed when she deliberately switched off from Bob's repetitive questions. Insight into the enormity of the adaptation required by the changes that Bob's disease necessitated relieved some of Jean's guilt. In therapy it was important that her feelings for Bob, the reality of their shared life together, be preserved. What Jean hated some days was the *disease* that Bob had; Jean's behaviors were an outcome of a person trapped and tired, sometimes frightened of what was happening.

> "I SHOULD NOT FEEL ANGRY OR RESENTFUL. LOOK AT WHAT BOB IS GOING THROUGH."

Jean's idea of the caregiver's role involved a lot of "shoulds": "I should not feel angry or resentful. Look at what Bob is going through." Jean was belittling the extraordinary personal demands and dynamics that were part of her life. To expose the background of her internal conflicts, these demands were examined in therapy, such as the particularly problematic times when Bob kept asking for things and she had to constantly get up. Her feelings required exploration. "How do those times make you feel?" At these times, Jean felt that she was Bob's mother: "I am a bottomless pit for his demands." With no feedback, Jean felt unloved.

Jean began to understand the dominance of the old patterns; her expectation to be loved by Bob was unrealistic and was creating too much havoc. She realized that she had, for a long time, been trying to *call* Bob back using old behavior patterns. When Bob had not responded, she had automatically seen him as selfish. As a corollary, she had felt unloved: "It is ridiculous to expect Bob to make me a cup of tea." Jean and the therapist worked up a list of the ways in which she had tried to call up old versions of Bob. Jean knew that she had to relinquish these behaviors and expectations. In fact, part of Jean had to relinquish her role as wife and become his caregiver. Jean understood that she had to seek some nurturing in order to replenish herself. Membership in self-help groups and social venues were options for companionship.

Trauma and grief were the backdrops to all of Jean's intense emotions. Why did she feel angry, bitter, resentful? The therapist explained the strength of models of "the world that should be." Jean's losses were happening all the time. Without expressing emotions, or working to assimilate some of the changes, there would be a buildup. Jean knew this feeling. "It's like a terrible feeling of helplessness. I feel sort of frightened. I have always dreaded being on my own. My worst fear has been a world without Bob." These shifts in mood found Jean wishing for someone to look after her: "It's too big. I'm not strong enough. What about me, my life? Where does all of this come from? Some days I'm fine." An explanation was required: When one becomes overwhelmed, often one feels helpless. In these situations, an individual easily slips into modes of dependency. In that mode of thinking or being, an individual is more likely to yearn for parent figures.

What could Jean do to armor herself? Jean's thinking was challenged. She was presently surviving her dreaded event—every minute and every day she had made it since Bob's disease had begun. "Well, if you put it like that, I guess I have done better than I expected," said Jean. Hoping to find corroborative strong versions of self in Jean's past, a search was undertaken. Encouraging, strong words and images appeared to stem from her father. Empathy for her feelings of weakness was given in tandem with continual reminders of her strengths. This was reinforced by marking where Jean had come from, what she had mastered so far. She was encouraged to review her progress.

Although Jean's emotional grieving was potentiated or more feasible when Bob went to live in the care facility, strengthening her perception of her ability to survive Bob's "loss" enabled her to acknowledge and express parts of her emotional pain along the way. Jean was able to tolerate facing some of her pain; she was no longer as frightened to put words to her loss. She was advised to write about her life at present, to create a fluid relationship with her feelings and pain. This would reduce the potential for times of buildup when she felt overwhelmed.

Considerations for Therapy

Explaining the dynamics of griefwork is important. It exposed the normality of Jean's internal conflict and reduced her anxiety. A therapist could ask her, "What is your brain trying to do? Look at your attachment to Bob, the life you took for granted, and the routines that have gone awry. It is not surprising that you feel numb, weak in your muscles, teary, unable to sleep. What can be done to support and restore your physical and emotional systems?"

Jean was interested in her survival, if only to ensure that she was able to look after Bob. Routines were devised and a set of weekly services were set into place. A key component was to reduce the emotional aspect of decision making and make decisions nonnegotiable. Another component was to divide Jean's caregiving tasks into goals that she would recognize as achievable. Respite, both short- and long-term, was fixed as part of the routine. In this instance, because respite decisions were taken out of Jean's hands, her guilt could be reduced. Camouflaging the relentlessness of her role as caregiver was vitally important. If an individual senses no punctuation or reprieve in this role, it is an overwhelming burden. The making of plans around respite was organized. (For further insight into issues surrounding family caregivers, the reader is referred to Schultz, C.L., & Schultz, N.C., 1997, 1998; Schultz, N.C., & Schultz, C.L., 1997; and Schultz et al., 1993.)

Amid all of this, when can loss be regarded as irrevocable, so that grieving can proceed? Only over time—through numerous, unmet expectations—would Jean learn that Bob would not be restored. For Jean, the dynamics of the attachment meant it would take a long time before she relinquished her hope that Bob would recover. In the end, it was Jean's ability to use her intellect that allowed her, as she put it, to "abandon her ideals." In therapy, Jean had done a lot of work exposing the images and triggers that led her to be repeatedly disappointed. These stemmed from a version of herself as a caregiver who could be selfless, perfect; and about romantic versions of devoted partners. Building her knowledge of the mixed signals inherent in Bob's condition and how they would collude with her wishes kept Jean on guard. As she became more realistic in her expectations, she became less angry and frustrated with Bob. The relationship, albeit different, was salvaged. Less likely to be persuaded of Bob's recovery, Jean could begin making some sad but necessary plans that would secure her husband's safety should anything adverse happen to her.

It was not until Jean placed Bob into care that she fathomed the depth of her losses. Up until then, Jean had been adamant that she still had Bob: "Bob is not dead. It feels wrong to grieve." After placement, some of this seemed to change. Placement was a marker. Perhaps for the first time the death of who Bob had been was formally acknowledged. There was a sense that placement marked an end. Although it also marked the end of Jean's role as a full-time caregiver, in this release, for Jean, her freedom was at Bob's cost. The pain of Jean's decision meant that its permanence still had to be kept in some psychological abeyance. Whether in the short or long term, however, Jean's pursued ideals were clearly lost. In this loss, Jean had forgone a version of self that had been intricately important. Her grief was deep and extremely painful. In therapy Jean was encouraged to memorialize what she and Bob had endured. She framed pictures and memories. Her attachment to Bob as an integral part of the patterns in her life continued unabated, and on certain occasions she revisited a daydream of having him return home. Over time, the placement drifted into permanency, with Jean sometimes contemplating Bob's possible return. In fact, the contemplations provided a psychological harbor from facing the irrevocability of her loss.

Apart from the multitude of losses that contextualized Bob's disease, there were two crucial ones: the loss of self that had slowly taken place during the course of Bob's illness, and the loss of Bob. Within this, Jean saw the strength she had mounted to endure what had been 2 years of grueling sadness and frustration. Jean had recognized her ability to survive without Bob. The therapist mentioned this to Jean. This was no recompense for what she had lost: "I have lost 2 good years that I should have shared with my husband."

CASE STUDY 7: LORNA AND THE NEED TO LOCATE SELF

Therapeutic Focus: Attending to Generalized Separation Anxiety

The day of Lorna's stroke had marked a significant ending for her. Possibly, she knew instinctively of the seriousness of what had happened and its threat. One day, around morning tea-time, Lorna had sensed a strangeness in herself. She described a fogginess to her thoughts, her surroundings—the kitchen looked dull as though covered in film. It was as though a mist or cloud had descended on her. Her right hand failed to move and her words failed to come out. She could not explain it, she just felt frightened! Lorna had begun the first strange steps into the process of degenerative cognitive disability. The experience can be likened to what it feels like to come out of anesthesia. From what is described, however, in the case of cerebral disease the feeling is more one of a relentless, frighteningly groggy confusion, interspersed with flashes of lucidity.

Amid what she described as "having a permanent cloud" around her, Lorna's learned defenses persisted. When Lorna was approximately 5 years old she had been put into a boarding school. According to Lorna, as she had watched her mother disappear down the path, she had not cried. Again according to Lorna, the manager of the boarding school had remarked: "How marvelous; you are so brave." Similarly, when the neurologist presented her with the proof of the bleeding that had taken place in her brain, Lorna made light of it. Well-worn tracts of words spilled forth: "It will mend itself, I expect." Keeping up an appearance of being fine and not letting herself come face-to-face with fear was one of Lorna's lifelong strategies. Although Lorna's response had sounded naive, the neurologist had let it drop.

Barry, her husband, had a naive belief in the ability to fix things. He believed in the omnipotence of doctors. When the neurologist made a somewhat offhand remark about the possibility that physical therapy might help Lorna improve, Barry heard no more. Latching onto what therapy might achieve, Barry had mounted the program of recovery. A "doing response" allowed him to establish a different relationship with this tragedy. Physiotherapy and social occasions, exercise and playing cards—all shielded what the outcome of this cognitive decline would inevitably hold. Lorna's recovery was Barry's mission. Lorna followed his lead, but without the same conviction; she just wanted to please Barry. This was an old pattern in their relationship, the familiarity of which would act as a temporary guide for Lorna's derailment.

But the changes, some blatant, some obscure, were relentless. Day by day Lorna was learning what she was up against. Lorna's hands would not take instruction, she could no longer write her name. Her bladder was not under control; she had little physiological sense of it. Lorna no longer knew the time. She would find herself dressing at odd hours in the middle of the night: "If I'm right in my thinking, it should be about 7:00 A.M., shouldn't it? "

While attempting to cook, Lorna would find herself unable to hold the instructions in her head; the end product of her cooking would be a concoction as confused as her thoughts. Reading, knitting, previously important pastimes, no longer provided any comfort as Lorna was unable to hold the sequence of either for long enough to succeed at them. She would make fun of herself: "I'm just a stupid person," a defense established far back in her childhood in response to a critical father. For Lorna, her ability to persist in completing things—a mainstay of her relationship with life—was gone. It was only the fogginess that came in and out that dulled the harshness of this reality. Depression was an inevitable outcome of the relentless series of activities that no longer reaped a result. She was put on medication soon thereafter.

Lorna began feeling embarrassed by her confusion; she began to disguise her lack of knowledge. Only to some people would she reveal the extent of her awareness; her pride remained intact at this stage. In and out of the mist, Lorna kept up the appearances for which she had received acclamation as a child.

The changes in Lorna's brain functioning took her to different time frames in her life in an instant. She would find herself transported to homes and times in her past. Her mother and father were there, animals she had had, her brother who had died when Lorna was in her twenties. In between these uncontrollable shifts in time frames of reality, the predominant state for Lorna was one of extreme anxiety—specifically separation anxiety, the fear of being abandoned and helpless. As a result, Lorna would constantly search for Barry. He would provide safety from her fear of being unable to fend for herself. In this extreme state of dependence, Lorna's relationship with Barry was compromised. No longer could she risk his anger and possible abandonment of her. How would she survive if he left her for even an hour? Without the ability to check her own safety and be satisfied of Barry's whereabouts, Lorna was given medication for anxiety.

In her states of clarity, of which there were many, Lorna was aware of her disheveled state. Much of Lorna's relationship with Barry revolved around physical attractiveness. Holding on to the last bastions, Lorna attempted to attend to her appearance, but her psychological state meant that Barry felt claustrophobic. Predominantly, Barry's feelings for her were a mixture of frustration and weariness. Over time, these feelings led him to seek increasing distance from Lorna—for his own survival. Sensing Barry's need for separation, Lorna's own separation anxiety heightened. Amid this insecurity, Lorna could find secure versions of her self in the past. Returning to the dependency of a child, Lorna sought unconditional love. This anxiety diminished when Lorna became lost in old photographs of herself, her mother, and her father. The photographs, a large part of therapy with Lorna, reminded her of who she was, her value to others, and her self-esteem. They helped her to locate a valuable version of herself.

Anxiety, fear, and damage to ego are key features of any disability. Without the establishment of a strong feeling of familiarity to surround and support oneself with, anxiety and fear amplify ego deficits. Lorna required the creation of an environment that would provide a high level of familiarity. In turn, familiarity would foster safety and provide the best

possible chance for her ego to be strengthened. It would mask her inabili-
ties. Unfortunately, this was terribly difficult because optimally, it was up
to Barry to create much of that familiarity. It was a tall order for Barry to
provide predictable, nonthreatening responses and behaviors to Lorna
and to live by a set of tight routines. Barry was advised to surround Lorna
with tools that would make her feel safe. Precoded telephone numbers,
personalized emergency buttons, regularly scheduled visits from caregivers and visitors all guaranteed that Lorna was surrounded by human
contact. If Lorna's fear of abandonment could be reduced and the environment generally seen to be safe, Lorna's physiological system should
theoretically go off alert.

Although the creation of this background might somewhat dull
Lorna's anxiety levels, her ego required further protection. Given her de-
teriorating condition, what activities were feasible for her? The selection
of tasks that Lorna could realisti-
cally achieve required interviews
with friends and family members.
These significant people in her life
could provide clues as to how her
past interests could be woven into
the present. Essentially, the therapist looked to find anything that
could occupy Lorna and give her a
feeling that she could "do" things.

"HE WAS A NICE-ENOUGH GUY, BUT
WHAT HE WAS ACTUALLY SAYING,
WELL I DIDN'T ASK QUESTIONS. TO
TELL YOU THE TRUTH, I DIDN'T
WANT TO HEAR ANY MORE."

Like many women from her era, fastidiousness related to housework,
specifically cleaning, stood out among others.

It was apparent that much of what Lorna did made no sense to her
but rather, was just what she "found herself doing." She would clean a
tray of silverware, fiddle for ages with the untangling of a ball of wool,
pick up threads from the carpet, pull dead leaves or spent blooms off pot-
ted plants, and methodically fold a paper bag or napkin into squares, over
and over. Barry was urged to encourage these activities because they
would occupy Lorna, divert her attention from him, and give her a sense
of completion.

A central problem was that Barry, similar to Jean in the previous case
study, really did not intellectually grasp what had happened to Lorna.
Speaking of the neurologist, Barry reflected, "He was a nice-enough guy,
but what he was actually saying, well I didn't ask questions. To tell you
the truth, I didn't want to hear any more." The neurologist's report to
them both had been far too traumatic. Barry had not been able to fathom
how it would actually translate into home life with Lorna. In many respects, Barry's lack of fundamental knowledge made him much less patient with Lorna's inability to do tasks. Often, he felt that she was not

really trying, that she actually could do more. Why Lorna would be in the present one moment and in the next, be mumbling about her past, was incomprehensible to Barry. To avoid further deterioration of the relationship and Lorna's sense of security, Barry needed to be educated quickly about what Lorna could feasibly manage. First, Barry needed to understand the facts surrounding what was happening in those moments. He needed to know enough to help him understand, but not so much that he was flooded with information.

Toward this goal, Barry was taught skills to manage Lorna's ego. He began giving her feedback that respected her cognitive disability. Barry also began respecting the different time frames that Lorna found herself in. When she returned to talking about her mother and father, long-since dead, Barry would no longer remind her of their death. Instead, he allowed her reality to exist uncriticized. Wandering with her into her thoughts, instead of focusing on the anxiety and fear that permeated the present, Barry found some time in which he could see the old Lorna. Laughing together about a shared memory, their relationship was momentarily reconnected and affirmed.

Although Lorna's emotions clearly were tangible, talking about them was terribly difficult. In an instant her mind could be captured by a noise outside the window or a piece of plastic on the floor; her mind would be elsewhere. Lorna had well-used distracting techniques and offhand comments that would shift attention away from her feelings. A gentle inquiry regarding whether she would like to talk about what had happened to her was met with well-worn, familiar phrases: "What would I want to do that for? I'm all right." That and the recurrent use of sayings that had served as anxiety relievers throughout her life predominated: "I expect things will get better; they have in the past!" These phrases, almost just a group of reflex statements, masked somewhat the enormity of Lorna's emotional and physical world. Irrespective of the veracity of these patterned responses, all of these defenses seemed to create a calming effect on Lorna.

Lorna's cognitive abilities continued to decline, and she was soon moved into a nursing home. Despite her dementia having progressed to a stage in which she seldom clearly knew that she was actually residing in a nursing home, the patterns of her attachment to Barry prevailed in her dementia and Lorna spent the days and nights searching for Barry. The anxiety created by this strange environment and the loss of her protector and attachment figure was of such intensity that sedatives were prescribed. The therapist worked with Barry to enhance Lorna's perception that she was at home.

As Lorna was at the point in which her losses could be camouflaged, associations of home and safety could easily be created. Barry was advised to shift significant bits of furniture into her nursing-home room.

Eventually, according to Lorna, the kitchen was in the next room. Guests were told to "let themselves in" and her cat, actually a stuffed animal, was beside her. To relieve Lorna's anxiety even more, the therapist recommended the use of audiotapes and videotapes (Woods & Ashley, 1995) in which familiar people would talk to her. A reminder board with messages such as "Back in 5 minutes" accentuated the idea that Lorna was being circled by her family and friends. "Everyone is safe" was another message that reassured Lorna of the safety of the people she needed to protect her.

Lorna expressed pockets of sadness, hopelessness, and anger. In flashes, she would suddenly refuse to respond to pleasantries made by the staff. She would speak of "the silly state of her mind" and how she was not able to say what she wanted. Now and then she would comment almost robotically, "How would you like being like this?" On some days, Lorna relived earlier experiences of intense sadness or fear: "They were trying to tie me down last night." Here, she was referring to the nurses, but it was clear that it was primarily an association in her mind with early childhood experience in a boarding school. Neither instance could be disentangled from the other.

On some occasions, when she felt in need of comfort, Lorna would make immediate reference to her mother: "Where's my mom? She should be here by now. We were just together." Taking advantage of Lorna's perception that her mother was nearby, a therapist was able to lend some comfort by replying: "Well, she will be here soon." Fuelled by this knowledge, Lorna's anxiety was visibly diminished, although it may have been only for a short period of time. The therapist took the opportunity to educate the nursing staff to accept and respect that Lorna lived in a series of parallel realities, many of which could be used to help her. The staff did not need to remind her that her parents were dead, the therapist advised them. Reminders of her parents, trinkets and photos, would result in a diminishing of anxiety and support Lorna through this period of her life.

Strangely enough, even in this nursing-home environment, before her further decline, Lorna was still able to make social comparisons that allowed her to view herself as coping better than others. She would remark on another resident, Kevin, who had the same cognitive disability: "He is doing much worse than me. I am doing well!" In these comparisons there was some positive feedback for Lorna. The therapist used the comparison to reassure Lorna that the extreme difficulty of what she faced was not going unnoticed: "You are managing to pull off a remarkable task, Lorna. Many people could not have done it." By doing so the therapist had paid deference to an important version of Lorna's self: her ability to cope well in adversity. The magnitude of the task had been legitimized, as well.

Considerations for Therapy

As Lorna's cognitive ability continued its decline, it became possible to surround her with her friends. Her memory allowed them to be there even when they were not. The therapist prompted Barry and his family to keep reminding Lorna that she was loved and remembered: "Beryl said to send her love. She will drop in on you today. She is really fond of you."

Given the lack of control she had over her thoughts, could Lorna grieve for what had happened to her? Theoretically, because of Lorna's inability to direct her thoughts or capture a single true and present reality, reality testing was impossible. Through her uncontrolled memory sequences, a multiplicity of "realities" was available to her. In this case, the intellectual component and thus the emotional component of griefwork could not take place. This is evident in the continuing separation anxiety that dominated her early days in the nursing home.

Barry died 6 months after Lorna had entered the nursing home. She was told that he had died; however, in an instant, Barry's death was lost in the death of her father 15 years earlier—and then that was gone. A valentine card from Barry declaring his love for her was positioned on the notice-board and some of his clothes were moved into her room. The information about Barry did not stay with Lorna: "Where's Barry?" she would ask. "I was just lying on the bed with him."

As time passed, however, Lorna's mind arrived at memories that would evoke Barry. In this case, the emotional sequelae that originally engendered separation anxiety surrounding her protector, Barry, had now diminished. That is, as her mind landed on an episode of when she was with Barry, her yearning could be subdued by a memory or a shared moment with another gentleman resident. It is interesting to note that Lorna's physiological state, although adapting slowly to her changed conditions, varied in relation to the place in her memory in which she found herself. For example, Lorna could be extremely agitated during the late afternoon. For 30 years, this was the time when Barry usually returned from work. Only a year after the original stroke, however, Lorna could be enticed into thinking of her mother at this time, which simultaneously brought her physiological state into balance.

Throughout her therapy, attention focused on two aspects. First, there was the likelihood that she would have constant separation anxiety. This was not just to do with the loss of her protector, but a review of her biography and developmental patterns indicated this separation anxiety would be accentuated by her boarding-school experience. Lorna's sense of safety needed to be secured. As she was easily distracted, a range of triggers, pictures, trinkets, and objects were strategically placed in her room. All had the potential to return her instantly to more secure time frames associated with feelings of safety and love.

Second, there were patterns in Lorna's developmental background that would assist in assuaging some of her anxiety. What Lorna historically had done to respond to situations of personal adversity in her past and the coping strategies she had internalized were identified. They played a central role in Lorna's ability to manage the anxiety that surrounded her situation and supported her ego. At the end, the importance of these patterns diminished. Lying in bed all day, with no demands to face threatening social interactions, Lorna found an emotional sanctuary. This sanctuary held only memories of safety and caring and exerted no pressure on Lorna to respond to others.

CASE STUDY 8: JASON AND THE NEED TO STOP BEING "CHEERED UP"

Therapeutic Focus: Attending to the Need to Legitimize a Feeling of Having Lost Something

"Black, black, black—that is the color inside me. But I just don't get it, why now? I have never felt like this, been like this before. I didn't feel it coming. All of a sudden everything was black." Jason, the speaker of these words, could best be described as having a nondescript appearance. Unlike most 16-year-olds who showed up for therapy in clothes selected to make a statement (specially placed earrings, T-shirts), Jason's clothes might have adorned a middle-age man going off to a golf game—no strong statements. In fact the only thing individualistic about him was his wheelchair.

Jason had cerebral palsy. His muscular strength and physical abilities were limited to his upper torso. He was intelligent and articulate. At an age when most individuals ponder their potential, however, Jason predominantly reflected on his lack thereof. The most disconcerting and threatening aspect of Jason when he came to therapy was his lack of drive. Jason was confined by a perceived lack of potential in his life. He had come to a full stop at 16 years of age.

Leaning his head back, staring at the roof, Jason began: "I hate my body. I hate being me, being dependent on my folks. There's no privacy. When it's not my folks I have this aide at school; he even takes me to the toilet. I don't even like him. I don't trust him but I have him helping me with this part of me. I can't hide anything without my family finding it. I have no friends. At least, I mean I don't know if they are really my friends—do they like me, or just feel sorry for me? I do favors for the ones who help me. It's sort of to thank them but I guess I'm buying their friendship. I'm afraid they'll get fed up with me, sick of me and my wheelchair and then they'll stop helping me. I can't tell my friends how I feel. I mean, they consider not being picked for the swimming squad as worth dying about. I begin to tell them that I'm sick of it—they tell me to 'get over it.'" This response by Jason's friends seemed incredible: "To get over this! Like I would, like I actually could, just get over it. They have no idea. I'd like to see them live my life, just do this for a day!" Jason could not "just get over it," and his friends, as far as he was concerned, were demanding some justification for a depression that had now taken up the larger part of a year.

In fact, as one of only five adolescents with disabilities at his school, Jason was coming face to face with how "different" he was. The isolation was staring him in the face. Not only could he not do what his friends could do, but a more frightening demarcation line had become patently clear. His peers were, according to Jason, seemingly oblivious to the "blackness" in him. He and his friends did not speak the same thoughts or have the same feelings. The outcome was that Jason was left with a dark feeling that he could not share. In fact, when Jason even touched on this blackness, his friends tried to cheer him out of it. Most likely they were daunted by Jason's life. According to Jason, there was and has always been a deceit in that cheering up. For once, he could not be diverted away from his thoughts and feelings. Jason deciphered this almost protective stance by his friends as dismissing what "he was about."

> "I CAN'T TELL MY FRIENDS HOW I FEEL. I MEAN, THEY CONSIDER NOT BEING PICKED FOR THE SWIMMING SQUAD AS WORTH DYING ABOUT. I BEGIN TO TELL THEM THAT I'M SICK OF IT—THEY TELL ME TO 'GET OVER IT.'"

Not wanting to come face to face with "it," Jason's disability had never become easy to talk about. Throughout his life, he had been cheered up or talked out of most of his feelings: "I don't tell my mom or my dad about my feelings. Never have. I don't want to lay this on them. If I even started to, my mom always looked upset. They've had enough, enough of looking after me!" The feelings had been there, but when he was young, he could not name them. In adolescence, instead of beginning to name them, he had tried to protect his parents from what he sensed as a bottomless pit of emotions. About to launch into his feelings, he would watch his parents' faces and would stop before he started. It was threatening to see his parents dissolve into anguish or anger. Left inside, the feelings gathered momentum. Jason had not *learned* that he could have a relationship with his pain, that he could legitimately express it and the world would not cave in, and that he and his parents would survive.

At this stage in his life, Jason clearly identified that he was no longer "one of them." Accompanying this insight, Jason wondered whether, in fact, he was ever one of them. He was in the midst of an identity crisis. Searching not only for who he is, he had also begun reviewing who he was. In this review, he had become frightened of who he may be. He announced, "I *am* one of them—the people in wheelchairs—the very people whom my friends and even my brother make fun of. When they have been mocking them, they have been talking about me. I can't believe that they don't catch on that they are offending me."

Again this is incredible to Jason; he felt that all along he had been living a delusion: "I never saw myself as one of them, but now when my friends say bad things about them, they're really talking about me. Before, just a year or so ago—sometimes I actually would join in." Feeling like an outcast from his familiar group of friends, and fearing the "them" who he has now just strongly connected with for perhaps the first time in his life, Jason saw clearly the two worlds. He was swinging between them.

As dimensions of reality opened up for Jason, individuals were becoming increasingly difficult to trust. In this stage of development, he had become aware of the nuances of adult behavior. All was not what it had seemed. In childhood, the outward appearance of adults *was* what they were. If the teacher smiled kindly, the teacher was kind; if the teacher got angry, the teacher was mean. In adolescence, finding out that people may actually *play* a role becomes clear. Jason had become privy to the idea of platitudes, that some statements may be insincere. What is said *to* you may not be said later *about* you.

Because Jason often had been relegated to sit with teachers, he had in fact been privy to their other opinions. In particular, Jason had listened to what teachers said about their students in the lunchroom. He had sensed insincerity and had begun contemplating whether their remarks to him were along the same lines. Did they just say those things to him because they felt sorry for him? This was a crucially important issue to address, for Jason needed to trust people; he needed them to help with his daily physical tasks.

During adolescence, the veil on the more simplistic thinking that is characteristic of earlier stages of development is lifted. For some individuals such as Jason it comes as a rude shock. Not only had he started to question his naive acceptance of adults, but Jason perceived he had become who his friends had disparaged in the past. On these grounds, who was to be trusted and who were really his friends? He would ask himself, "What do they think about me? Do they just feel sorry for me?"

Unfortunately, while Jason's cognitive development had allowed this view to become available, his models of disability were all negative.

In effect, Jason had begun to reject himself. The stage of adolescence marked a time when identity issues were paramount. For children with physical disabilities it represents something of a watershed. Whereas throughout childhood, Jason had incrementally absorbed the limitations his disability had made on his life, now as he faced this stage of development it is as if this absorption was no longer cushioned. Jason looked his disability squarely in the face. As he felt an increasing urge to separate from his parents, he contemplated the notions of loneliness and of being unprotected. Prior cognitive abilities of earlier stages of development never actually allowed this contemplation before, and it was painful and scary for Jason. "Who would love me?" he asked himself. He could not imagine being loved or admired by others.

At the same time, as he mentioned in therapy, his innate need for privacy and independence was directly sabotaged by his disability. Jason could not secure psychological or physical independence from his parents. For instance, he could not angrily reject his parents; what if they were to fight? Jason still needed them for very basic needs; he even needed them to help him shower. Jason could not even storm off angrily. In fact, what emerged was a short-circuiting of his identity development. Obviously, in this case, Jason had become sensitive to any behaviors that further demeaned his adulthood. What were well-meaning efforts to help before now became further threats to his emerging adult identity. A teacher leaned down to straighten his collar. Jason angrily shoved his arm away: "Get off me!" The teacher had offended Jason's boundaries, accentuated his helplessness, and diminished his ability to feel like an adult.

In retrospect, the creation of Jason's perception of disability needed to be merged and integrated into his view of the world and himself from day one. Disability needed to be framed in ways that would not represent such a threat to Jason during his adolescence. Instead, he had learned just the opposite. Essentially he had been "conditioned" to think otherwise. He did not admire people with disabilities and subsequently he did not admire himself. Such potential role models, say, individuals who had become airline pilots despite their paraplegia, were like a race apart from Jason. Rather than creating possibilities, these models only further served to exemplify the ingredients that Jason could not find in himself. They were the exception: "I'm not like them."

Therapy focused on reframing Jason's view of self. The creation of a self that was to be respected and admired, rather than feared, was crucial. Broadening and balancing Jason's perception of disability by introducing people, stories, and biographies bit by bit would begin some of this work. This was extremely difficult as he had not been allowed to cultivate dreams about who he might be—he was defined in relation to his limitations. His parents, worried that their son would experience a series of disappointments if he entertained what they saw as unrealistic dreams, had kept pulling his dreams into line: "You couldn't possibly do that!" Now Jason saw these words as the ultimate truth of the matter. They had become realized threats. In some respects, Jason was now battling with the fact that what his parents had said might be true.

The effect of cutting off potential was to cut off the buoyancy that dreams offer in development. Jason, rather than experimenting with the world, tasting samples of what the world may offer him, lived his limitations. In the meantime he had become frightened of sharing dreams about his world. If he did they immediately became too fragile. What others might say, or how they might react, was too great a risk.

Therapy looked toward the cultivation of Jason's dreams, personalizing and recognizing what was unique in him that was not solely about being in a wheelchair. Like many individuals who have experienced isolation from others, one of Jason's passions was to write to the world, to help others who might experience his reality. He could be reminded of certain professions that could be extrapolated from this area of interest, such as lawyers and politicians. Separating this young man out from his disability, from the "them" that he identified as a disparaging identification, and his parents' need to protect him, required an effort to clearly demarcate and make solid a different version of Jason. In talking about the fears of his parents, he could begin to realize that he had absorbed much of their fear. Discussing with the therapist how little his parents had actually known about the intricacies of his world was useful, as it exposed their fears as basically irrelevant; they had not lived his reality. All these discussions helped to demarcate a separation point from his parents and set the foundation for an adult version of self.

For Jason, who felt limited by his wheelchair, there had been very few opportunities for rituals that represented separation and evolving adulthood. Because adults tended to "help" him, he could not distinguish and mark his adult boundaries. Jason and his therapist began to talk about communication and assertiveness techniques that would allow him to teach others about his adulthood. He slowly began entertaining the idea that he could educate others about how he wished to be helped as an adult. This was directed toward helping him establish some control and opening the possibility for him to recognize an evolving sense of self that might offer potential for his future. There were childhood traps in his thinking that could, if changed, open up some form of freedom.

Paralleling and integral to this therapeutic work was giving Jason continuing permission to grieve. Although adolescence is a stage that involves the grieving of childhood, the relationships, and the world characterized by naiveté, for Jason, coming out of this naive state introduced a huge challenge in terms of his view of himself. Jason's emotional world had largely been suffocated by his parents, siblings, and friends. Feeling the need to protect Jason from the blackness, instead of allowing him to express his feelings at length and as often as he wanted to to parents, siblings, and friends had distracted him by making light of it.

Separating Jason from this suffocation took time. On first meeting him, it was agreed that the emotional spot that he found himself in needed to be respected. Now these feelings were to be legitimized. For the first time in his 16 years, Jason actually was grieving, not just feeling sad, but endeavoring to make sense of his feelings and who he was. Therapy gave him permission to tell it how it had been: the operations, the kids who had bullied him, the stares, the places he could not go, the walking he would like to try. The act of enhancing the respect for his loss revealed the possibility of some ritual specific to what Jason the child had endured. This would increase the legitimization and deference to what he had gone through, and it would also be extremely useful in amplifying a stronger sense of self—one not about being in a wheelchair.

According to Jason, not only had there been deceit in such cheering up, he had tried to deceive himself. Focusing exclusively on his physical development, Jason's emotional world had been side-stepped. What he was going through, really, at school had not been talked about in terms of its overwhelming nature; no strategies had ever been discussed. It had always been about his intellect, and his therapy. As though "it" (i.e., the disability) wasn't there, Jason, too, learned to cut this side of himself off. Thus, for Jason, revealing his emotional world was personally threatening. He had never road-tested his ability to express strong emotions.

In therapy, he shared his innermost dreams: "I often think how it might have been. I find myself fantasizing what it might have been like to walk. You know, I can't even imagine it. Sometimes my mind wanders to cures." Jason quickly added: "To which I know there are none!" Once again, it was clear that Jason had never dared to talk about this; his parents would cut him off. The central place that dreams and wishes play is often seen as threats to an individual's acceptance. This is particularly so in the case of disability.

The therapist looked for opportunities to suggest certain of Jason's characteristics that distinguished him from people with and without disability—challenges about who he might become. How would all of Jason's childhood experiences come together? Gentle suggestions, simple comments, and questions served as bait that would allow him to extricate some firm ground for a future. Carefully placed, these suggestions and feedback provided a place for Jason to reach. Optimally, because he might realize that there was a place for him in the future, Jason would not be as frightened to grieve as he had been previously. That is, Jason could continue to express his grief *because* there was someone or something after that grief. This capability might be usefully equated with an intuition that Jason needed, that he would survive if he plumbed the depths of his feelings of loss.

Integral to Jason's therapy here was the facilitating and co-creating of a strong adult self in whom Jason might have confidence. The therapist helped him see that he had already been strong. Yet the placement of these words must not ring of cheering up. Jason needed to discern for himself that they were valid and that these words were not platitudes. Observing his body language, the therapist could discern that Jason had come to fear that all adults spoke in platitudes. Jason weighed and slowly digested every comment the therapist made and threw some of it out that was not considered valid. It was important that if Jason was to continue respecting the therapist, then the depth of his experience and the realness of his disability needed to be continually acknowledged. Here, words had to be carefully chosen.

As mentioned previously, Jason began venting his hate for his body, the limitations it had set on his life: "I have been robbed," he protested. Allowing this process to proceed to its fruition was crucial. In the quest to touch some of his emotional pain, Jason employed strong, painful images; symbols; and emotionally laden, wrenching words. Each time the therapist used less emotionally wrenching words, Jason corrected and replaced them with his words. At the same time, it was equally crucial to manage the emotional outpouring so that Jason could perceive that he might survive the hate he was unloading on his body. Carefully, nearing the close of each session, seeds of survival and Jason's attributes were planted, not to replace or dismiss the grief but to provide a suggestion that there was a road out of it. During therapy, certain attributes that Jason could call his own were agreed on: characteristics such as resilience, patience, intuitional intellect, and emotional intelligence.

Against this background, some careful work was done with Jason's fear of rejection. He was challenged to critically examine and broaden the notion of rejection—what it meant about other people: Were people rejecting him, or were they rejecting the difficulties they felt inadequate to handle? If the latter was true, then educating the people in question might be beneficial.

Working with Jason, or any person with extensive disabilities, is extremely challenging. Jason had not been encouraged to mold his own dreams. A severe and limiting psychological context had prevented him from creating a unique identity. The well-meaning advice of his parents had been threaded into his life like a fear: Why bother to try, to dream, to aspire; there were no options.

This context had been further amplified by an understandably enmeshed relationship between Jason and his parents. One outcome was that Jason resisted learning new skills that might create greater independence. Instead, he routinely avoided any new opportunities. The idea of increasing skill bases had become something that he feared—symbolic of letting go of the world as he knew it and having to trust himself and other adults. Perhaps Jason felt that his parents would no longer be there if he gave up this connection with them.

The situation was more complex than that, however. Jason was still trying to communicate the depth of his emotional pain and respect his personal grief. According to this young man, if he returned to learning new skills, others would interpret that everything was now okay—just like his school friends wanted it to be. If the depression was short-lived, then as far as the world was concerned, the pain he felt was minimal and eminently able to go away. The black hole had not been adequately represented to his parents and friends. "If I started going out, they [parents and others] would think it was gone, that these feelings were gone. That I had gotten over it. But it can't just be gotten over!"

In summary, Jason's therapy revolved around the concept of a black hole. To help him deal with this, respect was mounted for its continuing place in his life; it would never, in fact, be adequately expressed. Jason came to understand that he did not have to accept what had happened to him—he just needed to continue to adapt to it. Talking about this in therapy, he agreed that what had happened to him was indeed unacceptable. He reached a conclusion that to educate his friends about his world was impossible; they would never understand until something like this happened to them.

Considerations for Therapy

For Jason, adolescence had presented a stark reality; he had become fearful of who he was and what that meant for his future. In evaluating his self and his world, he felt intense grief. In between tasks of therapy aimed at building some firm ground for his future, Jason's story was reviewed again and again. Using what words and imagery he could from all vantage points, he described the pictures of his life. He was given permission to understand his grief and to respect this time in his life. Several parallel processes were being woven throughout therapy: the creation of a sense of a safe world that he could trust; a sense that his friends were, as far as they were capable given their experiences, real friends; and a more independent version of self. The mastering of psychological techniques to deal with his personal grief throughout his life will be an ongoing challenge for Jason.

IN CONCLUSION

In developing, describing, and advocating therapy that directs attention
to traumatic loss and continuing grief, the extreme suffering that surrounds all personal adversity remains foremost in our minds. It is
paramount that our readers remain fully aware of the difficulties involved
in the undertaking of many of the psychoeducational tasks outlined in this
book. For many individuals, these tasks may prove too great and too
soon. Nevertheless, to borrow the words of William Shakespeare, the
most central and consistent therapeutic task to be accomplished in grieving nonfinite loss is to

"GIVE SORROW WORDS; THE GRIEF

THAT DOES NOT SPEAK

KNITS UP THE OVERWROUGHT

HEART AND BIDS IT BREAK."

—WILLIAM SHAKESPEARE,

MACBETH, ACT IV, SCENE 3,

LINE 209; AS CITED IN CRAIG,

1943, P. 865

REFERENCES

Ainsworth, M.D. (1969). Object relations, dependency and attachment: A theo-
retical review of the infant-mother relationship. *Child Development, 40,*
969–1025.
Alford, B.A., & Beck., A.T. (1997). *The integrative power of cognitive therapy.* New
York: Guilford Press.
American Psychiatric Association. (1994). *Diagnostic and statistical manual of mental
disorders* (4th ed.). Washington, DC: Author.
Averill, J.R. (1968). Grief: Its nature and significance. *Psychological Bulletin, 70,*
721–748.
Bandura, A. (1983). Self-efficacy determinants of anticipated fears and calamities.
Journal of Personal and Social Psychology, 45, 464–469.
Becker, E. (1962). Towards a comprehensive theory of depression: A cross disci-
plinary appraisal of objects, games and meaning. *Journal of Nervous and Mental
Disorders, 135,* 26–35.
Becker, E. (1973). *The denial of death.* New York: The Free Press.
Berger, P.L., & Luckmann, T. (1966). *The social construction of reality.* London:
Penguin Press.
Bloom-Feschbach, J., & Bloom-Feschbach, S. (1987). *The psychology of separation
and loss.* San Francisco: Jossey-Bass.
Blum, D. (1998, May/June). Finding strength. How to overcome anything.
Psychology Today, 32–38, 69–72.
Bowlby, J. (1960). Grief and mourning in infancy and early childhood. In R.S.
Eissler et al. (Eds.), *The psychoanalytic study of the child: Vol. XV.* Madison, CT:
International Universities Press.
Bowlby, J. (1961). Processes of mourning. *The International Journal of Psycho-
analysis, XLII,* 317–340.
Bowlby, J. (1973). *Separation: Anxiety and anger. Vol. 2: Attachment and loss.*
London: Penguin Press.
Bowlby, J. (1977). The making and breaking of affectional bonds. *British Journal
of Psychiatry, 130,* 201–210.
Bowlby, J. (1980). *Loss: Sadness and depression. Vol. 3: Attachment and loss.* London:
Penguin Press.
Bowlby, J. (1988). *A secure base: Clinical application of attachment theory.* London:
Routledge.
Breur, J., & Freud, S. (1955). Studies on hysteria. In *The standard edition of the
complete works of Sigmund Freud:* Vol. II. London: Hogarth Press
Bruce, E.J. (1994). *A longitudinal investigation of loss and grief for mothers and fathers
of children with intellectual disability.* Unpublished doctoral dissertation,
LaTrobe University, Melbourne, Victoria, Australia.
Bruce, E.J., & Schultz, C.L. (1992). Complicated loss: Considerations in coun-
selling the parents of a child with an intellectual disability. *The Australian
Counselling Psychologist, 8,* 8–20.
Bruce, E.J., & Schultz, C.L. (1994). A cross-sectional study of parenting percep-
tions: Caring for children with intellectual disability. *Australian Journal of
Marriage & Family, 15,* 56–65.

Bruce, E.J., Schultz, C.L., Smyrnios, K.X., & Schultz, N.C. (1993). Discrepancy and loss in parenting: A comparative study of mothers and fathers of children with and without intellectual disability. *Children Australia, 18,* 18–24.

Bruce, E.J., Schultz, C.L., Smyrnios, K.X., & Schultz, N.C. (1994). Grieving related to development: A preliminary comparison of three age cohorts of parents of children with intellectual disability. *British Journal of Medical Psychology, 67,* 37–52.

Bruce, E.J., Schultz, C.L., & Smyrnios, K.X. (1996). A longitudinal study of the grief of mothers and fathers of children with an intellectual disability. *British Journal of Medical Psychology, 69,* 33–45.

Bruce, E.J., & Shears, B. (2000). *Early intervention for mothers of children with chronic disability or illness: A pilot program focusing on parental trauma and grief and its implications for parent–child relationships.* Manuscript submitted for publication.

Canetti, E. (1973). *Crowds and power.* London: Penguin Press.

Cantril, H. (1950). *The "why" of man's experience.* New York: Macmillan.

Cheston, R. (1998). Psychotherapeutic work with people with dementia: A review of the literature. *British Journal of Medical Psychology, 71,* 211–231.

Clayton, P., Desmaris, L., & Winokur, G. (1968). A study of normal bereavement. *American Journal of Psychiatry, 125,* 168–177.

Collins, M.S. (1982). Parental reactions to a visually handicapped child: A mourning process. *Dissertation Abstracts International, 43*(3–B), 867.

Condon, J.T. (1986). Psychological disability in women who relinquish a baby for adoption. *The Medical Journal of Australia, 144,* 117–119.

Cooley, C.H. (1902). *Human nature and the social order.* New York: Scribner.

Crittenden, P.M. (1995). Attachment and psychopathology. In S. Goldberg, R. Muir, & J. Kerr (Eds.), *Attachment theory: Social, developmental, and clinical perspectives* (pp. 370–392). Hillsdale, NJ: The Analytic Press.

Crosby, F.J. (1982). *Relative deprivation and working women.* New York: Oxford University Press.

Davis, F. (1963). Uncertainty in medical prognosis, clinical and functional. *American Journal of Sociology, 66,* 41–47.

Deutsch, H. (1937). Absence of grief. *Psychoanalytic Quarterly, 6,* 12–22.

Deykin, E.Y., Campbell, L., & Patti, P. (1984). The postadoption experience of surrendering parents. *American Journal of Orthopsychiatry, 54,* 271–280.

Dietrich, D.R. (1989). Early childhood parent death, psychic trauma and organization, and object relations. In D.R. Dietrich & P.C. Shabad (Eds.), *The problem of loss and mourning. Psychoanalytic perspectives* (pp. 277–336). Madison, CT: International Universities Press.

Doka, K.J. (Ed.). (1989). *Disenfranchsied grief.* Lanham, MD: Lexington Books.

Elliott, T.R., Witty, T.E., Herrick, S., & Hoffman, J.T. (1991). Negotiating reality after physical loss: Hope, depression, and disability. *American Journal of Personality and Social Psychology, 61,* 608–613.

Engel, G.L. (1961). Is grief a disease? A challenge for medical research. *Psychosomatic Medicine, 23,* 18–22.

Erikson, E. (1965). *Childhood and society* (Rev. ed.). London: Paladin.

Fenichel, O. (1946). *The psychoanalytic theory of neurosis.* London: Routledge & Kegan Paul.

Fiske, S.T., & Taylor, S.E. (1984). *Social cognition.* Reading, MA: Addison Wesley.

Fitzgerald, R.G. (1970). Reactions to blindness: An exploratory study of adults with recent loss of sight. *Archives of General Psychiatry, 22,* 370–379.

Flavell, J.H., Miller, P.H., & Miller, S.A. (1993). *Cognitive development.* Upper Saddle River, NJ: Prentice Hall.

Freud, A. (1960). Discussion of Dr. John Bowlby's paper. *The Psychoanalytic Study of the Child, 15,* 53–62.

Freud, S. (1917). Mourning and melancholia. In *Sigmund Freud: Collected papers (Vol. 4).* New York: Basic Books.

Fried, M. (1963). Grieving for a lost home. In L.J. Duhl (Ed.); *The urban condition, People and policy in the metropolis* (pp. 151–170). New York: Basic Books.

Ganiban, J., Barnett, D., & Cicchetti, D. (2000). Negative reactivity and attachment: Down syndrome's contribution to the attachment–temperament debate. *Development and Psychopathology, 12,* 1–21.

Gloor, P. (1992). Role of the amygdala in temporal lobe epilepsy. In J. Aggleton (Ed.), *The amygdala: Neurobiological aspects of emotion, memory and mental dysfunction.* New York: Wiley-Liss.

Goffman, E. (1959). *The presentation of self in everyday life.* London: Penguin Press.

Goffman, E. (1963). *Stigma: Notes on the management of spoiled identity.* London: Penguin Press.

Grayson, H. (1970). Grief reactions to the relinquishment of unfulfilled wishes. *American Journal of Psychotherapy, 24,* 287–295.

Grollman, E.A. (1967). *Explaining death to children.* Boston: Beacon Press.

Grotberg, E.H. (1999). *Tapping your inner strength.* Oakland, CA: New Harbinger.

Groveman, A.M., & Brown, E.W. (1985). Family therapy with closed-head injured patients: Utilizing Kübler-Ross's model. *Family Systems Medicine, 3,* 440–446.

Guidano, V.F., & Liotti, G. (1983). *Cognitive processes and emotional disorders.* New York: Guilford Press.

Haan, N. (1977). *Coping and defending.* New York: Academic Press.

Harris, J.E. (1998). *How the brain talks to itself: A clinical primer of psychotherapeutic neuroscience.* Binghamton, NY: The Haworth Press.

Harris, P.L. (1989). *Children and emotion.* Oxford: Blackwell.

Harter, S., Bresnick, S., Bouchey, H.A., & Whitesell, N.R. (1997). The development of multiple role-related selves during adolescence. *Development and Psychopathology, 9,* 835–853.

Herman, J.L. (1992). *Trauma and recovery.* New York: Basic Books.

Hofer, M.F. (1995). Hidden regulators. Implications for a new understanding of attachment, separation, and loss. In S. Goldberg, R. Muir, & J. Kerr (Eds.), *Attachment theory. Social, developmental and clinical perspectives* (pp. 203–232). Hillsdale, NJ: The Analytic Press.

Horowitz, M.J. (1983). Psychological response to serious life events. In S. Breznitze (Ed.), *The denial of stress* (pp. 129–159). Madison, CT: International Universities Press.

Horowitz, M.J. (1986). *Stress response syndromes* (2nd ed.). Leonia, NJ: Jason Aronson Publishers.

Horowitz, M.J. (1988). *Introduction to psychodynamics: A new synthesis.* New York: Basic Books.

Horowitz, M.J. (1990). A model of mourning: Change in schemas of self and other. *Journal of the American Psychoanalytic Association, 38,* 297–324.

Jacobs, S.C. (1987). Measures of the psychological distress of bereavement. In S. Zisook (Ed.), *Biopsychosocial aspects of bereavement* (pp. 125–138). Washington, DC: American Psychiatric Press.

Jacobs, S., Kasl, S.V., Ostfeld, A.M., Berkman, L., Kosten, T.R., & Charpentier, P. (1987). The measurement of grief: Bereaved versus non-bereaved. *The Hospice Journal, 2,* 21–36.

Jacobson, E. (1957). Normal and pathological moods: Their nature and function. *Psychoanalytic Study of the Child, 12,* 73–113.

James, W. (1890). *Principles of psychology.* New York: Henry Holt & Co.

Kelly, G.A. (1955). *The psychology of personal constructs (Vol. 1).* New York: W.W. Norton & Co.

Kierkegaard, S. (1957). *The concept of dread.* Princeton: University Press. (Original work published 1844)

Kübler-Ross, E. (1969). *On death and dying.* New York: Macmillan.

Lee, H. (1960). *To kill a mockingbird.* New York: HarperCollins.

Leick, N., & Davidsen-Nielson, M. (1991). *Healing pain. Attachment, loss and grief therapy.* London: Routledge.

Lewin, K.A. (1935). *A dynamic theory of personality.* New York: McGraw-Hill.

Lewis, C.S. (1961). *A grief observed.* London: Faber and Faber.

Lewis, E., & Page, A. (1978). Failure to mourn a stillbirth: An overlooked catastrophe. *British Journal of Medical Psychology, 51,* 237–241.

Lindemann, E. (1944). Symptomatology and management of acute grief. *American Journal of Psychiatry, 101,* 141–148.

Lorenz, K. (1954). *Man meets dog.* London: Methuen.

McHugh, P. (1968). *Defining the situation.* Indianapolis: Bobbs-Merrill.

Mahler, M., Pine, F., & Bergman, A. (1975). *The psychological birth of the human infant.* New York: Basic Books.

Main, M. (1995). Recent studies in attachment: Overview with selected implications for clinical work. In S. Goldberg, R. Muir, & J. Kerr (Eds.), *Attachment theory: Social, developmental and clinical perspectives* (pp. 407–76). Hillsdale, NJ: The Analytic Press.

Marks, I.M. (1987). *Fears, phobias and rituals: Panic, anxiety, and their disorders.* New York: Oxford University Press.

Marris, P. (1982). The social construction of uncertainty. In C.M. Parkes, J. Stevenson-Hinde, & P. Marris (Eds.), *The place of attachment in human behavior* (pp. 76–90). New York: Basic Books.

Marris, P. (1986). *Loss and change* (2nd ed.). London: Routledge & Kegan Paul.

Mead, G.H. (1934). *Mind, self and society: From the standpoint of a social behaviorist.* Chicago: University of Chicago Press.

Merton, R.K. (1957). *Social theory and social structure* (Rev. ed.). New York: The Free Press.

Merton, R.K., & Rossi, A.K. (1968). Contributions to the theory of reference group behavior. In H.H. Hyman & E. Singer (Eds.), *Readings in reference group theory and research* (pp. 69–76). New York: The Free Press.

Mestrovic, S.G. (1985). A sociological conceptualisation of trauma. *Social Science and Medicine, 21,* 835–848.

Mistry, R. (1996). *A fine balance.* London: Faber and Faber.

Moore, T. (1991). *Cry of the damaged man.* Sydney, Australia: Picador.

Nagera, H. (1970). Children's reactions to the death of important objects: A developmental approach. *The Psychoanalytic Study of the Child, 25,* 360–400.

Neugarten, B.L. (1976). Adaptation and the life cycle. *The Counselling Psychologist, 6,* 16–20.

Olshansky, S. (1962). Chronic sorrow: A response to having a mentally defective child. *Social Casework, 43,* 190–193.

Ondaatje, M. (2000). *Anil's ghost*. New York: Alfred A. Knopf.

Opie, I. (1993). *The people in the playground*. Oxford: Oxford University Press.

Ortega y Gasset, J. (1957). *The revolt of the masses*. New York: W.W. Norton & Co.

Parkes, C.M. (1965). Bereavement and mental illness: Part 2. A classification of bereavement reactions. *British Journal of Medical Psychology, 38*, 13–26.

Parkes, C.M. (1971). Psycho-social transitions: A field for study. *Social Science and Medicine, 5*, 101–115.

Parkes, C.M. (1972). Components of the reaction to loss of a limb, spouse or home. *Journal of Psychosomatic Research, 16*, 343–349.

Parkes, C.M. (1975). What becomes of redundant world models? A contribution to the study of adaptation to change. *British Journal of Medical Psychology, 48*, 131–137.

Parkes, C.M. (1988). Bereavement as a psychosocial transition: Processes of adaptation to change. *Journal of Social Issues, 44*, 53–65.

Parkes, C.M., & Weiss, R.S. (1983). Recovery from bereavement. New York: Basic Books.

Parsons, T. (1955). Family structure and socialization of the child. In T. Parsons & R.F. Bales (Eds.), *Family: Socialization and interaction processes* (pp. 35–132). New York: The Free Press.

Peppers, L.G., & Knapp, R.J. (1980). *Motherhood and mourning perinatal death*. New York: Praeger Publishers.

Perlman, E. (1998). *Three dollars*. Sydney, Australia: Picador.

Pettigrew, T. (1968). Actual gains and psychological losses. In H.H. Hyman & E. Singer (Ed.), *Readings in reference group theory and research* (pp. 330–349). New York: Free Press.

Piaget, J. (1951). The child's conception of the world. Savage, Maryland: Littlefield Adams. (Original work published 1929)

Piaget, J. (1954). *The construction of reality in the child*. New York: Basic Books.

Piaget, J. (1962). *Play, dreams and imitation in childhood*. New York: W.W. Norton.

Piaget, J. (1970). *Genetic epistemology*. New York: Columbia University Press.

Pollock, G.H. (1970). Anniversary reactions, trauma and mourning. *Psychoanalytic Quarterly, 39*, 347–371.

Pollock, G.H. (1978). Process and affect: Mourning and grief. *International Journal of Psycho-analysis, 59*, 225–276.

Popper, K.R., & Eccles, J.C. (1977). *The self and its brain*. New York: Springer International.

Rank, O. (1961). *Psychology and the soul*. New York: Perpetua Books. (Original work published 1931)

Raphael, B. (1984). *The anatomy of bereavement*. London: Routledge.

Robinson, L.W., & DeRosa, S.M. (1980). *Parent needs inventory* (Rev. ed.). Austin, TX: Parent Consultants.

Rochlin, G. (1965). *Grief and discontents: The forces of change*. London: J. & A. Churchill.

Roskies, E. (1972). *Abnormality and normality: The mothering of thalidomide children*. London: Cornell University Press.

Rubin, S.S. (1983, January). *Beyond adjustment: Parameters of successful resolution of bereavement*. Paper presented at Third International Congress on Psychological Stress and Adjustment in Time of War and Peace, Tel Aviv, Israel.

Rubin, S.S. (1984). Mourning distinct from melancholia: The resolution of bereavement. *British Journal of Medical Psychology, 57*, 339–345.

Rubin, S.S. (1989). Death of the future? An outcome study of bereaved parents in Israel. *Omega, 20,* 323–339.

Rutter, M., & Rutter, M. (1993). *Developing minds: Challenge and continuity across the lifespan.* London: Penguin Press.

Sacks, O. (1991). *A leg to stand on.* London: Picador.

Sapolsky, R.M. (1992). *Stress, the aging brain and the mechanisms of neuron death.* Cambridge: MIT Press.

Schneider, J. (1984). *Stress, loss, and grief.* Baltimore: University Park Press.

Schultz, C.L., & Schultz, N.C. (1997). *Care for caring parents.* Melbourne: Australian Council for Educational Research.

Schultz, C.L., & Schultz, N.C. (1998). *The caregiving years.* Melbourne: Australian Council for Educational Research.

Schultz, C.L., Schultz, N.C., Bruce, E.J., Smyrnios, K.X., Carey, L., & Carey, C. (1993). Psychoeducational support for parents of children with intellectual disability: An outcome study. *International Journal of Disability, Development and Education, 40,* 205–216.

Schultz, N.C., & Schultz, C.L. (1997). *Care for caring parents: Leader's manual.* Melbourne: Australian Council for Educational Research.

Sekaer, C. (1987). Towards a definition of childhood mourning. *American Journal of Psychotherapy, XIV,* 201–219.

Seligman, M.E.P. (1995). *The optimistic child.* Boston: Houghton Mifflin.

Shabad, P.C. (1989). Vicissitudes of psychic loss of a physically present parent. In D.R. Dietrich & P.C. Shabad (Eds.), *The problem of loss and mourning. Psychoanalytic perspectives* (pp. 101–128) Madison CT: International Universities Press.

Shakespeare, W. (1943). Much ado about nothing. In W.J. Craig (Ed.), *The complete works of William Shakespeare* (Rev. ed.). London: Oxford University Press.

Shakespeare, W. (1943). Macbeth. In W.J. Craig (Ed.), *The complete works of William Shakespeare* (Rev. ed.). London: Oxford University Press.

Shibutani, T. (1955). Reference groups as perspectives. In J.G. Manis & B.N. Meltzer (Eds.), *Symbolic interaction: A reader in social psychology* (2nd ed., pp. 160–170). Needham Heights, MA: Allyn & Bacon.

Shields, C. (1997). *Larry's party.* London: Fourth Estate.

Silverman, P.R., Nickman, S., & Worden, J.W. (1992). Detachment revisited: The child's reconstruction of a dead parent. *American Journal of Orthopsychiatry, 62,* 494–503.

Snyder, C.R. (1989). Reality negotiation: From excuses to hope and beyond. *Journal of Social and Clinical Psychology, 8,* 130–157.

Stern, D. (1985). *The interpersonal world of the infant. A view from psychoanalysis and developmental psychology.* New York: Basic Books.

Sullender, R.C. (1985). *Grief and growth: Pastoral resources for emotional and spiritual growth.* New Jersey: Paulist Press.

Terr, L.C. (1985). Children traumatized in small groups. In S. Eth & R.S. Pynoos (Eds.), *Post-traumatic stress disorder in children* (pp. 45–70). Washington, DC: American Psychiatric Press.

Volkan, V. (1970). Typical findings in pathological grief. *Psychiatric Quarterly, 44,* 231–250.

Voysey, M. (1970). Impression management by parents with disabled children. *Journal of Health and Social Behavior, 13,* 80–89.

Voysey, M. (1975). *A constant burden: The reconstruction of family life.* London: Routledge and Kegan Paul.

Waller, W. (1938). *The family: A dynamic interpretation.* New York: Cordon Co.

Warner, M. (2000). *No go the bogeyman.* London: Vintage.

Winkler, R., & van Keppel, M. (1984). *Relinquishing mothers in adoption.* Melbourne, Australia: Institute of Family Studies.

Wolfenstein, M. (1966). How is mourning possible? *Psychoanalytic Study of the Child, 21,* 93–123.

Woods, P., & Ashley, J. (1995). Simulated presence therapy: Using selected memories to manage problem behaviors in Alzheimer's disease patients. *Geriatric Nursing, 16,* 9–13, 16.

Woolf, V. (1985). Sketch of the past. In J. Schulkind (Ed.), *Moments of being.* New York: Harvest Books.

Worden, J.W. (1991). *Grief counseling and grief therapy.* (2nd ed.) New York: Springer.

INDEX

Page numbers followed by *f* indicate figures; those followed by *t* indicate tables.